THE FATHERS OF THE CHURCH

A NEW TRANSLATION

VOLUME 44

THE FATHERS OF THE CHURCH

A NEW TRANSLATION

EDITORIAL BOARD

SAINT AMBROSE

THEOLOGICAL AND DOGMATIC WORKS

Translated by

ROY J. DEFERRARI, PH.D.
The Catholic University of America

THE CATHOLIC UNIVERSITY OF AMERICA PRESS
Washington 17, D. C.
1963

NIHIL OBSTAT:

HARRY A. ECHLE

Censor librorum

IMPRIMATUR:

✠ PATRICK A. O'BOYLE

Archbishop of Washington

August 1, 1962

Lithographed by
Sauls Lithograph Company, Inc.
Washington, D. C.

CONTENTS

v

INTRODUCTION

S T. AMBROSE WAS BORN in 339 in Augusta Trevero-
rum, the modern Trier or Trèves, famous for its size
and beauty and as a residence of emperors and as
the political capital of the Roman territory west of the Alps.

His family was both Roman and distinguished. It had given
consuls and prefects to the Empire, and at least one martyr,
a virgin named Soteris, to the Church. At the time of Ambrose's birth, his father, Aurelius Ambrose, held the high
office of Pretorian Prefect of the Gauls.

There were already two children in the family: the older
Marcellina, a girl of great strength of character and always
inclined to the religious life; the younger a boy, Uranius
Satyrus, of delicate health and excessively shy, between whom
and Ambrose there developed an intense brotherly affection.

Paulinus, St. Ambrose's biographer, tells little about the
early life of Ambrose. After his father died, his mother, whose
name is nowhere mentioned, went with her family to live in
Rome, where Marcellina received the veil from Pope Liberius
in the Basilica of St. Peter on the Feast of the Epiphany,
January 6, 353. St. Ambrose in *De virginibus* (3.11-14)

summarizes the address which Pope Liberius gave on this occasion. Since at this time there were no convents of virgins in Rome, Marcellina together with another consecrated virgin continued to live in her mother's house.

In the meantime, St. Ambrose and Satyrus had begun their schooling, which was divided into three parts: training in the elementary school; in the school of the grammaticus, which consisted of the critical study of the chief masterpieces of Greek and Latin literature; and in the school of the rhetor, which included instruction in the theory of oratory and oratorical composition, and in the practice of the application of these rules. In addition to this program, certain supplementary studies were available to youth of great promise. It appears that Ambrose studied philosophy and mathematics. Although he claims to be only an amateur in the field, he also exhibits some knowledge of medicine.

After completing their education, Ambrose and Satyrus left Rome in 365 and went to Sirmium as advocates attached to the Court of the Italian Prefecture. The prefect, Vulcatius Rufinus, was an old man of a distinguished family and honorable career. They soon attracted his attention by the brilliance of their oratory. In 368, Rufinus died and was succeeded by very rich and generous Sextus Petronius Probus, a young man of thirty-four years. He promoted the brothers to the Prefect's Judicial Committee. Probably in 370, Satyrus was a provincial governor, and Ambrose was named 'Consular,' or Governor, of the province of Aemelia Liguria.

After some years, probably in October, 373, Auxentius, the intended Arian Bishop of Milan, died. The exiled Catholic Bishop Dionysius by this time was also dead. It was necessary to elect a new bishop, and the Catholics and Arians contended violently to supply the winning candidate. Suddenly, with surprising unanimity, both parties agreed on Ambrose as bishop. St. Ambrose resorted to all sorts of subterfuges to avoid the appointment, but he finally yielded, as Paulinus says, 'recognizing the Divine Will concerning him.' The consecration was performed on December 1 by the bishops of the province, the principal consecrator being the Bishop of Aquileia. He had been baptized on November 24.

After his consecration, St. Ambrose made a donation of his acquired property to the Church, but retained his inherited property under his own control, although devoting the bulk of the income to charitable purposes. This was in accord with his own regulations for his clergy. He committed such property as he retained to the charge of his brother Satyrus, except a life interest for his sister. Satyrus gave up his own office to come to Ambrose's assistance, and to enable him to devote himself entirely to theological study and his other episcopal duties.

St. Ambrose spent much of his time in prayer, laying special stress on the duty of prayer at night. Next to prayer he valued the discipline of fasting. He strongly urged his people to practice fasting, especially in Lent, and he himself was scrupulous in this observance. He also considered fine clothes unsuitable for the clergy, and he himself cultivated simplicity in attire.

St. Ambrose held daily audiences which were attended by crowds of people of all classes and conditions, even by strangers from distant countries. When the long receptions were over, he devoted himself to study. It was probably at this time, chiefly, that Ambrose became acquainted with the works of various Jewish and Christian writers, on some of whom he leaned extensively in his own compositions. His favorite authors clearly were Philo, Origen, and Basil, but he shows some knowledge of the various works of Josephus, Eusebius, Hippolytus, Didymus, and Athanasius. He even studied the works of certain heretics, in order to be better able to refute their erroneous views.

His work as bishop of a great city was varied and extremely arduous. The following duties are noteworthy:

1. The administration of baptism and penance. He took great care to give adequate instruction to catechumens, the most famous of whom was St. Augustine. He was equally conscientious with the exercise of penitential discipline.

2. The superintendence of the charities of the Church. The details of this work were entrusted to the deacons, but the final responsibility rested with the bishop. He also was consulted directly on special cases.

3. The defence of the oppressed.

4. The hearing and determining of civil causes.

5. The discipline of his clergy.

In addition, as the sole metropolitan of northern Italy, he had the general supervision of the various dioceses of the province. He convoked ordinary and extraordinary provincial councils, heard appeals, issued directions as to the proper day for observing Easter, and consecrated bishops to the vacant sees.

During the fourth century the position of women had materially improved. The State gave them more protection against unjust and cruel treatment, and the Church held them in high honor, even allowing them to minister as deaconesses. The women of this period seem to have been more deeply influenced by Christianity than paganism, and in the Church they found many opportunities for the exercise of their energies. Pure marriage, widowhood, and virginity are the three degrees of the virtue of chastity. According to St. Ambrose, there is room in the Church for all three, although they are not of equal excellence.

Probably in February, 375, Uranius Satyrus, Ambrose's beloved elder brother, died.[1] The day of his death (September 17) as given in the Roman Martyrology is clearly wrong. They were very close. They shared everything: their property, thoughts and feelings, care and pleasures, even their very sickness and health. According to Ambrose, death is not an evil and should not be lamented: first, because it is the law of nature and the common lot of all men; secondly, because it brings release from the miseries of this life; and thirdly, because of the sure and certain hope of the resurrection of the body and the life of the world to come.

All the Arian activity in Milan, his own city, must have embarassed and distressed Ambrose greatly. The Empress mother Justina was still an Arian by religion and she detested Ambrose. Moreover, she was a very ambitious woman, who was determined to exercise supreme power by means of influence over her son, the child emperor, Valentinian II. She saw in Ambrose an energetic enemy of her faith and also a dangerous political rival. The empress gathered round herself a party of opposition to the bishop, whose aim was to discredit, and, if possible, to bring about the removal of the too powerful bishop. The point around which the battle would be waged was the question of providing facilities for Arian worship in Milan, which at that moment were nonexistent. Outside the walls of Milan there was a Catholic church called Portiana or the Basilica of Portius, and Justina was resolved to place this building at the disposal of the Arians. When this was refused, a second application was made

---

1 See Vol. 22 of this series for an English version of the two sermons St. Ambrose delivered on this occasion.

for the larger and newer basilica within the city. When asked to give this church over, Ambrose replied: 'The emperor has his palaces, let him leave the churches to the bishops.' The emperor sent soldiers to secure the delivery of the basilica, but St. Ambrose with some of his faithful followers occupied it first, and remained in it, singing psalms and hymns until the soldiers were ordered to retire.

St. Ambrose was destined to play an equally important part in the struggle between Christianity and paganism. It is important to note that Milan, not Rome, Ambrose, not Pope Damasus, determined the final victory of Christianity over paganism. One of the many remains at that time of heathen worship was the Altar of Victory in the senate house at Rome, which had been removed under Gratian. Symmachus, the Prefect of Rome, himself a pagan although a friend of St. Ambrose, petitioned Valentinian II to restore it, but Ambrose succeeded in defeating this petition by two letters (17 and 18) addressed to the young emperor. When Theodosius took over the imperial power in 387, still another attempt was made, but to no avail. Still later, the usurper Eugenius considered it good politics to cultivate the good will of the pagans and so ordered the Altar of Victory to be set up once more and the temples to remain open as of old. This triumph, however, was very short lived. When in the spring of 394 Theodosius defeated Eugenius at Aquileia, he brought paganism to an end, at least as a public religion. Naturally it lingered for a long time in private in the midst of indifferences, toleration, and sometimes persecution.

St. Ambrose was not only ready to exert his influence on the rulers of his day, but, as the occasion demanded, to make use of rebuke and Church discipline. Shortly after his consecration, St. Ambrose remonstrated with Valentinian I on the severity of his reign and a number of abuses within his government. The emperor made the following famous reply: 'Well, if I have offended, prescribe for me the remedies which the law of God requires.' In 390, Theodosius had a mild sedition in Thessalonica put down with undue severity, bringing about the slaughter of some 7,000 persons. St. Ambrose at once disregarded any serious consequence for himself, and wrote him the now famous letter 51, exhorting him to repentance, and declaring that he could not be present at any celebration of the Mass until he had publicly expressed repentance. He complied with this condition at once. On another occasion the same Theodosius, following the practice in the East, entered the sanctuary of the church, a privilege reserved only for the clergy in the West. St. Ambrose rebuked him severely and made him retire to another section of the church with the laity.

Ambrose, however, was of great assistance to the imperial family in temporal affairs. To cite briefly only a few of these occasions, he undertook two different missions on behalf of Valentinian II to Trèves for the purpose of warding off an invasion by the usurper Maximus. When Valentinian II died, Ambrose delivered the eulogy which stands as one of the finest examples of early Christian funeral orations. He performed a similar service for Theodosius in 395. On several occasions, too, he interceded for the Roman emperor with the Goths. Perhaps the most important achievement of St. Ambrose in his dealings with the Roman emperors was the establishment of the principle that the Church and the State are two independent authorities, each autonomous within its own sphere, but each rendering general assistance and support to the other.

St. Ambrose's contribution to the music of the Western

Church must not be left unmentioned. He improved the song itself by introducing a more lively and melodious song, which was now rendered not by professional singers alone, but by the whole congregation, singing alternately in two choirs. He also supplied new hymns of his own composition. While Hilary of Poitiers was the first Latin hymn writer and composer of a hymn book, he did not succeed in getting his people to sing his compositions. They were excessively dull and ill adapted for congregational singing. Thus Ambrose may very properly be regarded as the father and founder of Latin hymnody.

Only two years after the death of Theodosius in 395, St. Ambrose died very early in the morning of Easter eve. Within an hour after death, his body was taken to the cathedral to lie in state that day and throughout the following night. On Easter Sunday after Mass, it was taken from the cathedral to the Ambrosian Basilica, where it was buried close to the relics of Saints Gervasius and Protasius. The church of Sant'Ambrogio in Milan still shelters the dust of St. Ambrose.

The present volume contains four of the six treatises of St. Ambrose usually classified under the general title of Dogmatic and Controversial Works. These are *De mysteriis, De Spiritu Sancto, De incarnationis dominicae sacramento,* and *De sacramentis.* The last has been held of doubtful authenticity, but Fr. O. Faller, S.J., now convincingly establishes its Ambrosian authorship. The other two works of this group, *De fide* and *De poenitentia* will appear in another volume of this series.

Our translation of *De mysteriis* and the *De sacramentis* is based on the recent text by Fr. Faller in the *Corpus Scriptorum Ecclesiasticorum Latinorum;* the other two, on the Benedictine text, reprinted in Migne. All the treatises of this volume, with the exception of *De sacramentis,* have been translated by H. de Romeston in the Nicene and Post-Nicene Fathers 10 (New York 1896). *De sacramentis* and *De mysteriis* have been translated by Thompson and Srawley (London 1950). Of great value, also, is the unprinted master's dissertation of Brother Louis Cavell of the Brothers of the Sacred Heart, entitled *Sancti Ambrosii 'De Incarnationis Dominicae Sacramento Liber,' A Translation with Introduction and Commentary* (Washington 1955). The translations of passages from Scripture in this volume are taken or adapted from the Challoner-Rheims Version in the Confraternity edition. Each treatise will have a brief introduction of importance for itself.

CHRONOLOGICAL TABLE OF THE TIMES AND WORKS OF ST. AMBROSE

339 St. Ambrose born at Trèves early in this year.

343 Beginning of heresy of Photinus.

348 Birth of Prudentius, the Christian Vergil.

349 Synod of Sirmium against Photinus.

350 Death of Emperor Constans. St. Hilary, Bishop of Poitiers. Magnentius declared Emperor of West.

351 Condemnation of Photinus by a semi-Arian synod.

352 Liberius succeeds Julius as Pope.

353-4 St. Ambrose taken by mother to live in Rome. His sister Marcellina receives veil from Liberius at Christmas. Emperor Magnentius commits suicide.

354 Birth of St. Augustine on November 13. Death of Emperor Gallus.

355   Arian synod at Milan banishes Pope Liberius, Dionysius, Bishop of Milan, and Lucifer, Bishop of Cagliari.

356   St. Hilary of Poitiers is banished.

357   According to Arians, Liberius subscribes an Arian Creed, and returns to Rome 358. Between April 28 and May 29, Emperor Constantius visits Rome.

359   Council of Ariminum. Birth of Gratian on April 18.

361   Julian made emperor on November 3.

363   Emperor Julian dies on June 26. Felix becomes pope.

364   Emperor Jovinian dies. Valentinian and Valens become emperors.

365   Having completed education, Ambrose and Satyrus leave Rome and go to Sirmium as advocates.

366   Liberius dies in September. Damasus is elected in his place, but Ursinus also claims see.

367   Gratian, still a boy, declared Augustus on August 24 by Valentinian, his father.

370   Ambrose named 'Consular' or Governor of province of Aemilia-Liguria.

372   Conspiracy of Theodorus against Valens.

373   Auxentius, Arian bishop of Milan, dies sometime in October. St. Ambrose, still a catechumen, elected Bishop of Milan by acclamation, and consecrated on December 1. He was baptized on November 24, and on the following six days was made to pass formally through the successive grades of the ministry. St. Martin Bishop of Tours.

374-5 St. Ambrose sends delegation of clerics to St. Basil, Bishop of Caesarea, to ask for body of St. Dionysius, late Catholic Bishop of Milan. Cf. St. Basil, Letter 197.

375   Valentinian dies in November. His son Valentinian, though only four years old, recognized by Gratian as

Emperor of East. Gratian refuses title of Pontifex
Maximus. Satyrus, brother of St. Ambrose, dies in February. Two treatises on his death (*De Excessu fratris sui
Satyri*) are written. Some hymns are written in September.

376 St. Ambrose writes *De virginibus* in three books and
De viduis in one. Goths cross Danube.

377 St. Ambrose writes *De paradiso* and *De Cain,* also *De
virginitate* (June). The Goths rebel at Marcianople.

378 First two books of *De fide* are written during August
and September at request of Gratian, who sets out to
support Valens against Goths. *De Noe* is written in
autumn. Valens is killed at Adrianople. St. Ambrose
sells church plate to redeem the many Christians made
captives.

379-380 Disastrous famine in Rome. Cf. *De officiis* 3.46-48.

379 Theodosius is proclaimed Augustus at Sirmium. Con-
sulship of Ausonius. Gratian, on way back from Thrace,
asks Ambrose to come and meet him. He receives first
two books of the *De fide* and asks for one on Holy
Spirit. The latter is written two years later. In July
the sequestrated basilica at Milan is restored to Catholics
by Gratian. Maximus the Cynic goes to Constantinople.

380 Emperor Theodosius is baptized at Thessalonica. Books
3 and 4 of the *De fide* are written. St. Ambrose attends
synod at Rome under Damasus. He consecrates Anamius
Bishop of Sirmium, although Arians oppose. Council of
Zaragossa in autumn. Theodosius enter Constantinople
on November 24. On November 26 the Arians are expelled from the churches of Constantinople.

381 Athanaricus, leader of the Goths, dies at Constantinople.
De Spiritu Sancto in three books is written. Peter, Bishop

of Alexandria, dies. Ecumenical Council of Constantinople under Meletius of Antioch opens. At Aquileia a council, in which St. Ambrose takes leading part, opens against heretics Palladius and Secundianus. Cf. Letters 9-12 of Ambrose. Nectarius consecrated Bishop of Constantinople, and Flavian Bishop of Antioch. Toward the end of the year the *De incarnationis dominicae sacramento* is written.

382   Council of Italian bishops under Ambrose's direction meets to consider difficulties at Antioch and Constantinople. Cf. Letters 13, to Theodosius, and 14, his reply. Theodosius calls similar council at Constantinople. On October 3, Theodosius makes peace with the Goths. Emperor Gratian orders the removal of statue of Victory from Roman Forum. Cf. Letters 17 and 18. Acholius, Bishop of Thessalonica, dies during winter and is succeeded by Anysius.

383   Priscillianists visit Rome in vain effort to win Pope Damasus and St. Ambrose to their cause. Gratian, through plot directed by Maximus, is assassinated at Lyons on August 25. Famine in Rome. Cf. *De officiis* 3.7 and 49; Letter 18.

383-4 St. Ambrose sends first legation to Maximus in behalf of Empress Justina and her son Valentinian II.

384   Symmachus, prefect of city, appeals to Valentinian for restoration of Altar of Victory. St. Ambrose makes reply. Cf. Letters 17 and 18. A synod is held at Bordeaux against the Priscillianists. Pope Damasus dies and is succeeded by Siricius. *De poenitentia* probably written in this year.

385   The Spanish Bishops Idacius and Ithacius instigate death sentence against Priscillian and his followers at Trèves.

Ithacians consecrate Felix as Bishop. Cf. Letters 42-51.
Persecution of Catholics at Milan by Justina during
Holy Week. Cf. Letter 20. Valentinian II passes law
granting Arians equal rights with Catholics. Auxentius
lays claim to see of Milan. Cf. Sermon against Auxentius and Letter 21. St. Ambrose succeeds in procuring
restitution of deposit which a widow had entrusted to
the Church at Trent and which had been carried off
by imperial order. Cf. *De officiis* 2.29, 150, 151. Consecration of new basilica at Milan.

386 Discovery of bodies of St. Gervasius and St. Protasius.
Cf. Letter 22. St. Ambrose writes Letter 23 to the
bishops of province of Aemilia, regarding right day for
observing Easter. In spring, St. Ambrose writes the
Sermo contra Auxentium and *De Iacob,* and in middle
of year *De officiis.*

387 St. Augustine is baptized by St. Ambrose at Milan on
Easter. Second mission of St. Ambrose to Maximus. Cf.
Letter 24. St. Ambrose is expelled from Trèves because
he refuses to communicate with murderer of his sov-
ereign. Maximus crosses into Italy and enters Milan.
In this year St. Ambrose writes *In psalm. 61 enarratio,
Hexaemeron, Apologia prophetiae David,* and possibly
De mysteriis. De sacramentis was in all probability
written earlier.

388 Arians destroy residence of Bishop Nectarius at Constantinople. Cf. Letter 30 sec. 13. Empress Justina dies.
Valentinian II is converted by Theodosius. Theodosius
wages war against Maximus, who is thoroughly defeated
(cf. Letter 40, sec. 23), and is executed at Aquileia.
Third application is made for restoration of Altar of
Victory. St. Ambrose composes *De Ioseph* and *De inter-*

pellatione Iob et David. In December St. Ambrose and Theodosius collide on affair at Collinicum.

389 *De elia et ieiunio* is composed before Lent, and from May until February 390 the series of sermons, *Expositio psalmi CXVIII.*

390 Theodosius punishes a sedition at Thessalonica with excessive cruelty. St. Ambrose rebukes him severely and excludes him from communion. The Emperor repents and is readmitted to communion. Synod against Ithacian heretics and Felix, Bishop of Trèves, is held at Milan. Cf. Letter 51. Publication of *Expositio evangelii secundum Lucam* and the *In psalm. I enarratio.*

391-2 Anti-pagan edict for Rome (Cod. Theod. XVI 10.10) promulgated on February 24; for Egypt (Cod. Theod. XVI 10.11), on June 16. Part of Roman senate approaches Valentinian to request restoration of the Altar of Victory in Forum. Cf. Letter 57, sec. 5. *De institutione virginis* was written at about this time. Council of Capua was held in winter.

392 *De institutione virginis* published at Easter time. Valentinian II killed at Vienne by Arbogast. Cf. Letter 53 sec. 2; *De ob. Valent.* 25ff. His body is brought to Milan. St. Ambrose delivers *Consolatio de obitu Valent.* Still another delegation regarding Altar of Victory is sent by senate to Eugenius. Cf. Letter 57, sec. 6ff. Condemnation of Jovinian by Pope Siricius and Roman synod.

393 When Eugenius arrives at Milan, St. Ambrose leaves for Bononia Faventia and Florence. He writes letters to Eugenius and Sabinus. On January 10, Honorius, who was born September 9, 384, was created emperor.

393-4 In Florence St. Ambrose dedicates a basilica and deposits therein the bodies of martyrs Vitalis and Agricola he brought from Bononia. Delivers *Exhortatio virginitatis*; also writes Letter 59.

394 Theodosius sets out against Eugenius from Constantinople. Early in August St. Ambrose returns to Milan. On September 6, Theodosius defeats and slays Eugenius. St. Ambrose intercedes and wins pardon for followers of Eugenius. St. Ambrose writes *Enarrationes in Psalmos* 35-40; also Letters 61 and 62. Arbogast commits suicide on September 8. Toward end of year, Paulinus, later Bishop of Nola, and his wife Therasia renounce world. Theodosius becomes ill, and Honorius arrives at Milan.

395 Theodosius dies in Milan. St. Ambrose delivers *De obitu Theodosii.* Honorius and Arcadius become emperors. St. Augustine made Bishop of Hippo. Arcadius marries Eudoxia on April 27. On November 27, Rufinus is murdered. Remains of Saint Nazarius and Celsus are discovered by St. Ambrose and brought to Basilica of Apostles. Composition of *De nabuthe Iezraelita.*

396 Affair of Cresconius and Ambrose's correspondence with Queen Fritigil. Because of dissensions at Vercellae, St. Ambrose visits Church there and writes Letter 63.

397 St. Ambrose consecrates a bishop at Ticinum. A little later he falls ill. He commences but is unable to finish *Enarratio in Psalm. 43.* He recommends Simplicianus as his successor and dies very early in the morning of Easter Eve. He is buried in Ambrosian Basilica on April 5.

Some of the more important letters of St. Ambrose have been listed in the table above. The entire collection of ninety-one extant letters is presented in an English version by Sister Mary Melchior Beyenka, O. P., in Volume 26 of this series.

Sister Mary Melchior divides the collection into the following groups: Letters to Emperors; Letters to Bishops; Synodal Letters; Letters to Priests; Letters to His Sister; Letters to Laymen.

BIBLIOGRAPHY

Primary Sources:

The important sources for the life of St. Ambrose, besides his complete works, are the following:

Life of St. Ambrose, by his secretary Paulinus. It is probably the most reliable of all the biographies of saints belonging to this period.

Rufinus, *Ecclesiastical History.* This is independent of Paulinus, and has its information from a friend of St. Ambrose, Bishop Chromatius of Aquileia; its substantial accuracy is unquestioned.

St. Augustine, who knew Ambrose and was baptized by him in 387. Cf. St. Augustine: *Confess.* 5.13 and 14; 6.1-4; 9.5-7; *Epp.* 36, 44, 54, 147; *De civitate Dei* 22.8; *De cura pro mort.* 21; *De gratia Christi* 47; *Contr. Julian. Pelagi* 1.10; *Serm.* 286.4.

St. Jerome, *De viris. illustribus* 124; *Chronicon, Olymp.* 288; *Epp.* 15.4; 22.22; 48.14 and 18; 84.7; 121.6; *Apol. adv. Rufinum,* 1,2; *Transl. Hom.* XXXIX *Origenis in ev. Luc. Prolog.*

Sulpicius Severus, *Chron.* 2.48; Orosius, *Hist. adv. paganos,* 7.36; Anonymous, *Gallican Chronicle* A.D. 452 in *Chronica Minora,* ed. Mommsen, M.G.H. 9.646; Prosper 375 and 380; Idatius 382 and 385; Ennodius, ed. F. Vogel, 195, 346; Cassiodorus, *Instit. Div. Litt.* 20; *Chron.* 380; Marcellinus 398; Gregory of Tours, *De miraculis sancti Martini* 1.5; *De glor. martyrum* 47.

Socrates, *Ecclesiastical History* 4.30; 5.11. This is regarded as of little value; its chronology is especially confused.

Sozomen, *Ecclesiastical History* 6.24; 7.13,25. His sources are Rufinus and Socrates.

Theodoret, *Ecclesiastical History* 4.6-7; 5.13,17,18. The chief source appears to be Sozomen.

St. Basil, *Ep.* 197. Written to St. Ambrose, who had been elevated to archepiscopate of Milan only the year before, this letter is an answer to a request that the relics of St. Dionysius of Milan, who died in Cappadocia, be returned to his native city.

Editions and Translations:

Botte, Dom Bernard, Ambroise de Milan, *Des sacrements des Mystères* (Paris 1949).

Faller, O., *Corpus Scriptorum Ecclesiasticorum Latinorum* 73, containing among other works *De sacramentis* and *De mysteriis* (Vienna 1955).

Frisch, J. du, et N. le Nourry, *Sancti Ambrosii Mediolanensis Episcopi Opera*, 2 vols. (Paris 1686-1690).

Migne J., *Patrologiae Latinae Cursus Completus* (3rd reprint of the Benedictine edition), (Paris 1845).

Romestin, H. de, in *Nicene and Post-Nicene Fathers*, ser. 2 (New York 1896) 10.

General Works:

Broglie, Duc de, *Saint Ambrose*, trans. Margaret Maitland (London 1899).

Dudden, F. Homes, *The Life and Times of St. Ambrose*, 2 vols. (Oxford 1935).

Labriolle, Pierre de, *The Life and Times of St. Ambrose*, trans. Herbert Wilson (St. Louis 1928).

Loughlin, J. F., 'Saint Ambrose,' in *Catholic Encyclopedia* (London 1907).

Nagl, Maria Assunta, *Der Heilige Ambrosius* (Münster 1951).

Palanque, Jean Remy, *Saint Ambroise et l'empire romain* (Paris 1933).

Ratti, A., 'The Ambrosian Church of Milan,' in *Essays in History* (London 1933) 1-110.

Thompson, T. and J. H. Srawley, *St. Ambrose On the Sacraments and On the Mysteries* (London 1950).

THE MYSTERIES

Translated by

ROY J. DEFERRARI, PH.D.
The Catholic University of America

INTRODUCTION

HE TITLE OF THIS TREATISE varies in the manuscripts. Some have *De mysteriis sive initiandis.* The most ancient, however, have *De divinis mysteriis,* or simply *De mysteriis.*

Some scholars have tried to show that this treatise has been falsely ascribed to St. Ambrose. Their arguments, however, have little weight. Many parallels and points of contact between *De mysteriis* and well established works of St. Ambrose, as well as strong manuscript evidence, leave no doubt as to its Ambrosian authorship. The date of the treatise, however, is uncertain.[1]

The work consists of addresses given to the newly baptized during Easter week. They treat of the rites and meaning of the sacraments of baptism, confirmation, and Holy Eucharist. At two points (35-41; 55-58), a mystical commentary on certain passages of the Canticle of Canticles is brought in.

1 Dudden 697-698; Faller 51-60.

THE MYSTERIES[1]

Chapter 1

E HAVE GIVEN a daily sermon on morals, when the deeds of the Patriarchs or the precepts of the Proverbs were read, in order that, being informed and instructed by them, you might become accustomed to enter upon the ways of our forefathers and to pursue their road, and to obey the divine commands, whereby renewed by baptism you might hold to that manner of life which befits those who are washed.

(2) Now time warns us to speak of the mysteries and to set forth the very purpose of the sacraments. If we had thought that this should have been taught those not yet initiated before baptism, we would be considered to have betrayed rather than to have portrayed the mysteries; then there is the consideration that the light of the mysteries will infuse itself better in the unsuspecting than if some sermon had preceded them.

---

1 The word *mysteria* ('mysteries') has its usual general meaning in the writings of the Fathers, also the special Christian meaning as here, a synonym of *sacramenta* ('sacraments'). In the Greek Church today 'the mysteries' rather than 'the sacraments' is regularly used.

(3) So open your ears and enjoy the good odor of eternal life which has been breathed upon you by the grace of the sacraments. This we pointed out to you as we celebrated the mystery of the opening[2] and said: ' "Ephpheta," that is, "Be thou opened," '[3] so that everyone about to come to grace might know what he was asked and might necessarily remember what he responded.

(4) Christ celebrated this mystery in the Gospel,[4] as we have read, when He healed the deaf and dumb man. But He touched the mouth because He was curing both a dumb person and a man, in the one case, that his mouth might open with the sound of the infused voice, in the other, because this touch befitted a man and would not have befitted a woman.

Chapter 2

(5) After this Holy of holies[1] was opened to you, you entered the sanctuary of regeneration. Recall what you were asked; recall what you responded! You renounced the Devil and his works, the world with its luxury and pleasures. Your words are kept not in the tomb of the dead, but in the book of the living.

(6) There you saw the Levite,[2] you saw the priest, you saw the highest priest.[3] Do not consider the bodily forms, but the grace of their ministrations. You have spoken in the

---

2 A symbolical act, as explained in the next section.
3 Mark 7.34.
4 Cf. Mark 7.32.37.

---

1 A figurative name for the baptistery.
2 The deacon.
3 The bishop.

presence of the angels, as it is written: 'For the lips of the priest guard knowledge, and they seek the law from his mouth, because he is an angel of the Lord Almighty.'[4] There is no deceiving; there is no denying. He is an angel, who announces the kingdom of Christ, who announces life eternal, to be esteemed by you not according to appearance, but according to office. Consider what he has given over; reflect on his experience; recognize his position.

(7) Having entered, therefore, that you might recognize your adversary, whom you think you should renounce to his face, you turn toward the east. For he who renounces the devil, turns toward Christ, recognizes Him by a direct glance.

Chapter 3

(8) What have you seen? Water, certainly, but not this alone; the Levites (deacons) ministering there, the highest priest (bishop) questioning and consecrating. First of all, the Apostle taught you that 'we are not to consider the things that are seen, but the things that are not seen, for the things that are seen are temporal, but the things that are not seen are eternal.'[1] For elsewhere you have: 'The invisible things of God from the creation of the world are understood through the things that have been made; His eternal power also and divinity are estimated by His works.'[2] Therefore, too, the Lord Himself says: 'If you do not believe me, at least believe

---

4 Cf. Mal. 2.7.

1 Cf. 2 Cor. 4.18.
2 Cf. Rom. 1.20.

the works.'[3] Believe, therefore, that the presence of Divinity is at hand there. Do you believe the operation? Do you not believe the presence? Whence would the operation follow, unless the presence went before?

(9) Consider, moreover, how old the mystery is and prefigured in the origin of the world itself. In the very beginning, when God made heaven and earth, it says: 'The Spirit moved over the waters.'[4] He who was moving over the waters, was He not working over the waters? Why should I say: 'He was working'? As regards His presence, He was moving. Was He not working who was moving? Recognize that He was working in that making of the world, when the Prophet says to you: 'By the word of the Lord the heavens were made and all their strength by the breath of His mouth.'[5] Each statement relies on the testimony of the Prophet, both that He was moving over and that He was working. That He was moving over, Moses says; that He was working, David testifies.

(10) Accept another testimony. All flesh was corrupted by its iniquities. 'My Spirit,' says God, 'shall not remain in men, for they are flesh.'[6] By this, God shows that spiritual grace is turned aside by carnal impurity and by the stain of more serious sin. Therefore, God in His desire to repair what He had given caused the flood, and ordered Noe the just man to embark on the ark. When, as the flood subsided, he first sent forth a raven which did not return; he afterwards sent forth a dove, which is said to have returned with an olive twig.[7] You see the water; you see the wood; you perceive the dove—and do you doubt the mystery?

---

3 John 10.38.
4 Cf. Gen. 1.2.
5 Cf. Ps. 32.6.
6 Cf. Gen. 6.3.
7 Cf. Gen. 6.12; 8.12.

(11) The water is that in which the flesh is immersed, that all carnal sin may be washed away. All disgrace is buried there. The wood is that on which the Lord Jesus was fastened, when He suffered for us. The dove is that in whose form the Holy Spirit descended, as you have learned in the New Testament, who inspires peace of soul and tranquility of mind in us. The raven is the figure of sin, which goes out and does not return, if in you also the custody and form of justice be preserved.

(12) There is also a third testimony, as the Apostle teaches you: 'That our fathers were all under the cloud, and all passed through the sea, and all were baptized in Moses in the cloud and in the sea.'[8] And finally Moses himself says in his canticle: 'You sent your wind and the sea covered them.'[9] You notice that in that crossing of the Hebrews the figure of holy baptism even then was prefigured, wherein the Egyptian perished and the Hebrew escaped. For what else are we taught daily in this sacrament but that sin is overwhelmed and error abolished, but piety and innocence continue on entire?

(13) You hear that our fathers were under a cloud, that is, a good cloud which cooled the fires of carnal passions, a good cloud; it overshadows those whom the Holy Spirit visits. Finally it came upon the Virgin Mary, and the power of the Most High overshadowed her,[10] when she conceived the Redemption for the human race. And that miracle was performed in a figure by Moses. If then the Spirit was in a figure, He is now present in truth, when Scripture says to you: 'For the law was given by Moses, but grace and truth came by Jesus Christ.'[11]

---

8 1 Cor. 10.1,2.
9 Cf. Exod. 15.10.
10 Cf. Luke 1.35.
11 John 1.17.

(14) Marra was a bitter fountain. Moses cast the wood in it, and it became sweet.[12] For water without the preaching of the cross of the Lord is to no advantage for future salvation; but when it has been consecrated by the mystery of the saving cross, then it is ordered for the use of the spiritual laver and the cup of salvation. So, just as Moses, that is, the Prophet, cast wood into that fountain, also into this fountain the priest casts the message of the cross of the Lord, and the water becomes sweet for grace.

(15) Therefore, you should not trust only in the eyes of your body. Rather is that seen which is not seen, for the one is temporal, the other eternal. Rather is that seen which is not comprehended by the eyes, but is discerned by the spirit and the mind.

(16) Finally, let the reading from Kings[13] which we have just gone over teach you. Naaman was a Syrian and he had leprosy and he could not be cleansed by anyone. Then a maiden from among the captives said that there was a prophet in Israel who could cleanse him of the pollution of leprosy. The account says that having taken gold and silver he went forth to the king of Israel. This one, when he learned the reason for his coming, tore his garments, saying that he rather was being tried, since those things were being demanded of him which were not within the power of a king. Helisaeus, however, made known to the king that he should direct the Syrian to himself, in order that he might learn that there was a God in Israel. And when he had come, he ordered him to dip seven times in the Jordan river.

(17) Then he began to reflect that the rivers of his own country had better waters, in which he had often dipped and

---

12 Cf. Exod. 15.23-25.
13 Cf. 4 Kings 5.1-19.

he had never been cleansed of leprosy, and being induced by this he did not obey the commands of the Prophet. However, on the advice and persuasion of his servants he acquiesced and dipped, and when he was immediately cleansed he understood that one's being cleansed was not connected with the waters, but with grace.

(18) Understand now who that 'maiden of the captives' is! Obviously, the younger congregation of the Gentiles, that is, the Church of the Lord formerly weighed down by the captivity of sin, when it did not yet possess the liberty of grace, by whose counsel that foolish people of the Gentiles heard the word of prophecy which long before it had doubted;[14] afterwards, however, when it believed that it should obey, it was washed of every pollution of sin. And this man[15] doubted before he was healed; you have already been healed and so ought not to doubt.

Chapter 4

(19) On this account it was formerly foretold you that you should not believe this alone which you saw, lest perchance you, too, might say: 'Is this that great mystery which the eye has not seen nor the ear heard nor has it entered into the heart of man?[1] I see waters which I used to see daily; are these able to cleanse me, into which I have often descended and have never been cleansed?' From this learn that water cleanses not without the Spirit.[2]

---

14 Cf. Rom. 7.23-25.
15 Naaman.

1 Cf. 1 Cor. 29.
2 Cf. John 3.5.

(20) And so you have read that the three witnesses in baptism are one: the water, the blood, and the Spirit, for, if you take away one of these, the sacrament of baptism does not stand.[3] For what is water without the cross of Christ except a common element without any sacramental effect? And again without water there is no mystery of regeneration. For 'unless a man be born again of water and the Spirit, he cannot enter into the kingdom of God.'[4] Moreover, even a catechumen believes in the cross of the Lord Jesus, with which he, too, is signed, but, unless he be baptized 'in the name of the Father and of the Son and of the Holy Spirit,'[5] he cannot receive remission of sins nor drink in the benefit of spiritual grace.

(21) Therefore, that Syrian dipped seven times[6] under the law, but you were baptized in the name of the Trinity, you confessed the Father (recall what you did), you confessed the Son, you confessed the Spirit. Retain the order of things. In this faith you died to the world, you arose to God, and, as if buried in that element of the world, dead to sin you were revived to eternal life.[7] Believe, therefore, that these waters are not without power.

(22) Therefore, it is said to you: 'An angel of the Lord used to come down at certain times into the pool and the water was moved, and the first to go down into the pool after the troubling of the water was healed of whatever infirmity he had.'[8] This pool was in Jerusalem, in which one was healed every year. But no one was healed before the angel had

---

3 Cf. 1 John 5.8.
4 John 3.5.
5 Cf. Matt. 28.19.
6 Cf. 4 Kings 5.14.
7 Cf. Rom. 6.11,4.
8 John 5.4.

descended. So the angel descended, and, that there might be a sign that the angel had descended, the water was moved. The water was moved because of the unbelievers, for them a sign, for you faith; for them an angel came down, for you the Holy Spirit; for them a creature was moved, for you Christ operates, the Lord of the creature.

23) Then one was cured; now all are healed, or at least one Christian people alone. For there is in some even a 'deceitful water';[9] the baptism of unbelievers does not heal, does not cleanse, but pollutes. The Jew washes pots and cups, as if insensible things could receive either blame or grace; but do you baptize this insensible cup of yours, in which your good deeds may shine, in which the splendor of your grace may gleam forth. Therefore, that pool also is by way of a figure, that you may believe that the power of God also descends into this fountain.[10]

(24) Finally, the paralytic was awaiting a man. Who was He but the Lord Jesus born of the Virgin, at whose coming no longer would the shadow heal men one by one, but the truth all men together? This, then, was the one whose descent was being waited for, of whom God the Father said to John the Baptist: 'Upon whom thou wilt see the Spirit descending from heaven and abiding upon Him, He it is who baptizes with the Holy Spirit,' of whom John has testified, saying: 'I saw the Spirit descending from heaven as a dove and remaining upon Him.'[11] Why did the Spirit here descend like a dove, except that you might see, except that you might know that the dove, also, which the just Noe sent forth from the ark, was likeness of this dove, that you might recognize the type of the mystery?

---

9 Cf. Jer. 15.18.
10 Cf. John 5.7.
11 John 1.33,32.

(25) Perhaps you may say: 'Since that was a true dove, which was sent forth, and this One descended like a dove, how do we say that it was a likeness in one place, and truth in another, when according to the Greeks it is written that the Spirit descended "in the likeness of a dove"?' But what is so true as the Divinity, which remains always?[12] Moreover, the creature cannot be the truth, but a likeness which is easily destroyed and changed. At the same time the simplicity of those who are baptized should not be in likeness but should be true. Therefore, the Lord also says: 'Be therefore wise as servants, and guileless as doves.'[13] Rightly, then, did He descend like a dove to admonish us that we should have the simplicity of a dove. Moreover, we read that the likeness is to be accepted as the truth both with regard to Christ: 'And was found in likeness as a man,' and with regard to God the Father: 'Nor have you seen His likeness.'[14]

Chapter 5

(26) Is there still some reason for you to doubt, when the Father clearly calls out to you in the Gospel, saying: 'This is my Son in whom I am well pleased'; the Son calls out, upon whom the Holy Spirit showed Himself as a dove; the Holy Spirit also calls out, who descended as a dove; David calls out: 'The voice of the Lord is upon the waters, the God of majesty has thundered, the Lord upon many waters';[1] when Scripture testifies to you that, in response to the prayers

12 Cf. Luke 3.22; John 1.33.
13 Matt. 10.16.
14 Cf. Phil. 2.7; John 5.37.

1 Ps. 28.3.

of Jerobaal, fire came down from heaven, and, again, when Elias prayed, fire was sent which consecrated the sacrifice.'[2]

(27) You should consider not the merits of persons, but the duties of priests. And if you regard merits, just as you consider Elias, regard, also, the merits of Peter or of Paul, who handed down to us this mystery which they had received from the Lord Jesus. A visible fire was sent to them that they might believe, an invisible one works for us who believe; for them it was as a figure, for us as a warning. Believe, then, that the Lord Jesus is present, invoked by the prayers of priests, who said: 'Where two or three shall be, there am I also.'[3] How much more does He deign to impart His presence there where the Church is, where the mysteries are!

(28) You have descended then [into the water]; remember what you replied [to the questions], that you believe in the Father, you believe in the Son, you believe in the Holy Spirit. You do not have in your response: 'I believe in a greater and a lesser and a lowest [person].' But you are bound by the same guarantee of your own voice to believe in the Son exactly as you believe in the Father, to believe in the Spirit exactly as you believe in the Son, with this only exception, that you confess that you must believe in the cross of the Lord Jesus alone.

Chapter 6

(29) After this, of course, you went up to the priest. Consider what followed. Was it not that which David says: 'Like the ointment on the head, that ran down upon the

---

2 Cf. Judges 6.19-21; 3 Kings 18.36-38.
3 Cf. Matt. 18.20.

beard, the beard of Aaron.'[1] This is the ointment of which Solomon also says:[2] 'Thy name is as ointment poured out; therefore young maidens have loved thee and drawn thee.' How many souls renewed today have loved Thee Lord Jesus, saying: 'Draw us after thee; let us run to the odor of thy garments,' that they may drink in the odor of the Resurrection.

(30) Understand why this is done: 'For the eyes of a wise man are in his head.'[3] Therefore, it flows upon the beard, that is, upon the grace of youth; therefore, 'upon the beard of Aaron,' that you may become 'a chosen race,'[4] sacerdotal, precious; for we all are anointed unto the kingdom of God and unto the priesthood with spiritual grace.

(31) You went up from the font; remember the lesson of the Gospel.[5] For our Lord Jesus in the Gospel washed the feet of His disciples. When He came to Simon Peter, and Peter said: 'Thou shalt never wash my feet,' he did not notice the mystery, and so refused the ministry, because he believed that the humility of the servant was being overtaxed, if he should patiently permit the ministry of the Lord. And the Lord answered him: 'If I do not wash your feet, you will not have a part with me.' On hearing this, Peter said: 'Lord not only my feet, but also my hands and my head.' The Lord replied: 'He who is washed needs only to wash his feet, but is wholly clean.'

(32) Peter was clean, but he should have washed his feet, for he had the sin of the first man by succession, when the serpent overthrew him and persuaded him to error. So his feet are washed, that hereditary sins may be taken away; for our own sins are remitted through baptism.

---

1 Cf. Ps. 132.2.
2 Cant. 1.2,3.
3 Eccle. 2.14.
4 Cf. 1 Peter 2.9.
5 Cf. John 13.8-10.

(33) At the same time note that the mystery itself consists in the ministry of humility. For He says: 'If I have
washed your feet, I the Lord and Master,' how much more
'ought you also to wash one another's feet.'[6] For since the
very Author of salvation has redeemed us through obedience,
how much more ought we, His servants, to offer the service
of humility and obedience.

Chapter 7

(34) After this you received white garments as a sign
that you had put off the covering of sins, and had put on the
chaste robes of innocence, of which the prophet said: 'Sprinkle
me with hyssop and I shall be cleansed, wash me and I shall
be whiter than snow.'[1] For he who is baptized is seen to have
been cleansed both according to the law and according to
the Gospel; according to the law, because Moses sprinkled
the blood of a lamb with a bunch of hyssop;[2] according to
the Gospel, because the garments of Christ were white as
snow,[3] when in the Gospel He showed the glory of His Resurrection. He whose sin is forgiven is made whiter than snow;
and so the Lord said through Isaias: 'If your sins be as
scarlet, I shall make them white as snow.'[4]

(35) The Church, having assumed these vestments through
the laver of regeneration, says in the Canticles:[5] 'I am black
but beautiful, O ye daughters of Jerusalem,' black through the

---

6 Cf. John 13.14.

1 Ps. 50.9.
2 Cf. Exod. 12.22.
3 Cf. Matt. 17.2.
4 Isa. 1.18.
5 Cant. 1.4; 8.5.

frailty of human condition, beautiful through grace; black, because I am made up of sinners, beautiful by the sacrament of faith. Perceiving these vestments, the daughters of Jerusalem in amazement say: 'Who is this that cometh up made white?' She was black; how was she suddenly made white?

(36) For the angels also doubted, when Christ rose again; the powers of heaven when they saw doubted that flesh was coming up into heaven. Finally they said: 'Who is this king of glory?' And when some said: 'Lift up the gates, ye princes, and be ye lifted up, ye everlasting gates, and the king of glory will come in,' others doubted, saying: 'Who is this king of glory?'[6] In Isaias, also, you have it that the powers of the heavens doubted and said: 'Who is this that cometh from Edom, the redness of his garments from Bosra, beautiful in his white robe?'[7]

(37) Christ, moreover, on seeing His Church in white vestments—for whom He himself, as you have it in the book of Zacharias the Prophet, had put on 'filthy garments'[8]—that is, a soul pure and washed by the laver of regeneration, says: 'Behold, thou art fair, my love, behold thou art fair, thy eyes are as a dove's,'[9] in whose likeness the Holy Spirit descended from heaven. Beautiful are the eyes, because, as we said above, He descended as a dove.

(38) And below: 'Thy teeth are as flocks of sheep, that are shorn, which came up from the washing, all with twins, and there is none barren among them; thy lips are as a scarlet lace.'[10] No ordinary praise is this, first by the pleasing comparison with the shorn sheep; for we know that goats feed

6 Cf. Ps. 23.7,8,7.
7 Isa. 63.1.
8 Zach. 3.3.
9 Cant. 4.1.
10 Cf. Cant. 4.2,3.

in high places without danger and securely take food in steep places; then, when they are shorn, are relieved of the superfluous. The Church is compared to a flock of these, having within herself the many virtues of souls, that put aside through the laver superfluous sins, that offer to Christ the mystic faith and the moral grace, that speak of the cross of the Lord Jesus.

(39) In these the Church is beautiful. Therefore, God the Word says to her: 'Thou art all fair, my love, and there is not a spot in thee,' because sin has been washed away; 'Come hither from Libanus, my spouse, come hither from Libanus; from the beginning of faith thou shalt pass over and pass on,'[11] because, renouncing the world, she passed over temporal things and passed on to Christ. And again God the Word says to her: 'Why art thou made beautiful and sweet, O love, in thy delights? Thy stature has become like the palm, and thy breasts as clusters of grapes.'[12]

(40) And the Church answers Him: 'Who shall give thee to me, my brother, sucking the breasts of my mother? I shall find thee without and shall kiss thee, and no one shall despise me. I shall take hold of thee and bring thee into my mother's house, and into the secret place of her who conceived me. You will teach me.'[13] Do you see how, delighted with the gift of grace she desires to attain to the interior mysteries and to consecrate all her affections to Christ? She still seeks, she still rouses His love and asks that it be roused for her by the daughters of Jerusalem, by whose grace, that is, the grace of faithful souls, she desires that her spouse be provoked to a richer love for her.

(41) Therefore, the Lord Jesus himself, invited by the

11 Cant. 4.7; cf. 4.1,8.
12 Cant. 7.6,7.
13 Cant. 8.1,2.

zeal of such great love, by the beauty of elegance and grace, because now no sins of defilement were among the baptized, says to the Church: 'Put me as a seal upon thy heart as a sign upon thy arm,'[14] that is, 'Thou art elegant, my beloved, thou art all fair, nothing is lacking to thee. Place me as a seal upon thy heart,' that thy faith may shine with the fulness of the sacrament. Let your works also shine and bring forth the image of God, according to whose image you were made. Let not your love be diminished by any persecution, a love which many waters, cannot shut off, nor rivers overflow.'

(42) So recall that you have received a spiritual seal, 'the spirit of wisdom and of understanding, the spirit of counsel and of fortitude, the spirit of knowledge and of piety, the spirit of holy fear,'[15] and preserve what you have received. God the Father sealed you; Christ the Lord confirmed you, and gave a pledge, the Spirit, in your hearts, as you have learned in the lesson of the Apostle.[16]

Chapter 8

(43) The cleansed people, rich in these insignia, hasten to the altar of Christ, saying: 'And I shall go unto the altar of God who gives joy to my youth.'[1] For the people, having put aside the defilements of ancient error, renewed in the youth of an eagle, hasten to approach that heavenly banquet.

14 Cf. Cant. 8.6.
15 Cf. Isa. 11.2-3.
16 Cf. 2 Cor. 5.5. In the early Church, just as in the Eastern Church today, confirmation was given immediately after baptism. The reference here seems to be to confirmation.

1 Cf. Ps. 42.4.

They come, therefore, and, seeing the sacred altar arranged, exclaim saying: 'Thou hast prepared a table in my sight.' David introduces these people as speaking when he says: 'The Lord feeds me and I shall lack nothing; in a place of good feeding there he placed me; he led me beside the water of refreshment.' And below: 'For though I should walk in the midst of the shadow of death, I shall fear no evil, for thou art with me. Thy rod and thy staff these have comforted me. Thou doest prepare a table in my sight, against those who trouble me. Thou hast anointed my head with oil, and thy cup inebriating me is wonderful.'[2]

(44) Now let us consider this, lest anyone perchance seeing the visible—since the things that are invisible are not seen and cannot be comprehended by human eyes—may by chance say: 'For the Jews God rained manna; He rained quail,[3] but for this His Church well-beloved by Him, there are these things which He has prepared, concerning which it has been said: "That eye has not seen nor ear heard, nor has it entered into the heart of man what things God has prepared for those who love Him." '[4] Therefore, lest anyone say this, we wish with the highest zeal to prove that both the sacraments of the Church are more ancient than those of the synagogue and more excellent than manna is.

(45) The lesson from Genesis, which has been read, teaches them to be more ancient. For the synagogue took its beginning from the law of Moses, but Abraham was far earlier. After he had conquered his enemies and had received

---

2 Cf. Ps. 22.1-5. The baptistery was apart from the church. Here the newly 'enlightened' were baptized and confirmed, after which they were led in solemn procession into the church to attend the celebration of the mysteries and to receive their first Communion.
3 Cf. Exod. 16.13.
4 1 Cor. 2.9.

back his own nephew, when he was enjoying victory, then Melchisedech met him and brought forth those things, which Abraham venerated and received.[5] Abraham did not bring them forth, but Melchisedech, who is introduced 'without father, without mother, having neither beginning of days nor end, but like to the Son of God,' of whom Paul says to the Hebrews: 'He continues a priest for ever,'[6] who in the Latin version is called King of justice, King of peace.

(46) Do you not recognize who this is? Can a man be a king of justice, when he himself is scarcely just; can he be a king of peace, when he can scarcely be peaceable?—'Without a mother' according to Divinity, because He was begotten of God the Father, of one substance with the Father; 'without a father' according to the Incarnation, because He was born of the Virgin, 'having neither beginning nor end,' for He himself is 'the beginning and the end' of all things, 'the first and the last.' Therefore, the sacrament which you have received is not a gift of man but of God, brought forth by Him who blessed Abraham, the father of faith, him whose grace and deeds you admire.

(47) It has been proven that the sacraments of the Church are more ancient; now realize that they are more powerful. In very fact it is a marvelous thing that God rained manna on the fathers, and they were fed by daily nourishment from heaven. Therefore, it is said: 'Man has eaten the bread of angels.'[7] But yet all those who ate that bread died in the desert, but this food which you receive, this 'living bread, which came down from heaven,' furnishes the substance of

---

5 Gen. 14.14-18.
6 Heb. 7.3.
7 Ps. 77.25.

eternal life, and whoever eats this bread 'will not die forever'; for it is the body of Christ.[8]

(48) Consider now whether the bread of angels is more excellent or the flesh of Christ, which indeed is the body of life. That manna was from heaven, this is above the heavens; that was of heaven, this of the Lord of the heavens; that was subject to corruption, if it were kept for a second day, this is foreign to every corruption, because whosoever shall taste in a holy manner shall not be able to feel corruption. For them water flowed from the rock, for you blood [flowed] from Christ; water satisfied them for the hour, blood satiates you for eternity. The Jew drinks and is thirsty; when you drink, you will not be able to be thirsty; that was in a shadow, this in truth.

(49) If that which you admire is a shadow, how great is that whose shadow you admire? Hear that what came to pass among the fathers is a shadow. It is said: 'For they drank of the rock that followed, and the rock was Christ; but with many of them God was not well pleased; for they were laid low in the desert. Now these things came to pass in a figure for us.'[9] You recognize the more excellent things; for the light is more powerful than the shade, truth than figure, the body of its author than manna from heaven.

Chapter 9

(50) Perhaps you may say: 'I see something else; how do you tell me that I receive the Body of Christ?' This still remains for us to prove. Therefore, we make use of examples

---

8 Cf. John 6.49-58.
9 1 Cor. 10.4-6.

great enough to prove that this is not what nature formed but what benediction consecrated, and that the power of benediction is greater than that of nature, because even nature itself is changed by benediction.

(51) Moses held a rod; he cast it down and it became a serpent; again, he took hold of the tail of the serpent and it returned to the nature of a rod. You see then that by the grace of the Prophet the nature of the serpent and that of the rod were interchanged twice. The rivers of Egypt were flowing with a pure stream of water; suddenly, from the veins of the springs blood began to burst forth; there was no drinking water in the rivers. Again at the prayer of the Prophet the blood of the rivers ceased; the nature of the waters returned. The people of the Hebrews were hemmed in on all sides, shut off on the one side by the Egyptians, enclosed on the other by the sea. Moses raised his rod, the water divided and hardened like walls, and a way for travel appeared between the waters.[1] The Jordan turning back contrary to nature returned to the source of its stream. Is it not clear that the nature of the waters of the sea and of the course of the river was changed?[2] The people of the fathers were thirsty; Moses touched the rock; and water flowed forth from the rock. Did not grace work contrary to nature for the rock to throw forth water which its nature did not have:[3] The Mara was a very bitter stream, so that the people, although thirsty, were unable to drink it. Moses threw a piece of wood into the water, and the nature of the waters laid aside its bitterness, which grace when suddenly infused tempered.[4] In the time of Eliseus the Prophet, one of the sons of the prophets lost

---

1 Cf. Exod. 4.1-4; 7.19-21; 14.21-22.
2 Cf. Josue 3.16.
3 Cf. Exod. 17.5-6.
4 Cf. Exod. 15.22-25.

the head of his axe, and it sank immediately. He who had
lost his axe sought the help of Eliseus; Eliseus also threw
a piece of wood into the water, and the axe floated.[5] Surely
we realize that this also happened contrary to nature, for the
substance of iron is heavier than the liquid of waters.

(52) So we notice that grace is capable of accomplishing
more than is nature, and yet thus far we have mentioned
only the benediction of a prophet. But if the benediction of
man had such power as to change nature, what do we say
of divine consecration itself, in which the very words of our
Lord and Saviour function? For that sacrament, which you
receive, is effected by the words of Christ. But if the words
of Elias had such power as to call down fire from heaven,
will not the words of Christ have power enough to change
the nature of the elements? You have read about the works of
the world: 'that He spoke and they were done; He commanded and they were created.'[6] So, cannot the words of
Christ, which were able to make what was not out of nothing,
change those things that are into the things that were not?
For it is not of less importance to give things new natures
than to change natures.

(53) But why do we use arguments? Let us use His own examples, and by the mysteries of the Incarnation let us establish
the truth of the mysteries. Did the process of nature precede
when the Lord Jesus was born of Mary? If we seek the usual
course, a woman after mingling with a man usually conceives.
It is clear then that the Virgin conceived contrary to the
course of nature. And this body which we make is from the
Virgin. Why do you seek here the course of nature in the body
of Christ, when the Lord Jesus himself was born of the

5 Cf. 3 Kings 18.36-38.
6 Cf. Ps. 148.5

Virgin contrary to nature? Surely it is the true flesh of Christ, which was crucified, which was buried; therefore it is truly the sacrament of that flesh.

(54) The Lord Jesus himself declares: 'This is my body.'[7] Before the benediction of the heavenly words another species is mentioned; after the consecration the body is signified. He Himself speaks of His blood. Before the consecration it is mentioned as something else; after the consecration it is called blood. And you say 'Amen,' that is, 'It is true.' What the mouth speaks, let the mind within confess; what words utter, let the heart feel.

(55) Christ then feeds His Church on these sacraments, by which the substance of the soul is made strong, and, seeing the continuous advancement of her grace, rightly says to her: 'How beautiful thy breasts have become, my sister, my spouse, how beautiful they have become from wine, and the odor of thy garments as the odor of Libanus. A garden enclosed is my sister, my spouse, a garden enclosed, a fountain sealed.'[8] By this he signifies that the mystery should remain sealed with you, lest it be violated by the works of an evil life and by the adulteration of chastity; lest it be divulged to whom it is not fitting; lest it be spread abroad among infidels by garrulous conversation. So the custody of your faith should be good, that the integrity of your life and silence may continue undefiled.

(56) Therefore, the Church also, preserving the depth of the heavenly mysteries, hurls back the severe storms of the winds, and invites the sweetness of blooming grace; and knowing that her garden cannot displease Christ, she calls to the Bridegroom, saying: 'Arise, O northwind, and come, O south-

---

7 Matt. 26.26; Mark 14.22; Luke 22.19; 1 Cor. 11.24.
8 Cf. Cant. 4.10-12.

wind, blow through my garden and let my ointments flow down. Let my brother go down into his garden and eat the fruit of his apple-trees.'[9] For it has good trees and fruitful, which have touched their roots in the water of the sacred fountain[10] and have burst forth into good fruits with a growth of new richness, so as not to be cut now by the axe of the Prophet, but to abound with the fruitfulness of the Gospel.

(57) Finally, the Lord also, delighted with their fertility, replies: 'I have entered into my garden, my sister, my spouse. I have gathered my myrrh with my spices; I have eaten my food with my honey; I have drunk my drink with my milk.'[11] Understand, faithful one, why I have said 'food' and 'drink.' This, however, is not doubtful, that in us He himself eats and drinks, just as in us you read that He says that He is in prison.

(58) Therefore, the Church also, seeing so much grace, urges her sons, urges her neighbors to come together to the sacraments, saying: 'Eat, my neighbors, and drink and be inebriated, my brethren.'[12] What we eat, what we drink, the Holy Spirit expresses to you elsewhere, saying: 'Taste and see that the Lord is sweet: Blessed is the man who trusts in Him.'[13] Christ is in that sacrament, because the body is Christ's. So the food is not corporeal but spiritual. Therefore the Apostle also says of its type: 'Our fathers ate the spiritual food and drank the spiritual drink,'[14] for the body of God is a spiritual body; the body of Christ is the body of the Divine Spirit, for the Spirit is Christ, as we read: 'The Spirit before our face is Christ the Lord.'[15] And in the Epistles of

9 Cf. Cant. 4.16-51.
10 Cf. Vergil, *Georgics* 4.32.
11 Cf. Cant. 5.1.
12 *Ibid.*
13 Cf. Ps. 33.9.
14 Cf. 1 Cor. 10.3.
15 Cf. Lam. 4.20.

Peter we have: 'And Christ has died for you.'[16] Finally, that food strengthens our heart, and that drink 'rejoices the heart of man,'[17] as the Prophet has recalled.

(59) Thus, then, having obtained everything, let us know that we have been regenerated. Let us not say: 'How were we regenerated? We have not entered into the womb of our mother and been born again? I do not recognize the course of nature?'—But no order of nature is here, where there is the excellence of grace. Finally the course of nature does not always produce generation; we confess that Christ the Lord was conceived of a Virgin and we deny the order of nature. For Mary did not conceive of man, but received of the Holy Spirit in her womb, as Matthew says: 'She was found with child of the Holy Spirit.'[18] If, then, the Holy Spirit coming upon the Virgin effected conception, and effected the work of generation, surely there must be no doubt that the Spirit, coming upon the Font, or upon those who obtain baptism, effects the truth of regeneration.

---

16 Cf. 1 Peter 2.21.
17 Cf. Ps. 103.15.
18 Matt. 1.18.

THE HOLY SPIRIT

INTRODUCTION

HE THREE BOOKS of *The Holy Spirit* are a sequel to *The Faith,* and the two works are sometimes considered as one under the title of *The Trinity.* However, the two are definitely distinct works. *The Faith* was written in 378, and it was sometime after this that Emperor Gratian wrote to Ambrose requesting that he write something on the Holy Spirit. In reply, Ambrose asked for time to consider the matter. In the meantime also, Ambrose in 380 attended a council held by Damasus in Rome, where the chief topic of discussion was the orthodox faith concerning the Spirit. At this council also the heresy of the Macedonians, the so-called 'Contenders against the Spirit,' was condemned. Finally, probably in April, 381, Ambrose published his work in three books on the Holy Spirit.

The Holy Spirit is an attack on the Macedonians, who were so called after Macedonius, the semi-Arian bishop of Constantinople whose doctrine on the Holy Spirit they followed. Macedonius taught that the Holy Spirit 'had no claim to the divine honors which were attributed to the Son, being but a minister and a servant, as the holy angels may without

31

offence be called.'[1] With regard to the Second Person of the Trinity, the Macedonians might or might not be Arians.

In *The Holy Spirit,* St. Ambrose, who knew Greek very well, drew on such Greek sources as St. Basil, Didymus, and others. The Greek East had already been obliged to face this heresy and thus had accumulated a rather extensive literature on the subject. It was natural, therefore, for Ambrose to make use of it.

St. Jerome, however, took a dim view of St. Ambrose as a literary artist. In his work on famous men (124), Jerome says: 'Ambrose, Bishop of Milan, is writing to the present day. Of whom, since he is alive, I will reserve my judgment, lest I be blamed either for flattery or for speaking the truth!' St. Ambrose and his *Holy Spirit* are undoubtedly the author and work severely criticized by St. Jerome as quoted by Rufinus in his *Apology,*[2] where he compares St. Ambrose with a daw decked in another bird's plumage, and charges Ambrose with writing 'bad things in Latin taken from good things in Greek.' He characterized the book itself as 'flaccid and spiritless, sleek and pretty, decorated with purple patches, but defective in its logic, and lacking that restrained and manly force which compels the assent of the reader even against his will.'

St. Jerome is, of course, most unreasonably severe. Rufinus strongly defended St. Ambrose, saying: 'The saintly Ambrose wrote his book on the Holy Spirit not in words only but with his own blood, for he offered his life blood to his persecutors, and shed it within himself, though God preserved his life for future labors.' Finally, St. Augustine's testimony is most worthy of note. He says: 'St. Ambrose, when treating of the

---

1 Sozomen, *H.E.* 4.27; Cf. Socrates, *H.E.* 2.45.
2 *Apol. adv. Hieron.* 2.23-25.

deep subject of the Holy Spirit, and showing that He is equal with the Father and the Son, makes use of a simple style of discourse; inasmuch as his subject required not the embellishments of language, but proofs to move the minds of his readers.'[3]

An objective and impartial evaluation of St. Ambrose's work on the Holy Spirit will show that, while he borrowed extensively from his Greek sources, he did so with genuine discrimination. He not only selected his material carefully, but changed the order and arrangement to suit his purpose, and at times added much material of his own. To be sure, his logic may be regarded as less cogent than that of Didymus, and he is guilty of redundancies and other stylistic faults, but, as Dudden says, 'the treatise furnishes a clear, straightforward statement of the Catholic doctrine of the Holy Spirit, and is peculiarly important as the first attempt made in the West to deal systematically and exhaustively with this great topic.'[4]

---

3 *Christian Doctrine* 4.21.
4 St. Ambrose, *His Life and Times* 198.

THE HOLY SPIRIT

Book I

Prologue

WHEN JEROBAAL, AS WE READ, was beating out the harvest of wheat with a rod under an oak tree,[1] he received a message from God to free the people of God from the power of strangers. Nor is it any wonder that he was chosen for grace, since already then, being established under the shadow of the holy cross and of the adorable wisdom in the predestined mystery of the future Incarnation, he was producing perceptible grains of rich corn from their hiding places, and was separating the elect of the saints from the sweepings of the empty chaff. For these elect, disciplined by the rod of truth, laying aside the superfluities of the old man together with his actions, are thus gathered in the Church as in a wine-press; for the Church is the wine-press

---

1 Cf. Judges 6.11; also, *ibid.* 6.32: 'From that day Gedeon was called Jerobaal, because Joas had said: Let Baal revenge himself on him that hath cast down his altar.'

35

of the eternal fountain, in which the fruit of the heavenly vine overflows.

(2) And Gedeon, moved by this message, when he heard that, although thousands of people failed, the Lord would save his people from the enemy by one man,[2] offered the young of goats, according to the precept of the angel, and placed unleavened bread upon the rock, and covered them with broth, and, as soon as the angel of God touched these with the tip of the rod which he was carrying, fire burst forth from the rock; and so the sacrifice which was being offered was consumed.[3] By this sign it seems to have been declared that the rock possessed the figure of the body of Christ, because it is written: 'And they drank of the spiritual rock that followed them; and the rock was Christ.'[4] This surely referred not to His divinity but to His flesh, which flowed over the hearts of the thirsting people with the perpetual stream of His blood.

(3) Already at that time then it was declared in a mystery that the Lord Jesus in His flesh, when crucified, would destroy not only the sins of the doers but also the desires of souls. For the flesh of the kid is referred to the fault of the deed, the broth to the enticements of desires, as it is written: 'For the people burned with excessive desire, and said: Who shall give us flesh to eat'?[5] That the angel put forth the rod, and touched the rock, from which fire came forth,[6] shows that the flesh of the Lord, filled with the Divine Spirit, would burn away all the sins of mankind. Therefore, the Lord also says: 'I am come to send fire on the earth.'[7]

---

2 Cf. Judges 6.14.
3 Cf. Judges 6.19-21.
4 1 Cor. 10.4.
5 Num. 11.4.
6 Judges 6.21.
7 Luke 12.49.

(4) So the man who is learned and has foreknowledge of the future observes the heavenly mysteries, and therefore, according to the message from God, slew a bullock destined by his father for the idols, and he himself sacrificed another bullock of seven years to God.[8] By doing this he revealed very manifestly that after the coming of the Lord all the sacrifices of the Gentiles are to be abolished, and only the sacrifice of the Lord's passion is to be offered to God for the redemption of the people. For that bullock was in figure Christ, in whom, as Isaias said,[9] dwelt the fullness of the seven spiritual virtues. This bullock Abraham also offered when he saw the day of the Lord and was glad.[10] He it is who was offered now in the figure of a kid, now in that of a sheep, now in that of a bullock. Of a kid, because He is a sacrifice for sins; of a sheep, because He is a willing offering; of a bullock, because He is a victim without stain.

(5) Holy Gedeon then foresaw the mystery. Then he selected three hundred for battle that he might show that not by the number of the multitude but by the sacrament of the cross was the world to be freed from the attack of more serious enemies. And yet, although he was brave and faithful, he asked of the Lord still fuller proofs of future victory, saying: 'If thou wilt save Israel by my hand, as thou hast said O Lord, behold, I put this fleece of wool on the floor; if there be dew on the fleece, and it be dry on all the ground, I shall know that by my hand, as thou hast said, thou wilt deliver Israel. And it was so.' But afterwards he added that dew should again flow forth upon the whole earth, and that dryness be on the wool.[11]

---

8 Cf. Judges 6.25.
9 Cf. Isa. 11.2.
10 Cf. John 8.56.
11 Cf. Judges 7.6; 6.36-38.

(6) Someone asks, perchance, whether he does not seem to be as it were incredulous, who, although informed by many proofs, asked for still more. But how can he seem to have asked in doubt and uncertainty who was speaking mysteries? He was not then in doubt but careful less we be in doubt. For how could he be in doubt whose prayer was effective? Moreover, how could he have approached battle without anxiety, if he had not understood the message from God; for the dew on the fleece was the faith among the Jews, because the words of God descended like dew.[12]

(7) Therefore, when the whole world became withered by the unfruitful heat of Gentile superstition, then was that dew of heavenly visitation upon the fleece. But after the lost sheep of the house of Israel[13] (from whom I think that the figure of the Jewish fleece was foreshadowed), after those sheep, I say, refused the fountain of living water,[14] the dew of the moistening faith dried up in the breasts of the Jews, and that divine fountain turned away its course into the hearts of the Gentiles. Hence it is that now the whole world is moistened by the dew of faith, but the Jews indeed have lost their prophets and counselors.

(8) And it is no wonder that they undergo the dryness of unbelief, whom the Lord deprived of the fertility of the prophetic shower, saying: 'I shall command my clouds not to rain upon that vineyard.'[15] For there is the salutary rain of the prophetic cloud, as David also has said: 'He shall come down like rain upon the fleece and as showers falling gently upon the earth.'[16] This rain the divine Scriptures promised

---

12 Cf. Deut. 32.2.
13 Cf. Matt. 15.24.
14 Cf. Jer. 2.13.
15 Cf. Isa. 5.6.
16 Ps. 71.6.

us for the whole world to water the earth with the divine dew of the Spirit at the coming of the Lord and Saviour. So now the Lord has come, the rain also has come, the Lord has come bringing with Him the heavenly drops; and so now we drink, who before were thirsty, and we drink that divine Spirit with an interior draught.

(9) So holy Gedeon foresaw this, that the nations of the gentiles also were about to drink of the true and spiritual dew by the reception of the faith, and so he inquired more diligently; for the caution of the saints is necessary, since indeed Josue, the son of Nun, also asked, when he saw the leader of the heavenly host: 'Art thou one of ours or of our adversaries?'[17] lest perchance he might be deceived by some tricks of the adversary.

(10) Yet not without significance is the fact that he placed the fleece neither in a field nor in a meadow, but placed it in a threshing floor: 'For the harvest is great, but the laborers are few,'[18] because through faith in the Lord there was to be a harvest fruitful in virtues.

(11) Nor was this without significance, that he dried the fleece of the Jews, and poured its dew into a basin, so that it was filled with water, yet he himself did not wash his feet with that water.[19] The prerogative of so great a mystery was due another. He was being awaited who alone could wash away the squalor of all. Gedeon was not so great as to claim this mystery for himself. For not Gedeon but 'the Son of man came not to be ministered unto but to minister.'[20] And so let us learn in whom these mysteries are seen to be fulfilled. Not in holy Jerobaal, for they were still beginnings.

---

17 Jos. 5.13.
18 Luke 10.2.
19 Cf. Judges 6.39,40.
20 Matt. 20.28.

Therefore, the Gentiles were conquered, for the dryness was still upon the Gentiles; therefore, Israel conquered, because the dew then remained on the fleece.

(12) Let us come to the Gospel of God. I find the Lord divesting Himself of His garments, and girding Himself with a towel, pouring water into a basin, washing the feet of His disciples.[21] This water was that heavenly dew; this was prophesied: that the Lord Jesus would wash the feet of His disciples with that heavenly dew. And now let the feet of our souls be extended. The Lord Jesus wishes to wash our feet also, for not to Peter alone but to each one of the faithful does He say: 'If I wash not thy feet, thou shalt have no part with me.'[22]

(13) Come, therefore, O Lord Jesus, divest Yourself of Your garments which You have put on for my sake. Be You naked, that You may clothe us with your mercy. Gird Yourself with a towel for our sakes, that You may gird us with Your gift of immortality. Pour water into the basin; wash not only our feet but also the head, and not only the footprints of the body, but also of the mind. I wish to put off all the filth of our frailty, so that I, too, may say: 'I have put off my garment, how shall I put it on? I have washed my feet, how shall I defile them?'[23]

(14) How great is that majesty! As a servant, You wash the feet of Your disciples, as God You pour dew from heaven. Not only do you wash the feet, but You also invite us to recline with You, and You exhort us by the example of Your graciousness saying: 'You call me Master, and Lord; and you say well; for so I am. If I then, being Lord and Master,

21 Cf. John 13.4,5.
22 Cf. John 13.8.
23 Cant. 5.3.

have washed your feet; you also ought to wash one another's feet.'[24]

(15) I also, then, wish to wash the feet of my brethren; I wish to fulfil the mandate of the Lord; I do not wish to be ashamed of myself nor to disdain what He Himself did first. Good is the mystery of humility, because, while I wash the filth of others, I wash away my own. But not all were able to drink in this mystery. Indeed, Abraham also wished to wash feet, but because of a feeling of hospitality.[25] Gedeon, too, wished to wash the feet of the angel of the Lord who appeared to him;[26] but he wished to do this to one; he wished to do it as one who was offering obedience, not as one who was offering fellowship. This is a great mystery, which no one knows. Then He said to Peter: 'What I do thou knowest not now; but thou shalt know hereafter.'[27] This, I say, is a divine mystery, which even they who have washed will need. It is not then the simple water of a heavenly mystery, by which we succeed in deserving to have a part with Christ.

(16) There is also a kind of water which we pour into the basin of our soul, water from the fleece and from the Book of Judges, water from the Book of Psalms.[28] The water is the dew of the heavenly message. Therefore, Lord Jesus, let this water come into my soul, into my flesh, that by the moisture of this rain the valleys of our minds and the fields of our inmost heart may grow green.[29] Let Your drops come upon me, besprinkling grace and immortality. Wash the steps of my mind, that I may not sin again. Wash off the heel

---

24 John 13.13,14.
25 Cf. Gen. 18.4.
26 This reference cannot be identified.
27 John 13.7.
28 Cf. Ps. 22.2.
29 Cf. Ps. 71.6.

of my spirit,[30] that I may be able to abolish the curse, that
I may not feel the bite of the serpent on my inner foot,[31] but,
as You Yourself have ordered Your followers that I may
have the power with uninjured foot to tread upon the serpents
and scorpions.[32] You have redeemed the world; redeem the
soul of one sinner.

(17) This is the special prerogative of Your compassion,
by which You have redeemed the world through individuals.
Elias was sent to one widow, Eliseus cleansed one;[33] You,
O Lord Jesus, have today cleansed a thousand here for us.
How many in the city of Rome, how many in Alexandria,
how many in Antioch, how many also in Constantinople!
For Constantinople also has now received the word of God,
and has received the evident proofs of Your judgment. For
as long as she cherished the poisons of the Arians shut up in
her vitals, disturbed by wars with neighbors, her walls re-
echoed with the arms of the enemy. But as soon as she
rejected those alien from the faith, she saw the enemy himself, the judge of kings, whom she was always accustomed
to fear, surrender; she received him as a suppliant; she
buried him when he died; she possesses him entombed.[34]
How many then also have you cleansed at Constantinople,
how many finally today in the whole world.

(18) Damasus did not cleanse; Peter did not cleanse;
Ambrose did not cleanse; Gregory did not cleanse;[35] for ours

---

30 Cf. Gen. 3.15.
31 That is, the soul.
32 Cf. Luke 10.19.
33 Cf. 3 Kings 17.9; 4 Kings 5.14.
34 Athanaricus, king or *judex* (judge) of the West Goths in Dacia.
   Emperor Valens defeated him in 369.
35 Damasus of Rome, Peter of Alexandria (the news of whose death had
   probably not yet reached Milan), Gregory of Constantinople, and
   Ambrose of Milan.

are the services, but Yours are the sacraments. For it is not of human power to confer the divine; but it is Your gift, O Lord, and the Father's, who spoke through the Prophets, saying: 'I will pour out my spirit upon all flesh; and your sons and their daughters shall prophesy.'[36] This is the heavenly dew in figure; these those free rains, as we read: 'God separating free rain for His inheritance.[37] For the Holy Spirit is not subject to a foreign power or law, but is arbiter of His own freedom, dividing all things according to the authority of His own will, as we read, to each one, as He wills.[38]

Chapter 1

(19) So the Holy Spirit is not in the midst of all, but above all things. For, since, most merciful Emperor, you have been so fully instructed about the Son of God that you yourself may now teach, I shall not put you off any longer since you desire and demand to hear more explicitly about Him,[1] especially since you lately showed that you were so pleased by such an assertion that without any urging you ordered the Basilica to be restored to the Church.

(20) So, then, we hold the grace of your faith and the reward of ours; for we cannot say otherwise than that this grace was of the Holy Spirit, that, while all were unaware of it, you suddenly returned the Basilica. This, I say, is the gift, this the work of the Holy Spirit, who indeed was then preached by us, but was operating in you.

(21) Nor do I deplore the losses of the earlier time, since

36 Joel 2.28.
37 Cf. Ps. 97.10.
38 Cf. 1 Cor. 12.10.

1 The Holy Spirit.

that sequestration of the Basilica brought a kind of interest on a loan. For you sequestrated the Basilica that you might give proof of faith. Thus your piety fulfilled its purpose, which so sequestrated as to prove, and so proved as to restore. I have not lost the fruit, and I hold your judgment, and it has been made clear to all that in a kind of diversity of action you have never had a diversity of opinion. It has been made clear to all, I say, that when you sequestrated it had not been *your* deed, and that it was *your* deed when you restored.

(22) First, then, let us begin with the matters of less importance, that our treatise may ascend by certain steps, as it were, so that those who do not bear the faith may be influenced at least by reason. For they can say in the beginning: 'We do not say that the Spirit serves.' But when they say that Christ serves, how can they deny this with respect to the Spirit? But if they agree that Christ was in the form of a servant according to flesh, it is meet and fitting. So if according to His divinity Christ does not serve, the Spirit also does not serve. But if the Spirit does not serve, but all things serve, then above all things is the Spirit, who does not serve as all things do.

(23) Now this very matter which we have mentioned, let us establish by evidence. The beginning of the discussion is that all things serve. Moreover, it is clear that all things serve, since it is written: 'All things serve thee.'[2] The Spirit said this through the Prophet. He did not say: 'We serve' but 'they serve you,' that you might believe that He himself is excepted from serving. Therefore, since all things serve, and the Spirit does not serve, surely the Holy Spirit is not among all things.

---

2 Ps. 118.91.

(24) For if we say that the Holy Spirit is among all things, surely when we read that 'the Spirit searcheth the profound things of God,'[3] we deny that God the Father is above all things. For since the Spirit is from God, and is the Spirit of His mouth, how can we say that the Holy Spirit is among all things, when God is above all things, whose is the Spirit, certainly possessing full perfection and perfect power?

(25) But lest they think that the Apostle erred, let them accept whom he has followed as the authority of this belief. For the Lord in the Gospel said: 'When the Paraclete shall come, whom I will send you from the Father, the Spirit of truth, who proceedeth from the Father, he shall give testimony of me.'[4] So the Holy Spirit proceeds from the Father, and bears witness of the Son. A witness, both faithful and true, bears witness also of the Father, than whom nothing is more full for the expression of the divine majesty, nothing more clear regarding the unity of divine power, since the Spirit knows the same as the Son, who is the witness and the inseparable sharer of the Father's secrets.

(26) And so He excluded the society and the multitude of the creatures from the knowledge of God, but by not excluding the Holy Spirit He showed that He is not an associate of creatures. Thus that, too, which is read in the Gospel, 'No man hath seen God at any time; the only begotten Son who is in the bosom of the Father, he hath declared Him,'[5] pertains to the exclusion of the Holy Spirit. How has He not seen God who searcheth even the profound things of God? How has He not seen God who knows the things that are of

3 1 Cor. 2.10.
4 John 15.26.
5 John 1.18.

God.'[6] How has He not seen God who is of God? So, since it is laid down that 'no man hath seen God at any time,' but the Spirit has seen Him, surely the Spirit is excepted. He, then, is above all things who is excepted from all things.

Chapter 2

(27) Holy Emperor, the reason seems to be full of piety, but it does not seem so to the impious. Notice, then, what they labor to do. For the heretics are accustomed to say that the Holy Spirit is to be numbered among all things for this reason, because it is written of the Son of God: 'All things were made through Him.'[1]

(28) How badly is the deliberation confused which does not cling to the truth and is involved in a distorted order of statements! For this, then, would be valid, that they might say that the Holy Spirit is among all things, if they should prove that He was made. For Scripture says that all things that were made were made through the Son, but, since the Holy Spirit is not taught to have been made, surely He cannot be proved to be among all things, who was neither made nor created like all things. To me, then, this testimony is of benefit on two counts: that He is proved to be above all things because he is not made, and that because he is above all things that He is seen not to have been made, and is not to be numbered among those things which have been made.

(29) But if anyone, because the Evangelist stated that all things were made through the Word, does not except the Holy Spirit (although the Spirit of God, saying in John:

6 Cf. 1 Cor. 2.10.

1 John 1.3.

'All things were made by Him,' did not say: 'We were made all things,' when surely the Lord Himself showed that the Spirit of God spoke in the Evangelists, saying: 'For it is not you that will speak, but the spirit of your Father, that speaketh in you'[2]), nevertheless, if anyone, as I have said, does not except the Holy Spirit in this place, but numbers Him among all things, then neither does he except the Son of God in that place where the Apostle said: 'Yet to us, there is but one God, the Father, of whom are all things, and we through him.' But that he may know that the Son is not among all things, let him read what follows; for when he says: 'And one Lord Jesus Christ, through whom are all things,'[3] surely he excepts the Son of God from all things, who also excepted the Father.

(30) Moreover, it is of the same impiety to disparage either the Father or the Son or the Holy Spirit. For he does not believe in the Father who does not believe in the Son; nor does he believe in the Son of God who does not believe in the Spirit, nor can faith stand without the rule of truth. For he who has begun to deny the unity of power in the Father and the Son and the Holy Spirit surely cannot prove a divided faith there where there is no division. So, since the unity of piety is to believe well, the unity of impiety also is to believe badly.

(31) Thus, those who think that the Holy Spirit should be numbered among all things, because they read that all things were made through the Son, surely think also that the Son is to be numbered among all things, because they read: 'All things are of God.'[4] Consequently, moreover, they do not separate the Father from all things who do not separate the

---

2 Cf. Matt. 10.20.
3 1 Cor. 8.6.
4 2 Cor. 5.18.

Son from all creatures, because, just as all things are of the Father, so, too, are all things through the Son. The Apostle, foreseeing in the Spirit, said this very thing, lest he should seem to have placed the Son among all things, at least in the eyes of the impious who had heard that the Son had said: 'That which my Father hath given me is greater than all.'[5]

Chapter 3

(32) But perhaps some one may say: 'For what reason, when the Apostle said all things are of the Father, and all things through the Son, was he silent about the Holy Spirit,' and from this he may desire to establish a prejudice. But if he persists in malicious interpretation, in how many places will he find the power of the Holy Spirit declared, where Scripture has expressed nothing about either the Father or the Son, but has left it to be understood!

(40)[1] When, then, the grace of the Spirit is proclaimed, is that of God the Father or of the Only-begotten Son denied? This is not so, because, just as the Father is in the Son and the Son in the Father, so also he says: 'The charity of God is poured out into our hearts through the Holy Ghost who is given to us.'[2] And just as he who is blessed in Christ is blessed in the name of the Father and of the Son and of the Holy Spirit because there is one name, one power so, too, when some divine operation either of the Father or of the Son or of the Spirit is described, it is referred not only to the Holy

---

5 John 10.29.

1 The sequence of chapters continues thus in the editions, omitting eight numbers.
2 Rom. 5.5.

Spirit but also to the Father and to the Son, and it is referred not only to the Father but also to the Son and to the Spirit.

(41) Then the Ethiopian eunuch of the Queen Candace, when baptized in Christ,[3] obtained the full mystery. And those who denied that they knew the Holy Spirit, although they said that they were baptized in the baptism of John, were baptized afterwards, because John baptized unto the remission of sins in the name of the coming Jesus, not in his own name.[4] And so they did not know the Spirit, because they had not received baptism in the name of Christ, as John was accustomed to baptize. For John, although he did not baptize in the Spirit, nevertheless preached both Christ and the Spirit. Then when he was asked whether perchance he himself was Christ, he replied: 'I baptize you in water, but He will come stronger than I, whose shoes I am not worthy to carry; He will baptize you in the Holy Spirit and in fire.'[5] These, therefore, because they had not been baptized in the name of Christ nor with the faith of the Holy Spirit, were not able to receive the sacrament of baptism.

(42) And so they were baptized in the name of Jesus Christ,[6] and baptism was not repeated among these, but was received for the first time; for there is one baptism.[7] Moreover, where there is not the full sacrament of baptism, there is not considered to be a beginning or any kind of baptism. But baptism is full, if you confess the Father and the Son and the Holy Spirit. If you deny one, you will ruin the whole. And just as when

---

3 Cf. Acts 8.27.
4 Cf. Acts 19.2-5.
5 Cf. John 1.26-27; Matt. 3.11; Luke 4.16.
6 Ambrose is here merely referring to the passage in the Acts as implying Christian baptism. He is not to be taken, as some have done, as teaching that baptism is valid when the name of Christ alone is mentioned.
7 Cf. Eph. 4.5.

you comprehend one in words, either Father or Son or Holy Spirit, yet do not deny in faith either the Father or the Son or the Holy Spirit, the sacrament of faith is full, so also, although you mention the Father and the Son and the Holy Spirit, and reduce the power of the Father or of the Son or of the Holy Spirit, the entire mystery is void. Then, too, those very ones who had said: 'We have not heard whether there be a Holy Ghost,'[8] were afterwards baptized in the name of the Lord Jesus Christ. And this abounded unto grace, because they now knew the Holy Spirit by Paul's preaching.

(43)   Nor should it seem contradictory that, although even afterwards there was silence regarding the Spirit, yet there was belief in Him, and what had been unmentioned by words was expressed by faith. For when it is said 'In the name of our Lord Jesus Christ,' the mystery is completed by the unity of the name, and the Spirit is not separated from the baptism of Christ; for John baptized in penance, Christ in the Spirit.[9]

(44)   Now let us consider whether, just as we read that the sacrament of baptism is full in the name of Christ, so also, when only the Spirit is named, nothing is lacking to the fullness of the mystery. Let us follow through the argument that he who has said One has signified the Trinity. If you say Christ, you have designated also God the Father by whom the Son was anointed, and Him Himself who was anointed, the Son, and the Holy Spirit with whom He was anointed. For it is written: 'This Jesus of Nazareth, whom God anointed with the Holy Spirit.'[10] And if you say the Father, you have indicated alike both His Son and the Spirit of His mouth, if, moreover, you also comprehend this in your heart. And if

---

8 Acts 19.2.
9 Cf. Acts 19.4,6.
10 Cf. Acts 10.38.

you say the Spirit, you have named also God the Father, from whom the Spirit proceeds, and the Son, because the Spirit is also of the Son.

(45) Whereby authority may be joined with reason, Scripture indicates that we can also rightly be baptized in the Spirit, when the Lord says: 'But you shall be baptized with the Holy Ghost.'[11] And elsewhere the Apostle says: 'For in onè Spirit were we all baptized into one body.'[12] There is one work, because there is one mystery; there is one baptism, because there was one death for the world; there is a unity of prediction which cannot be separated.

(46) But if in this place the Spirit is separated from the operation of the Father and of the Son, because it is said: 'Of God are all things, and through the Son are all things,'[13] then, too, when the Apostle says of Christ: 'Who is over all things, God blessed forever,'[14] he set Him not only before all creatures, but (which is wicked to say) before the Father, also. But far from it, for the Father is not among all things, is not among a kind of crowd of His own creatures. Every creature is below; the divinity of the Father and of the Son and of the Holy Spirit is above. The one serves, the other rules; the one is subject, the other governs; the one is the work, the other is the author of the work; the one adores all, the other is adored by all.

(47) Then it is written of the Son: 'And let all the angels of God adore him.'[15] You do not have: 'Let the Holy Spirit adore.' And below: 'But to which of the angels said he at any time: Sit on my right hand, until I make thy enemies thy

11 Acts 1.5.
12 1 Cor. 12.13.
13 Cf. 1 Cor. 8.6.
14 Rom. 9.5.
15 Heb. 1.6.

footstool? Are they not all,' says he, 'ministering spirits sent to minister?'[16] When he says 'all,' he does not include the Holy Spirit, does he? Surely not, because Angels and other powers are destined to serve in the ministering and obedience to the Son of God.

(48) But indeed the Holy Spirit is not a minister, but a witness of the Son, just as the Son said of Him: 'He shall give testimony of me.'[17] So the Spirit is a witness of the Son. He who is a witness knows all things, just as God the Father is a witness. For thus you have it in later passages, for our salvation was confirmed, with God as witness, also by signs and wonders, and by diverse powers, and by divisions of the Holy Spirit.[18] He who divides as He wishes is surely above all things, not among all things; for to divide is the favor of the worker, not the material of the work.[19]

(49) If the Son is above all things, through whom our salvation received its beginning, that it might be preached, surely God the Father also, who testifies and gives proof to our salvation by signs and wonders, is excepted from all. Similarly, moreover, the Spirit also, who by His divisions bears testimony to our salvation, is not to be numbered in the crowd of creatures, but is to be considered with the Father and the Son, who Himself is not divided by a cutting of Himself when He divides; for since He is indivisible, He loses nothing when He bestows upon all, just as the Son also loses nothing when the Father receives the kingdom,[20] nor does the Father suffer loss when He gives what is His own to the

---

16 Heb. 1.13,14.
17 John 15.26.
18 Cf. Heb. 2.4.
19 Cf. 1 Cor. 12.11.
20 Cf. 1 Cor. 15.24.
21 Cf. 1 Cor. 15.6.

Son. We know thus that there was no loss in the division
of spiritual grace, on the testimony of the Lord,[21] for He
who breaths where He will[22] is everywhere without loss. We
shall speak about this more fully below.

(50) Meanwhile now, since it has been proposed to state
in its order that the Spirit is not to be computed among all
things, let us take up the author of this assertion, the Apostle
himself, on whose words they raise question. For what all
those things were, whether visible or invisible, he himself
pointed out, saying: 'For in Him were all things created in
heaven and on earth.'[23] You see that 'all things' was said of
those things which are either in heaven or on earth, for in
heaven there are also invisible things that were made.

(51) Yet lest it might be unknown to anyone, he added
about what he said in these words: 'Whether thrones, or
dominions, or principalities, or powers; all things were created
through him and in him; and he is before all; and by him all
things consist.'[24] Does he then include here the Holy Spirit
among creatures? Or when he says that the Son of God is
before all, is he to be thought to have said 'before the Father'?
Certainly not, for as he says here that all things were created
through the Son, and all things in heaven consist in Him,
so, too, it cannot be doubted that all heavenly things have
their strength in the Spirit, when it is read: 'By the word
of the Lord, the heavens were established; and all the power
of them by the spirit of his mouth?'[25] Above all things, then,
is He from whom is all the power of heavenly and earthly
things. He, then, who is above all things, surely does not

---

22 Cf. John 3.8.
23 Col. 1.16.
24 Col. 1.16,17.
25 Ps. 32.6.

serve; He who does not serve is free; He who is free holds the laws of sovereignty.

(52) If we had said this in the beginning, it would have been denied. But just as they deny the lesser that the greater may not be believed, so let us on our part set forth the lesser, so that they may either bring forth their perfidy even in the lesser, or if they consent to the lesser, we may gather the greater from the lesser.

(53) I think, most kindly Emperor, that they have been very fully refuted who dare to reckon the Holy Spirit among all things. But yet that they may know that they are pressed not only by the testimony of the Apostles, but also by that of the Lord, how do they dare to number the Holy Spirit among all things, when the Lord himself said: 'Whosoever shall blaspheme the Son of man, it shall be forgiven him; but to him who shall blaspheme the Holy Ghost, it shall be forgiven neither in this world nor in the world to come'?[26] How, then, does anyone dare to reckon the Spirit among creatures? Or who so binds himself as to think that, if he disparages any creature, this is not to be forgiven him by any pardon. For if the Jews, because they adored the host of heaven,[27] were deprived of divine help, but he who adores and confesses the Holy Spirit is acceptable to God, he who does not confess Him is condemned without forgiveness as guilty of a sacrilege, surely from this the Holy Spirit cannot be reckoned among all things, but to be above all things, any injury to Whom is expiated by eternal punishments.

(54) Moreover, observe carefully why the Lord has said: 'Whosoever shall blaspheme against the Son of man, it shall be forgiven him, but to him that shall blaspheme against

26 Cf. Luke 12.10.
27 Cf. 4 Kings 17.16.

the Holy Ghost it shall be forgiven neither in this world nor in the world to come.'[28] Is there one offence against the Son; another against the Holy Spirit? For just as there is one dignity, so there is one injury. But if anyone, deceived by the appearance of the human body, think more remissly than is fitting about the body of Christ (for it ought not to seem paltry to us, since it is the palace of virtue, the fruit of the Virgin), he possesses guilt, but he is not shut off from pardon, which he can receive by faith. If anyone indeed denies the dignity, majesty, and eternal power of the Holy Spirit, and thinks that demons are cast out not in the Spirit of God but in Beelzebub, there can be no entreaty for pardon there where is the fullness of sacrilege, because he who has denied the Spirit has denied God the Father and the Son, for the Spirit of God is the same as is the Spirit of Christ.

Chapter 4

(55) But no one will doubt that the Spirit is one, although many have doubted about the oneness of God. For many heretics have said that the God of the Old Testament is one, and that the God of the New is another. But just as the Father is one, who both spoke of old, as we read, to the Fathers by the Prophets, and in the last days spoke to us by the Son,[1] and as the Son is one, who according to the context of the Old Testament was offended by Adam, seen by Abraham, worshiped by Jacob, so, too, the Holy Spirit is one, who was active in the Prophets, was breathed upon the Apostles, was joined with the Father and the Son in the

---

28 Cf. Luke 12.10; Matt. 12.32.

---

1 Cf. Heb. 1.1,2.

sacrament of baptism.[2] For of Him David says: 'And take not thy holy spirit from me.' Of Him also he said elsewhere: 'Whither shall I go from thy spirit?'[3]

(56) That you may know that the Spirit of God is the same as is the Holy Spirit, as we also read in the Apostle: 'No man, speaking by the Spirit of God, saith anathema to Jesus. And no man can say, the Lord Jesus, but by the Holy Ghost,'[4] the Apostle called Him the Spirit of God. He called Him also the Spirit of Christ, as you have it: 'But you are not in the flesh, but in the spirit, if so be that the Spirit of God dwell in you. Now if any man have not the Spirit of Christ, he is none of his.' And below: 'And if the Spirit of him who raised up Jesus from the dead, dwell in you.'[5] He Himself, then, is the Spirit of God, who is the Spirit of Christ.

(57) He Himself is also the Spirit of life, as the Apostle says: 'For the law of the spirit of life, in Christ Jesus, hath delivered me from the law of sin and of death.'[6]

(58) Him then whom the Apostle called the Spirit of life, the Lord in the Gospel called the Paraclete, the Spirit of Truth, as you have it: 'And I will ask the Father, and he shall give you another Paraclete, that he may abide with you for ever. The Spirit of truth, whom the world cannot receive, because it seeth him not, nor knoweth him.'[7] You have, then, also the Paraclete Spirit, the same called both the Spirit of Truth and the invisible Spirit. How, then, do certain men think the Son visible in His divinity, when the world cannot see even the Spirit?

---

2 Cf. 2 Peter 1.21; John 20.22; Matt. 28.19.
3 Ps. 50.13; 138.7.
4 1 Cor. 12.3.
5 Rom. 8.9,11.
6 Rom. 8.2.
7 John 14.16,17.

(59) Receive now the word of the same Lord, that He is the Holy Spirit, who is the Spirit of Truth; for you have it at the end of this book: 'Receive ye the Holy Ghost.'[8] That the same is also the Holy Spirit who is the Spirit of the Lord, Peter teaches, saying: 'Ananias, why did you decide to tempt and to lie to the Holy Spirit?' And straightway he says to the wife of Ananias: 'Why have you [both] decided to tempt the Spirit of the Lord?'[9] When he says 'you [both],' he shows that his words were spoken of that Spirit of whom he had spoken to Ananias. He Himself, then, is the Spirit of the Lord who is the Holy Spirit.

(60) The Lord declared Him also the Holy Spirit, who is the Spirit of the Father, saying, according to Matthew, that what we say in persecution should not be considered: 'For it is not you that speak but the spirit of your Father, that speaketh in you.'[10] Likewise He says, according to Luke: 'Be not solicitous how or what you shall answer, or what you shall say. For the Holy Ghost shall teach you in the same hour what you ought to say.'[11] So, although many are called spirits, as it is said: 'Who makest thy Angels spirits,'[12] yet the Spirit of God is one.

(61) Therefore, both the Apostles and the Prophets have followed the one Spirit. Just as the vessel of election, the doctor of the Gentiles, says: 'For in one Spirit we have all been made to drink,'[13] Him, as it were, who cannot be divided, but is infused in our souls, and flows into our senses, that He may quench the ardor of worldly thirst.

---

8 John 20.22.
9 Cf. Acts 5.3,9.
10 Matt. 10.20.
11 Luke 12.11,12.
12 Ps. 103.4.
13 1 Cor. 12.13.

Chapter 5

(62) The Holy Spirit, then is not of the substance of corporeal things, for He infuses incorporeal grace into corporeal things, but neither is He of the substance of invisible creatures, for they, too, receive His sanctification, and through Him are superior to the other works of the universe. Whether you speak of Angels or Dominions or Powers, every creature waits for the grace of the Holy Spirit. For just as we are children through the Spirit, because 'God hath sent the Spirit of his Son into your hearts, crying: Abba, Father. Therefore now he is no more a servant, but a son.'[1] Thus, too every creature awaits the revelation of the sons of God, whom he makes sons of God by the grace of the Holy Spirit. Thus, also, every creature itself shall be changed by the revelation of the grace of the Spirit, 'and shall be delivered from the servitude of corruption into the liberty of the glory of the children of God.'[2]

(63) Every creature, then, is subject to change, not only that which already has been changed by some sin or condition of the elements, but also that which can be liable to corruption by the imperfection of nature, although it is not yet so because of the zeal of discipline. For as we have taught in earlier books,[3] the nature of angels also could have been changed. Surely it is fitting to think that as is the nature of one, so is the nature of others. Then the nature of the rest also is capable of change, but the discipline is better.

(64) Then every creature is capable of change, but the Holy Spirit is good and not capable of change; for He cannot be changed by some imperfection of nature, who does away

1 Gal. 4.6,7.
2 Rom. 8.21.
3 Cf. *Faith* 3.2.

with the imperfections of all, and pardons their sins. How, then, is He subject to change who by sanctifying changes others to grace and is not Himself changed?

(65) How is He subject to change who is always good? For the Holy Spirit is never evil, through Whom the things that are good are ministered to us. Thus the two Evangelists in one and the same place, in words differing from each other, yet designated the same things. For in Matthew you have: 'If you, then, being evil, know how to give good gifts to your children; how much more will your Father, who is in heaven give good things to them that ask him?'[4] But according to Luke you will find it written thus: 'How much more will your Father from heaven give the Holy Spirit to them that ask Him?'[5] We note then that the Holy Spirit is good in the judgment of the Lord, by the testimony of the evangelists, since the one has named good things for the Holy Spirit, the other the Holy Spirit for good things. If, then, the Holy Spirit is that which is good, how is He not good?

(66) Nor does it escape us that some manuscripts also have according to Luke: 'How much more will your Father from heaven give a good gift to them that ask Him?' This good gift is spiritual grace, which the Lord Jesus poured forth from heaven, after He had been transfixed to the gibbet of the cross and, bringing back the triumphal spoils of vanquished death, He arose from the dead as victor over death, as you have it written: 'Ascending on high, He hast led captivity captive; He hast given gifts to men.'[6] And well does he say 'gifts.' For as the Son was given, of Whom it is written: 'A child is born, a son is given to us,'[7] spiritual

---

4 Matt. 7.11.
5 Luke 11.13.
6 Cf. Ps. 67.19.
7 Isa. 9.6.

grace also is given. But why do I hesitate to say that the Holy Spirit also is given to us, when it is written: 'The charity of God is poured out into our hearts by the Holy Ghost who is given to us.'[8] Surely, since captive breasts could not receive Him, the Lord Jesus first lead captivity captive, that He might pour forth the gift of divine grace into our free affections.

(67) Moreover, he said it beautifully: 'led captivity captive.' For Christ's victory is the victory of liberty, which delivered all to grace, bound none to injury. So in the absolving of all, no one is captive. And because at the time of the Lord's passion injury alone was on a holiday, which dismissed all as captives whom it was holding, captivity itself, turning back upon itself, was made captive, not now devoted to Belial, but to Christ, to serve Whom is liberty. 'For he that is called in the Lord, being a bondman, is the freeman of the Lord.'[9]

(68) But to return to our purpose, He says: 'They are all gone aside, they are become unprofitable together; there is none that doeth good, no not one.'[10] If they except the Holy Spirit, even they themselves confess that He is not among all; if they do not except Him, then they also confess that He has gone aside among all.

(69) But let us see whether He has goodness, since He is the source and the principle of goodness. For just as the Father and the Son have goodness, so also the Holy Spirit has goodness. This the Apostle also taught when he said: 'But the fruit of the Spirit is peace, charity, joy, patience, goodness.'[11] But who doubts that He is good whose fruit is goodness? For 'a good tree yieldeth good fruit.'[12]

---

8 Rom. 5.5.
9 1 Cor. 7.22.
10 Ps. 13.3.
11 Cf. Gal. 5.22.
12 Cf. Matt. 7.17.

(70) And so if God is good, how is He not good who is the spirit of His mouth, who searches the deep things of God? Can the infection of evil enter into the deep things of God? From this it is understood how foolish they are who deny that the Son of God is good, when they cannot deny that the Spirit of Christ is good, of Whom the Son of God says: 'Therefore I said that he shall receive of mine.'[13]

(71) Or is the Spirit not good who makes the good of the worst, abolishes sin, destroys evil, shuts out crime, infuses the good gift, makes apostles of persecutors, priests of sinners? He says: 'You were heretofore darkness, but now light in the Lord.'[14]

(72) But why do we put them off? For if they demand words, since they do not deny facts, let them accept the Spirit as described as good, for David said: 'Thy good spirit shall lead me into the right way.'[15] For what is the Spirit if not full of goodness? Although He is inaccessible by nature, yet He can be received by us on account of His goodness, fitting all things by His power, but He is partaken of by the just alone, simple in substance, rich in virtues, present to everyone, dividing of His own with each one, and everywhere whole.

(73) And worthily did the Son of God say: 'Go ye, and baptize the nations in the name of the Father and of the Son and of the Holy Spirit,'[16] not disdaining association with the Holy Spirit. Why, then, do some now bear it ill that the Spirit, whom the Lord did not disdain in the sacrament of baptism, be joined in our devotion with the Father and the Son?

13 John 16.15.
14 Eph. 5.8.
15 Cf. Ps. 142.10.
16 Cf. Matt. 28.19.

(74) Good, then, is the Spirit, good not as acquiring, but as imparting goodness. For the Holy Spirit does not receive from creatures, but is received, just as He is not sanctified but He Himself sanctifies. For the creature is sanctified, but the Holy Spirit sanctifies. In this matter though there is a common use of the word, yet there is a difference of nature. For both the man who receives and God who gives sanctity are called holy, because we read: 'Be ye holy, because I too am holy.'[17] So sanctification and corruption cannot belong to one nature, and therefore the grace of the Holy Spirit and the creature cannot belong to one substance.

(75) Thus, since all invisible remaining nature whose substance some rightly think reasonable and incorporeal outside the Trinity does not impart spiritual grace but acquires it, does not share in it but takes it, surely the common nature of the creature is to be separated from association with the Holy Spirit. Let them believe, then, that the Holy Spirit is not a creature; or if they consider Him a creature, why do they join Him with the Father; or if they consider Him a creature, why do they join Him with the Son of God? But if they do not think that He is to be separated from the Father and the Son, let them not think Him a creature, because where there is one sanctification, there is one nature.

Chapter 6

(76) Yet there are many who, because we are baptized in water and in the Spirit, do not think that there is any difference in the offices of water and the Spirit, and so do not think that there is any difference in nature. Nor do they notice that we are buried in the element of water that renewed

17 Cf. Lev. 19.2.

through the Spirit we may rise again. For in the water is the representation of death, in the Spirit the pledge of life, that through water the body of sin may die, which as in a kind of tomb envelops the body, and through the power of the Spirit we may be renewed from the death of sin, reborn in God.

(77) And so these three witnesses are one, as John said: 'The water, the blood, and the Spirit.'[1] One in the mystery, not in nature. The water, then, is the witness of burial, the blood is the witness of death, the Spirit is the witness of life. If, then, there is any grace in water, it is not from the nature of water, but from the presence of the Holy Spirit.

(78) Do we live in the water as in the Spirit? Are we signed in the water as in the Spirit? For we live in Him, and He Himself is the pledge of our inheritance, just as also the Apostle said writing to the Ephesians: 'In whom also believing you were sealed with the holy Spirit of promise. Who is the pledge of our inheritance.'[2] So we were sealed by the Holy Spirit, not by nature but by God, for it is written: 'He that hath anointed us, is God: Who also hath sealed us, and given the pledge of the Spirit in our hearts.'[3]

(79) So we were sealed with the Spirit by God. For just as we die in Christ, that we may be born again, so, too, we are signed with the Spirit, that we may be able to possess His splendor and image and grace, which surely is the sign of the Spirit. For although apparently we are sealed in the body, yet truly we are sealed in the heart, that the Holy Spirit may set forth in us the likeness of the heavenly image.

(80) Who, then, shall dare to say that the Holy Spirit is separated from God the Father and from Christ, when

---

1 Cf. 1 John 5.8.
2 Eph. 1.13,14.
3 2 Cor. 1.21,22.

through Him we merit to be according to the image and likeness of God, and through Him it is brought about, as the Apostle Peter said, that we are sharers in the divine nature?[4] In this surely there is no heredity of carnal succession, but the spiritual connection of the grace of adoption. And that we may know that this seal is of our heart rather than of our body, the Prophet teaches, who says: 'The light of thy countenance, O Lord, is signed upon us; thou hast given gladness in my heart.'[5]

Chapter 7

(81) And so when the Lord appointed His servants the Apostles, that we might know that the creature is one thing, spiritual grace another, He appointed them to different places, because they could not all be everywhere at the same time. But to all He gave the Holy Spirit, who should pour forth the gift of inseparable graces upon the Apostles though separated. There were, then, different persons, but one effect of the operation in all, because one is the Holy Spirit, of whom it is said: 'You will receive the power of the Holy Ghost coming upon you, and you will be witnesses unto me in Jerusalem, and in all Judea, and Samaria, and even to the uttermost part of the earth.'[1]

(82) Therefore, the Holy Spirit is uncircumscribed and infinite, who infused Himself into the minds of the disciples through the separated divisions of distant regions and the remote confines of the whole world, whom nothing can pass

4 Cf. 2 Peter 1.4.
5 Ps. 4.7.

1 Acts 1.8.

by or deceive. And so holy David says: 'Whither shall I go from thy spirit? or whither shall I flee from thy face?'[2] Of what angel does Scripture say this? Of what Dominion? Of what Power? Of what angel do we find the power diffused over many? For angels were sent to few, but the Holy Spirit was infused upon peoples. Who then will doubt that that is divine which is infused upon many at the same time and is not seen, but that that is corporeal which is both seen and possessed by individuals?

(83) But just as the Spirit, sanctifying the Apostles, is not a sharer in human nature, so, too, He sanctifying Angels, Dominions, and Powers has no participation with creatures. But if some think that there is no spiritual sanctity in angels, but some other kind of grace according to the property of their nature, these will surely judge angels to be inferior to men. For since they themselves confess that they dare not compare angels with the Holy Spirit, and they cannot deny that the Holy Spirit is poured into men; moreover, since the sanctification of the Spirit is a divine gift and favor, surely men who have better sanctification will be found to be preferred to the angels. But since angels descend to the aid of men, it is to be understood that the creation of the angels is higher, since it receives more spiritual grace, yet the gift both to us and to them is of the same author.

(84) But how great is the grace, which makes the lower creation of the human state equal to the gifts of the Angels, as the Lord himself promised saying: 'You will be as the angels in heaven.'[3] Nor is it difficult. For He who made the angels in the Spirit, will also make men through the same grace the equal of the angels.[4]

---

2 Ps. 138.7.
3 Cf. Matt. 22.30.
4 Cf. Ps. 103.4.

(85) But of what creature can it be said that it has filled
the universe, as it is written of the Holy Spirit: 'I shall pour
out my spirit upon all flesh.'[5] This cannot be said of an angel.
Finally, Gabriel himself, when sent to Mary, said: 'Hail, full
of grace,' surely declaring spiritual grace in her, because the
Holy Spirit had come upon her, and was about to have her
womb full of grace with the heavenly Word.

(86) For it is of the Lord to fill all things, who says: 'I
fill heaven and earth.'[6] If, then, it is the Lord who fills heaven
and earth, who can judge the Holy Spirit to have no share
in the dominion and the divine power, who filled the world
and what is beyond the whole world, has filled Jesus, the
redeemer of the whole world? For it is written: 'And Jesus
being full of the Holy Ghost, returned from the Jordan.'[7]
Who other than He who was of the same fullness could fill
Him who fills all things?

(87) But lest they object that this was said according to
the flesh, although He alone was more than all, from whose
flesh virtue went forth to heal all, nevertheless, as the Lord
fills all, so, too, is it read of the Spirit: 'For the spirit of the
Lord hath filled the whole world.'[8] You also have it said of
all those who came together with the Apostles: 'Being filled
with the Holy Ghost, they spoke the word of God with
confidence.'[9] You see that the Holy Spirit gives both fullness
and confidence, whose operation the Archangel announces
to Mary, saying: 'The Holy Ghost shall come upon thee.'[10]

(88) You also have it in the Gospel that the angel at a
certain time went down into a pond, and the water was

---

5 Joel 2.28.
6 Cf. Jer. 23.24.
7 Luke 4.1.
8 Wisd. 1.7.
9 Cf. Acts 4.31.
10 Luke 1.35.

moved. And he that went down first into the pond was made whole.[11] What did the angel announce in this type but the descent of the Holy Spirit, which would take place in our time to consecrate the waters when invoked by sacerdotal prayers? That angel, then, was the herald of the Holy Spirit, because through spiritual grace medicine was to be applied to the infirmities of our soul and mind. The Spirit, too, then has the same ministers as God the Father and Christ. So He fills all things, so He possesses all things, so He operates all things and in all things, just as both God the Father and the Son operate.

(89) What, then, is more divine than the operation of the Holy Spirit, since God himself also bears witness to the Spirit as Him who presides over His blessings, when he says: 'I will pour out my spirit upon thy seed, and my blessing upon thy stock'?[12] For no blessing can be full except through the infusion of the Holy Spirit. Therefore, the Apostle also found nothing better to wish for us than this, as he himself said: 'We cease not to pray for you, and to beg that you may be filled with the knowledge of His will, in all wisdom and spiritual understanding, that you may walk worthy of God.'[13] So he taught this to be the will of God, that walking rather in good works and words and affections we be filled with the will of God, who places the Holy Spirit in our hearts. Therefore, if he who possesses the Holy Spirit is filled with the will of God, surely there is no difference of will between the Father and the Spirit.

11 Cf. John 5.4.
12 Isa. 44.3.
13 Col. 1.9.

Chapter 8

(90) At the same time note this, that God gives the Holy Spirit.[1] For this is no human deed, nor is it given by man, but He who is invoked by the priest is given by God, in which is the gift of God and the ministry of the priests. For if Paul the Apostle judged[2] that he could not grant the Holy Spirit by his own authority, and believed himself so unequal to this office that he desired us to be filled with the Spirit by God, who is so great as to dare to arrogate to himself the granting of this gift? And so the Apostle conveyed the wish in prayer; he did not claim the right by some authority; he wished to obtain, he did not presume to command. Peter also says that he was not sufficient to be able either to force or to prevent the Holy Spirit. For thus he spoke: 'If then God gave to them the same grace as to us also who have believed in the Lord Jesus Christ; who was I, that I could oppose God?'[3]

(91) But perhaps they are not moved by the example of Apostles, and so let us employ divine pronouncements. For it is written: 'Jacob is my servant; I will uphold him; my elect, my soul delighteth in him; I have given my spirit upon him.' The Lord, also through Isaias, said: 'The Spirit of the Lord is upon me, because the Lord hath anointed me.'[4]

(92) Who, then, shall dare to say that the substance of the Holy Spirit is created, at whose illumination of our hearts we perceive the beauty of divine truth and recognize the difference between the creature and the Godhead, so that the work is separated from the author? Or of what creature had

---

1 Cf. Rom. 5.5.
2 Cf. Eph. 5.18.
3 Acts 11.17.
4 Cf. Isa. 42.1; 61.1.

God so spoken as to pour out dominions or powers or angels?
But He says: 'I will pour out of my spirit.'[5] He did not say
'my Spirit,' but 'of my Spirit,' for we cannot take the fullness
of the Holy Spirit, but we receive so much as our Master
divides of His own according to His will. But just as the Son
of God 'thought it no robbery Himself to be equal to God;
but debased Himself,'[6] that we might be able to receive Him
in our minds, but He debased Himself not because He was
empty of His own fullness, but that He might pour Himself
in me, who could not sustain His fullness, according to the
measure of my capacity, so, too, the Father says that He pours
forth of the Holy Spirit upon all flesh, for He did not pour
Him forth entirely, but what He poured forth abounded
for all.

(93) Therefore, it was poured upon us of the Spirit, but
in truth the Spirit abode over the Lord Jesus, since He was
in the form of man, as it is written: 'He upon whom thou
shalt see the Spirit descending, and remaining on him, he it
is that baptizeth with the Holy Ghost.'[7] Around us from
abundant provision is the liberality of Him who bestows; in
him abides forever the fullness of the whole Spirit. Whatever
then He has judged as sufficient for us, He has poured forth;
and what has been poured forth, is not separated nor is it
divided; but He has a unity of fullness, whereby He illumines
the sight of our hearts according to the possibility of our
strength. Finally, we take as much as the progress of our
minds acquires; for the fullness of spiritual grace is indivisible,
but is shared by us according to the capability of our nature.

(94) So God pours forth of the Spirit; God's love is also

5 Joel 2.28.
6 Phil. 2.6.
7 John 1.33.

poured forth through the Spirit; by this argument we should recognize the unity of the operation and of the grace. For just as God pours forth of the Holy Spirit, so, too, 'The charity of God is poured out into our hearts through the Holy Ghost,'[8] that we may understand that the Holy Spirit is not a work, who is the arbiter and affluent source of divine love.

(95) Similarly that you may believe that that which is poured forth cannot be common to creatures, but peculiar to the Godhead, the name of the Son also is poured forth: 'Thy name is as oil poured out.'[9] Nothing can be superior to the force of this statement. For just as ointment inclosed in a vase keeps in its odor, which odor is held back as long as it is in the narrow confines of the vase, although it cannot reach many, yet it preserves its strength, but when the ointment has been poured forth, it is diffused far and wide; so, too, the name of Christ before His coming among the people of Israel, was inclosed in the minds of the Jews as in a vase. For 'in Judaea God is known; His name is great in Israel';[10] that is, this name which the vases of the Jews contained held back in their narrow confines.

(96) Surely the name was great then, also, when it clung to the confines of the infirm and the few, but it had not yet poured forth its greatness through the hearts of the Gentiles and into the confines of the whole world. But after by His coming He had shone throughout all the world, He spread that divine name of His throughout every creature, not filled up with something added (for fullness recognizes no increase), but filling empty spaces, that His name might be wonderful in the whole land. Therefore, the pouring out of this name

8 Rom. 5.5.
9 Cant. 1.2.
10 Ps. 75.1.

signifies a kind of abundant exuberance of graces, and a plenitude of heavenly blessings, for whatever is poured forth flows
forth from abundance.

(97) And so, just as Wisdom, which proceeds from the
mouth of God, cannot be said to be created, nor the Word,
which is uttered from His heart, nor the power, in which is
the eternal fullness of eternal majesty, so also the Spirit, which
is poured forth from the mouth of God, cannot be considered
to be created, since God Himself has shown such great unity
that He says that He pours forth of His Spirit. By this we may
understand that the grace of God the Father is the same as
that of the Holy Spirit, and that it is divided in the minds of
individuals without any severance or loss; therefore, that it
is poured forth from the Spirit of God, is neither broken off,
nor comprehended within any corporeal parts, nor is it
severed.

(98) For how is it credible that the Spirit is divided by
some sections? John says of God: 'In this we know that He
abideth in us from the Spirit which He hath given us.'[11]
Moreover, what abides always, surely is not changed; so if it
has no change, it has eternity. And on this account the Holy
Spirit is eternal, but the creature is subject to fault and on
this account is changeable. Moreover, what is changeable,
cannot be eternal;[12] and so there can be nothing in common
between the Holy Spirit and the creature, because the Spirit
is eternal, but every creature is temporal.

(99) But the Apostle also shows that the Holy Spirit is
eternal: 'For if the blood of goats and of oxen, and the ashes
of a heifer being sprinkled, sanctify such as are defiled, to the
cleansing of the flesh; how much more shall the blood of

11 1 John 3.24.
12 Cf. Rom. 8.20.

Christ, who through the Holy Ghost offered Himself without spot to God!'[13] Therefore, the Spirit is eternal.

Chapter 9

(100) Now many have thought that the Holy Spirit is the ointment of Christ. And well is He ointment, because He is called the oil of gladness, the joining together of many graces giving forth a fragrance. But God the Almighty Father anointed Him the chief of the priests, who was anointed not as others in a type under the law, but was both anointed according to the law in the body, and in truth was full of the virtue of the Holy Spirit from the Father above the law.

(101) This is the oil of gladness, of which the Prophet says: 'God, thy God hath anointed thee with the oil of gladness above thy fellows.'[1] Finally, Peter speaks of Jesus as anointed with the Spirit, as you have it: 'You know the word which hath been published through all Judea; for it began from Galilee, after the baptism which John preached, Jesus of Nazareth, how God anointed him with the Holy Ghost.'[2] So the Holy Spirit is the oil of gladness.

(102) And well did he say oil of gladness, lest you might think Him a creature, for the nature of the oil is such that it by no means mingles with the moisture of another nature. Gladness also does not anoint the body, but illumines the recesses of the heart, as the Prophet has said: 'Thou hast given gladness in my heart.'[3] So since he wastes his time

---

13 Heb. 9.13,14.

1 Ps. 44.8.
2 Acts 10.37,38.
3 Ps. 4.7.

who wishes to mingle oil with moister material, because, since the nature of oil is lighter than others, while other materials settle, it rises and is separated, how do those meanest of hucksters think that the oil of gladness can be fraudulently mingled with other creatures, when surely corporeal things cannot be mixed with the incorporeal, nor created things with the uncreated?

(102A) And well is that called the oil of gladness with which Christ was anointed, for no customary and common oil was to be sought for Him with which either wounds are refreshed or fever relieved, since the salvation of the world did not seek the alleviation of His wounds, nor did eternal might demand the refreshment of a tired body.

(103) Nor is it wonderful if He has the oil of gladness who caused those at the point of death to rejoice, relieved the world of sadness, and destroyed the stench of sorrowful death. And thus the Apostle says: 'For we are unto God the good odour of Christ,'[4] surely indicating that He spoke of spiritual things. But when the Son of God himself says: 'The Spirit of the Lord is upon me, wherefore he hath anointed me,'[5] He indicates a spiritual ointment. Therefore, the ointment of Christ is the Spirit.

(104) Or since the name of Jesus is as ointment poured out, if here they wish to understand Christ himself as expressed by the name of ointment, not the Spirit of Christ, surely, when Peter the Apostle said that the Lord Jesus was anointed by the Holy Spirit, it is undoubtedly clear that the Spirit also is called ointment.

(105) But what wonder, since both the Father and the Son are said to be Spirit? Of this indeed we shall speak more

---

4 2 Cor. 2.15.
5 Luke 4.18.

fully when we begin to speak of the Unity of the Name.[6] Yet since a most suitable place occurs here, also, that we may not seem to pass it by without a conclusion, let them accept that the Father also is called Spirit, as the Lord said in the Gospel: 'For God is a Spirit';[7] and Christ is called a Spirit, for Jeremias said: 'The Spirit before our face, Christ the Lord.'[8]

(106) Therefore, both the Father is Spirit and the Son is Spirit; for what is not the body of a creature, this is spirit, but the Holy Spirit is not mingled with the Father and the Son, but is distinct from the Father and from the Son. For the Holy Spirit did not die, who could not die, because He did not take on flesh, nor could the eternal Godhead have been capable of dying, but Christ died according to the flesh.

(107) Indeed He died in that which He took from the Virgin, not in that which He had from the Father, for Christ died in that in which He was crucified. But the Holy Spirit could not have been crucified, who had not flesh and bones. But the Son of God was crucified, who took on flesh and bones, that on that cross the temptations of our flesh might die. For He took on what He was not, that He might conceal what He was; He concealed what He was, that He might be tempted in it, and that that which He was not might be redeemed, that He might call us to that which He was, through that which He was not.

(108) Oh, the divine mystery of that cross, on which weakness hangs, might is free, vices are fixed, trophies are raised! Therefore, a certain saint said: 'Pierce thou my flesh with nails from fear of Thee;'[9] not with nails of iron, he says,

---

6 Cf. Chapter 14.
7 John 4.24.
8 Cf. Lam. 4.20.
9 Cf. Ps. 118.120.

but of fear and of faith; for the bonds of virtue are mightier than those of punishment. Finally, when Peter followed the Lord up to the palace of the high priest,[10] him whom no one had bound, faith fettered; and whom faith fettered, punishment did not loose. Again, when he was bound by the Jews, prayer loosed him, punishment did not hold him, because he did not recede from Christ.

(109) Therefore, crucify sin, that you may die to sin, for he who dies to sin lives to God. You should live for Him who did not spare His own son, that in His body He might crucify our passions. For Christ died for us, that we might live in His renewed body. Therefore, not our life but our guilt died in Him, 'who,' it is said, 'bore our sins in His body upon the tree, that we, being separated from our sins, should live with justice, by the wounds of whose stripes we have been healed.'[11]

(110) Therefore, that wood of the cross is our conveyance, as it were, the ship of our salvation, not a punishment, for there is no other salvation than the conveyance of eternal salvation. While seeking after death, I do not feel it; while contemning punishment, I do not suffer; while disregarding fear, I do not know it.

(111) Who is it, then, by the wounds of whose stripes we have been healed but Christ the Lord, of whom the same Isaias prophesied that His stripes were our remedy,[12] of whom the Apostle Paul in his Epistles wrote: 'He who knew no sin was made sin for us.'[13] This indeed was divine in Him, that His flesh did no sin, nor did the creature of the body taken on in Him commit sin. For what wonder is it, if the Godhead alone did not sin, since It had no incentives to sin? But if God alone

---

10 Cf. Matt. 26.58.
11 Cf. 1 Peter 2.24.
12 Cf. Isa. 53.5.
13 Cf. 2 Cor. 5.21.

is without sin, surely every creature by its own nature, as we have said, is subject to sin.

Chapter 10

(112) Tell me, then, whoever denies the divinity of the of the Holy Spirit. The Spirit, moreover, could not have been subject to sin, who rather forgives sin. Does an angel forgive? Does an archangel forgive? Surely not, but the Father alone forgives, the Son alone, the Holy Spirit alone.[1] No one, moreover, cannot avoid what he can forgive.

(113) But perhaps someone has said that the Seraph said to Isaias: 'Behold this hath touched thy lips, and shall take away thy iniquities, and shall cleanse thy sins.'[2] 'Shall take away,' it says, 'and shall cleanse.' Not I shall take away, but that fire from the altar of God, that is, spiritual grace. What else can we piously understand to be on the altar of God than the grace of the Spirit? Surely not the wood of trees, nor soot and coal. Or what is so pious as for us to believe according to the mystery that it was revealed by the mouth of Isaias that all men are to be cleansed through the passion of Christ, who according to the flesh like coal burned away our sins, as you have it in Zachary: 'Is not this a brand plucked out of the fire? And that was Jesus clothed with filthy garments.'[3]

(114) Finally, that we may know that this mystery of the common Redemption was very clearly revealed by the prophets you have it said also in this place: 'Behold He has taken away your sins,'[4] not because Christ put aside His sins,

---

1 Cf. Luke 5.21.
2 Cf. Isa. 6.7.
3 Cf. Zach. 3.2,3.
4 Cf. Zach. 3.4.

who did no sin, but because in the flesh of Christ the whole human race was absolved of its sins.

(115) But even if Seraph had taken away sin, it would have been destined for this mystery surely as one of the ministers of God. For thus did Isaias say: 'For one of the Seraphim was sent to me.'[5]

Chapter 11

(116) The Spirit indeed also is said to have been sent, but the Seraph to one, the Spirit to all.[1] The Seraph is sent to minister; the Spirit works a mystery. The Seraph performs what is ordered; the Spirit divides as he wishes.[2] The Seraph passes from place to place, for he does not fill all things, but is himself also filled by the Spirit. The Seraph descends with a passing according to his nature, but we cannot indeed think of this with respect to the Holy Spirit, of whom the Son of God said: 'When the Paraclete shall come, whom I shall send you from the Father, the Spirit of truth, who proceedeth from the Father.'[3]

(117) For if the Spirit proceeds from a place, and passes to a place, the Father also will be found in a place, and the Son. If He goes out of a place, whom the Father sends, or the Son, surely the Spirit passing and proceeding from a place seems to leave both the Father and the Son as a body, according to impious interpretations.

(118) I declare this with reference to those who say that

---

5 Cf. Isa. 6.6.

1 Cf. John 16.7.
2 Cf. 1 Cor. 12.11.
3 John 15.26.

the Spirit has motion by descending. But neither is the Father circumscribed in any place, who is over all things not only of a corporeal nature, but also of invisible creation, nor is the Son enclosed by the places and times of His works, who as the Worker of all creation is over every creature, nor is the Spirit of truth, namely the Spirit of God, circumscribed by any corporeal boundaries,[4] who, since He is incorporeal, is over all rational creation by the ineffable fullness of the Godhead, having the power over all things of breathing where He wishes and of inspiring as He wishes.[5]

(119) The Spirit, then, is not sent as from a place, nor does He proceed as from a place, when He proceeds from the Son, as the Son Himself, when He says: 'I came forth from the Father, and am come into the world,'[6] puts an end to all opinions, which can be considered as from place to place, as with some bodies. Moreover, similarly when we read that God is either within or without, surely we do not either include God within some body or separate Him from some body, but weighing this with a deep and ineffable estimation we understand the secret of the divine nature.

(120) Finally, Wisdom so says that she proceeded from the mouth[7] of the Most High not to be outside the Father but with the Father, because 'the Word was with God,'[8] not only with the Father, but also in the Father. For He says: 'I am in the Father, and the Father in me.'[9] But neither when He came out of the Father did He withdraw as from a place, nor is He separated as a body from a body; nor when He is

---

4 Cf. Wisd. 7.23.
5 Cf. John 3.8.
6 John 16.28.
7 Cf. Eccli. 24.5.
8 John 1.1.
9 John 14.10.

in the Father is He included as a body in a body. Also, when the Holy Spirit proceeds from the Father and the Son, He is not separated from the Father, nor is He separated from the Son. For how can He be separated from the Father who is the Spirit of His mouth?[10] This surely both is the proof of His eternity, and expresses the unity of the Godhead.

(121) He exists, then, and abides always, who is the Spirit of His mouth; but He seems to come down, when we receive Him, that He may dwell in us, lest we be alien to His grace. He seems to come down upon us, not because He comes down, but because our spirit goes up to Him. We would speak more fully of this, did we not recall that already in early works[11] there is set forth that the Father said: 'Let us go down, and there confound their tongue,'[12] and that the Son said: 'If anyone love me, he will keep my word; and my Father will love him, and we will come to him, and will make an abode with him.'[13]

(122) The Spirit, then, so comes as the Father comes, because, where the Father is, there is also the Son, and where the Son is, there is the Holy Spirit. The Holy Spirit, therefore, is not to be thought to come separately. Moreover, He does not come from place to place, but from the disposition of the order to the salvation of redemption, from the grace of vivification to the grace of sanctification, to transfer us from earth to heaven, from harm to glory, from servitude to kingdom.

(123) Thus, then, the Spirit comes as the Father comes. For the Son said: 'I and the Father will come, and will make an abode with him.' Does the Father come corporeally? Thus,

---

10 Ps. 32.6.
11 *De fide* 7.
12 Gen. 11.7.
13 John 14.23.

then, comes the Spirit, in whom, when He comes, is the full presence of the Father and the Son.

(124) For who can separate the Holy Spirit from the Father and the Son, when indeed we cannot name the Father and the Son without the Spirit? For 'no man can say, the Lord Jesus, but by the Holy Ghost.'[14] So if we cannot name the Lord Jesus without the Spirit, surely we cannot proclaim Him without the Spirit. But if the angels also proclaim the Lord Jesus, whom no one can proclaim without the Spirit, then in them also the office of the Holy Spirit functions.

(125) We have proved then that there is one presence, that there is one grace on the part of the Father and of the Son and of the Holy Spirit, which is so heavenly and divine that the Son gives thanks for this, saying: 'I give thanks to thee, O Father, Lord of heaven and earth, because thou hast hid these things from the wise and prudent, and hast revealed them to little ones.'[15]

Chapter 12

(126) Therefore, since the calling is one, the grace also is one. Then it is written: 'Grace to you and peace from God our Father, and from the Lord Jesus Christ.'[1] Behold we have it that there is one grace on the part of the Father and the Son, and that there is one peace on the part of the Father and the Son, but this grace and peace are the fruit of the Spirit, as the Apostle himself taught when he said: 'But the

14 1 Cor. 12.3.
15 Matt. 11.25.

1 Rom. 1.7.

fruit of the Spirit is charity, joy, peace, patience.'[2] Peace is both good and necessary, that no one may be disturbed by the uncertainties of disputations, and may be shaken by the storm of bodily passions, but that with simplicity of faith and tranquility of mind, the affections may persevere quietly about the worship of God.

(127) As to peace we have given proof, but as to grace the Prophet Zacharias says that God promised to pour the spirit of grace and mercy upon Jerusalem,[3] and the Apostle Peter says: 'Do penance, and be baptized every one of you in the name of Jesus Christ, for the remission of your sins; and you shall receive the grace of the Holy Ghost.'[4] Therefore, as grace is of the Father and of the Son, so also is it of the Holy Spirit. For how can there be grace without the Spirit when all divine grace is in the Holy Spirit?

(128) Not only do we read of the peace and grace of the Father and of the Son and of the Holy Spirit, but also of the charity and communion, faithful Augustus. For of charity it is said: 'The grace of our Lord Jesus Christ, and the charity of God.'[5] We have received the charity of the Father. The same charity which is of the Father, is also of the Son. For He Himself said: 'He that loveth me, shall be loved by my Father, and I will love him.'[6] For what is the charity of the Son, if not that He offered himself for us, and redeemed us with His blood.[7] Moreover, the same charity is also in the Father, for it is written: 'For God so loved the world, as to give His only begotten Son.'[8]

---

2 Gal. 5.22.
3 Cf. Zach. 12.10.
4 Acts 2.38.
5 2 Cor. 13.13.
6 John 14.21.
7 Cf. Eph. 5.2.
8 John 3.16.

(129)   So the Father gave His Son, and the Son Himself gave Himself. Charity is preserved, and devoutness is not harmed, for there can be no harm to devoutness, where there is no hardship in giving. He gave Him who was willing; He gave Him who offered Himself; surely the Father did not give the Son for punishment but for grace. If you enquire into the merit of the deed, question the word 'devoutness.' The vessel of election clearly shows this unity of divine charity, for both Father gave the Son, and the Son Himself gave Himself. The Father gave, who 'spared not even His own Son, but delivered Him up for us all.'[9] Of the Son also he says: 'Who delivered Himself for me.'[10] 'Delivered,' he says. If of grace, why do I find fault? If of injury, I owe more.

(130)   But as the Father gave the Son, and the Son Himself gave Himself, learn that the Spirit also gave Him. For it is written: 'Then Jesus was led by the Spirit into the desert, to be tempted by the devil.'[11] So the Spirit, too, loved the Son of God and gave Him. For just as the charity of the Father and of the Son is one, so have we declared that this charity of God is poured forth abroad through the Holy Spirit and is the fruit of the Holy Spirit, for 'the fruit of the Spirit is charity, joy, peace, patience.'[12]

(131)   Moreover, it is manifest that there is fellowship with the Father and with the Son, for it is written: 'Our fellowship with the Father and with His Son, Jesus Christ'; and elsewhere: 'The communication of the Holy Ghost with you all.'[13] If, then, there is one peace, one grace, one charity, one communication on the part of the Father and of the Son

9 Rom. 8.32.
10 Gal. 11.20.
11 Matt. 4.1.
12 Gal. 5.22.
13 1 John 1.3; 2 Cor. 13.13.

and of the Holy Spirit, surely there is one operation, and where there is one operation, certainly the power cannot be divided, and substance separated. For how can the grace of the same operation come together?

Chapter 13

(132) Who then shall dare to deny the unity of the name, when he sees the oneness of the operation? But why do I affirm the unity of the name with arguments when there is the evident proof of the divine voice that the Father and the Son and the Holy Spirit have one name? For it is written: 'Go baptize the nations in the name of the Father, and of the Son and of the Holy Ghost.'[1] 'In the name,' he said, not 'in the names.' So there is not one name for the Father, another name for the Son, another name for the Holy Spirit, because there is one God, not several names, because there are not two Gods, not three Gods.[2]

(133) And that He might disclose that there is one Godhead, one majesty, because there is one name of the Father and of the Son and of the Holy Spirit, and that the Son did not come in one name, and the Holy Spirit in another, the Lord Himself said: 'I am come in the name of my Father, and you receive me not. If another shall come in his own name, him you will receive.'[3]

(133A) Moreover, what the name of the Father is, this same name Scripture declares to be the Son's, for the Lord said in Exodus: 'I will go before thee in my name and I will

1 Cf. Matt. 28.19.
2 Cf. 1 Cor. 8.4.
3 John 5.43.

proclaim in the name of the Lord before thee.'[4] So the Lord said that He would proclaim the Lord in His name. So the Lord is the name both of the Father and of the Son.

(134) But since the name of the Father and of the Son is one, accept that the same name is that of the Holy Spirit also, for the Holy Spirit also came in the name of the Son, as it is written: 'But the Paraclete, the Holy Ghost, whom the Father will send in my name, he will teach you all things.'[5] For He who came in the name of the Son, surely also came in the name of the Father, for the name of the Father and of the Son is one. Thus it comes about that the name of the Father and of the Son and of the Holy Spirit is one. 'For there is no other name under heaven given to men, whereby we must be saved.'[6]

(135) At the same time He taught that the unity of the name is to be believed, not the disparity, for Christ came in the oneness of the name, but anti-Christ is to come in his own name, as it is written: 'I am come in the name of my Father; and you receive me not. If another shall come in his own name, him you will receive.'[7]

(136) It is taught, then, from these passages that there is no diversity of names in the Father and the Son and the Holy Spirit, Paraclete, and that what is the name of the Father, this also is the name of the Son; similarly, that what is the name of the Son, this also is that of the Holy Spirit, when the Son is also called Paraclete, as is the Holy Spirit. And so the Lord Jesus says in the Gospel: 'And I will ask the Father, and he shall give you another Paraclete, that he may abide

---

4 Cf. Exod. 33.19.
5 John 14.26.
6 Acts 4.12.
7 John 5.43.

with you for ever, the Spirit of Truth.'[8] And well did He say 'another' that you might not understand the Son Himself to be the Spirit Himself, for there is a unity of the name, and no Sabellian[9] confusion of the Son and of the Spirit.

(137) And so one Paraclete is the Son, another Paraclete the Holy Spirit, for John also called the Son a Paraclete, as you have it: 'If any man sin, we have an Advocate [Paraclete] with the Father, Jesus Christ.'[10] And so just as there is unity of name, so also is there unity of power; for where the Paraclete Spirit is, there also is the Son.

(138) For just as the Lord says here that the Spirit will be with the faithful forever, so too, does He show elsewhere regarding Himself that He will be with the Apostles forever, saying: 'Behold, I am with you all days, even to the consummation of the world.'[11] So the Son and the Spirit are one; the name of the Trinity is one; and there is one and indivisible Presence.

(139) Moreover, just as we show that the Son is named the Paraclete, so, too, we show that the Spirit is called the Truth. Christ is the Truth; the Spirit is the Truth; for you have it in John's epistle: 'That the Spirit is Truth.'[12] Not only is the Spirit called the Spirit of Truth, but also Truth, just as the Son is proclaimed Truth, who says: 'I am the way, and the truth, and the life.'[13]

---

8 John 14.16,17.
9 The Sabellians, anxious to maintain the unity of God, denied the differences in Persons and identified the Father and the Son.
10 1 John 2.1.
11 Matt. 28.20.
12 Cf. 1 John 5.6,7.
13 John 14.6.

Chapter 14

(140) But why should I add that just as the Father is light, so, too, the Son is light, and the Holy Spirit is light? This surely belongs to divine power. For God is light, as John said: 'That God is light; and that in Him there is no darkness.'[1]

(141) But the Son also is Light, because 'Life was the Light of men.'[2] And the Evangelist, that he might show that he spoke of the Son of God, says of John the Baptist: 'He was not the light, but was to bear witness to the light, that he was the true light, which enlighteneth every man that cometh into this world.'[3] Therefore, since God is the Light, and the Son of God is the true Light, without doubt the Son of God is true God.

(142) You have it also elsewhere that the Son of God is the Light: 'The people that dwelt in darkness and in the shadow of death have seen a great light.'[4] But what is more evident than this which says: 'For with thee is the fountain of life; and in thy light we shall see light.'[5] That is, that with Thee, God Omnipotent Father, who are the Fount of Life, in thy light the Son, we shall see the light of the Holy Spirit. Just as the Lord Himself shows when He says: 'Receive ye the Holy Ghost,' and elsewhere: 'Virtue went out from Him.'[6]

(143) Moreover, who will doubt that the Father Himself is light, when it is read of His Son that He is the splendor of eternal light?[7] For of whom if not of the eternal Father

1 1 John 1.5.
2 John 1.4.
3 John 1.8,9.
4 Cf. Isa. 9.2.
5 Ps. 35.10.
6 John 20.22; Luke 6.19.
7 Cf. Heb. 1.3.

is the Son the splendor, who both is always with the Father and always shines not with a dissimilar but with the same light?

(144) And Isaias points out that the Holy Spirit is not only light but is also fire, when he says: 'And the light of Israel shall be as fire.'[8] Thus the Prophets called Him a burning fire, because in those three points we notice more readily the majesty of the Godhead, for to sanctify is of the Godhead, and to illuminate is proper to fire and light, and to be expressed and to be seen in the appearance of fire is customary with the Godhead; 'for God is a consuming fire,'[9] as Moses said.

(145) For he himself saw the fire in the bush, and he had heard God at that time when a voice came from the flame of fire to him saying: 'I am the God of Abraham, and the God of Isaac, and the God of Jacob.'[10] The voice was from the flame, and the flame was in the bush, and the flame was not harmful. For the bush was burned, and was not burned up, because in that mystery the Lord represented that He would come to illuminate the thorns of our body; not to consume those beset with miseries but to mitigate the miseries; who would baptize with the Holy Spirit and with fire,[11] that He might distribute grace and consume sins. Thus in the appearance of fire God keeps His purpose.

(146) In the Acts of the Apostles also, when the Holy Spirit descended upon the faithful, the likeness of fire was seen, for thus you have it: 'And suddenly there came a sound from heaven, as though the Spirit were coming with great might; and it filled the whole house where they were sitting;

8 Isa. 10.17.
9 Cf. Deut. 4.24.
10 Cf. Exod. 3.15.
11 Cf. Matt. 3.11.

and there appeared to them cloven tongues as it were of fire.'[12]

(147) Therefore, too, did that take place, when Gedeon, about to overcome the Medianites, ordered three hundred men to take pitchers, and to hold lighted lamps in the pitchers, and in their right hands trumpets; thus our ancestors preserved what they had received from the Apostles, that the pitchers are our bodies, which, fashioned out of clay, know not how to fear, if they burn with the fervor of spiritual grace, and bear testimony to the passion of the Lord Jesus with a confession of a melodious voice.

(148) Who, then, will doubt of the Godhead of the Holy Spirit, when, where the grace of the Spirit is, there the likeness of the Godhead appears? By this testimony we gather not the diversity but the unity of the divine power. For how can there be a separation of power, where the effect of the operation in all is one? Neither indeed can there be grace of the sacraments, except where there was remission of sins.

(149) What, then, is that fire? Surely not fire made of common twigs, or roaring by the burning of the stubble of the forests, but that fire which, like gold, improves good deeds, and consumes sins like stubble. This surely is the Holy Spirit, who is called both the fire and the light of the Lord's countenance; the light, as we have said above: 'The light of thy countenance, O Lord, is signed upon us.'[13] What then is the light that is sealed, if not the light of that spiritual seal 'in whom believing,' he says, 'you were sealed with the holy Spirit of promise'?[14]

(150) And just as there is the light of the divine countenance, so fire flashes forth from the countenance of God,

12 Cf. Acts 2.2,3.
13 Ps. 4.7.
14 Eph. 1.13.

for it is written: 'A fire shall burn in His countenance.'[15]
For the grace of the day of judgment shines forth, that abso-
lution may follow, to reward the allegiance of the saints. O
the great richness of the Scriptures, which no one can comprehend with human nature! O greatest proof of the divine
Unity! For how many things are indicated by these two
verses!

Chapter 15

(151) We have said that the Father is Light, the Son is
Light, the Holy Spirit is Light. Let us accept also that the
Father is Life, the Son is Life, the Holy Spirit is Life. For
John said: 'That which was from the beginning, which we
have heard and which we have seen, and with our eyes have
diligently looked upon, and our hands have handled, concerning the word of life; and life was manifested, and we
have seen, and do bear witness, and declare unto you the life,
which was with the Father.'[1] And he said both the Word
of Life and the Life, that he might signify both the Father
and the Son as the Life. For what is the Word of Life, if not
the Word of God? And by this both God and the Word of
God are the Life. And just as He is called the Word of Life,
so is He the Spirit of Life. For it is written: 'For the Spirit of
Life was in the wheels.'[2] Therefore, just as the Word of Life
is Life, so the Spirit of Life is Life.

(152) Observe now that just as the Father is the Fountain of Life, so, too, many have declared that the Son also

---

15 Cf. Ps. 49.3.

1 Cf. 1 John 1.1,2.
2 Ezech. 1.20.

is signified as the Fountain of Life, because, He says, with
You, Almighty God, your Son is the Fountain of Life, that
is, the Fountain of the Holy Spirit, since the Spirit is the Life,
as the Lord says: 'The words that I have spoken to you,
are Spirit and Life,'[3] because where the Spirit is, Life also
is; and where Life is, the Holy Spirit also is.

(153) Yet many wish that the Father alone be indicated
in this passage by Fountain, although they see what Scripture
has said. It says: 'With thee is the fountain of life,'[4] that is,
with the Father is the Son, for the Word is with God, who was
in the beginning and was with God.

154) But whether one understands in this passage the
Father or the Son as the Fountain, surely we understand not
a fountain of water which is something created, but of that
divine grace, that is, of the Holy Spirit, for He is living water.
Thus the Lord says: 'If thou didst know the gift of God,
and who it is that saith to thee, give me to drink; thou, perhaps, wouldst have asked of him, and he would have given
thee living water.'[5]

(155) This water did the soul of David thirst for. The
fountain of these waters does the hart pant after,[6] not thirsting for the poisons of serpents. For the water of spiritual grace
is living, that it may purify the internal parts of the mind,
and wash away every sin of the soul, and cleanse hidden
errors.

---

3 John 6.64.
4 Ps. 35.10.
5 John 4.10.
6 Cf. Ps. 41.3,2.

Chapter 16

(156) But lest someone should disprove as it were of the littleness of the Spirit, and so wish to make a difference in magnitude, because the water seems to be a small portion of the fountain, although the examples of created things seem least of all suited for comparison with the Godhead, yet lest they have some prejudice also from this comparison with a created thing, let them learn that the Holy Spirit has been called not only water but also a river, according to what is written: 'Out of His belly shall flow rivers of living water. Now this he said of the Spirit which they should receive who believed in Him.'[1]

(157) Therefore, the Holy Spirit is a river, and a very large river, which according to the Hebrews flowed from Jesus in the lands, as we have received it in prophecy from the mouth of Isaias.[2] This river is great, which flows always, and never fails. Not only a river, but also one of profuse stream, and of overflowing greatness, just as David also said: 'The stream of the river maketh the city of God joyful.'[3]

(158) For that city, the heavenly Jerusalem, is not washed by the course of some earthly river, but the Holy Spirit proceeding from the Fountain of Life, by a short draught of which we are satiated, seems to flow more abundantly among those heavenly Thrones, Dominions and Powers, Angels and Archangels, boiling in the full course of seven spiritual virtues. For if the river spreading over the tops of its banks overflows, how much more does the Spirit, rising above every creature, when He touches the remaining lower fields of the mind, as

1 John 7.38,39.
2 Is. 66.12.
3 Ps. 45.5.

it were, delight that heavenly nature of creatures with a kind of more effusive fertility of His mind!

(159) Let it not cause disturbance that John has said here either 'rivers' or elsewhere 'seven Spirits';[4] for by these sanctifications of the gifts of the Spirit, as Isaias said, is signified the fullness of the virtues: the spirit of wisdom, and of understanding, the spirit of counsel, and of fortitude, the spirit of knowledge, and of godliness, the spirit of the fear of God.[5] So there is one river, but many streams of spiritual gifts. This river, then, goes forth from the Fountain of Life.

(160) Here again do not turn your understanding to the lower things, because there seems to be a kind of difference between a fountain and a river; and yet the sacred Scripture has provided for all things lest the weakness of human nature be caught by the lowliness of the language. Although you picture to yourself any river, it comes from a fountain; yet it is of one nature, of one splendor and grace. Do you also say that the Holy Spirit is of one substance with the Son of God and God the Father, of one brilliance and glory? I shall make a faithful summary of the unity of the power, and shall not fear any question as to the difference in greatness. For even in this Scripture looks out for us; for the Son of God says: 'He that shall drink of the water that I shall give him, there will become in him a fountain of water, springing up unto everlasting life.'[6] This Fountain indeed, spiritual grace, is a river proceeding from the living Fountain. The Holy Spirit, then, is also the Fountain of Life.

(161) You notice, then, from His words that the unity of the divine greatness is signified, and that Christ also cannot

4 John 7.38; Apoc. 5.6.
5 Cf. Isa. 11.2.
6 Cf. John 4.13,14.

be denied by the heretics as a Fountain, since the Spirit, too, is called a Fountain. And as the Spirit is called a river, so, too, the Father said: 'Behold, I shall come upon you like a river of peace, and as a torrent inundating the glory of the Gentiles.'[7] But who will doubt that the Son of God is the river of life, from whom the rivers of eternal life flowed forth?

(162) Good, then, is the water, spiritual grace. Who will give this Fountain to my breast? Let it spring up in me; let the bestower of eternal life flow upon me. Let that Fountain flow over upon us; let it now flow from us. For Wisdom says: 'Drink water out of thy own cistern, and the streams of thy own well, and let thy waters flow abroad in thy streets.'[8] How shall I hold this water from flowing forth, from slipping away? How shall I preserve my vessel, lest any crack of sin penetrating it let the moisture of eternal life trickle forth? Teach us, Lord Jesus, teach us as You taught your Apostles, saying: 'Lay not up for yourselves treasures on earth, where the rust, and the moth consume, and where thieves dig through, and steal.'[9]

(163) Clearly He indicates that the thief is the unclean spirit, who cannot steal upon those who walk in the light of good works, but if he should catch one midst the joys of earthly pleasures, despoils him of all the flower of eternal virtue. And so the Lord says: 'Lay up for yourselves treasures in heaven where neither the rust, nor the moth doth consume, and where thieves do not dig through, nor steal. For where thy treasure is, there is thy heart also.'[10]

(164) Our rust is lasciviousness; our rust is wantonness;

7 Cf. Isa. 66.12.
8 Prov. 5.15,16.
9 Matt. 6.19.
10 Matt. 16.20,21.

our rust is luxury, which obscure the sharpness of the mind with the filth of vices. Again our moth is Arius, our moth is Photinus, who cut the holy vestment of the Church with their impiety, and desiring to separate the indivisible unity of the divine power, gnaw the precious veil of faith by their sacrilegious bite. Water is spilled, if Arius has implanted his tooth; it flows forth if Photinus has fixed his sting in anyone's vessel. We are a base formation; we speedily feel vices. But no one says to the potter: 'Why hast thou made me thus?' For although our vessel is base, yet one is in honor, another in dishonor.[11] So do not open your pit, and do not dig with vices and crimes, lest some one say: 'He hath opened a pit and dug it; and he is fallen into the hole he made.'[12]

(165) If you seek Jesus, abandon broken pits; for Christ was not accustomed to sit near a pit, but near a well. There that Samaritan woman who believed, that woman who wished to draw water, found Him.[13] Although you ought to have come early in the morning, yet, even you should come later, you will find Jesus at the sixth hour tired from the journey. He is tired, but because of you, because He has sought you for a long time, your unbelief has long tired Him. Yet He is not offended, if only you come. He asks to drink, who is about to give. But He drinks not the water of a passing stream, but your salvation. He drinks your compassion; He drinks the cup, that is, that passion which is the redeemer of your crimes, that you may quench the thirst of this world by the drink of His sacred blood.

(166) Thus Abraham deserved God after he dug a well. Thus, Isaac, when he walked along the way to the well,

---

11 Rom. 9.20; cf. 9.21.
12 Ps. 7.16.
13 Cf. John 4.6,7.

received the wife who was coming as a type of the Church.[14] Faithful he was at the well; unfaithful at the pit. Then, too, Rebecca, as we read, found her seeker at the fountain, and the harlots washed themselves with blood in the pit of Jezebel.[15]

14 Cf. Gen. 21.30; 24.62,67.
15 Cf. 3 Kings 22.36.

THE HOLY SPIRIT

Book Two

Prologue

LTHOUGH IN THE FIRST BOOK of the ancient history it has been made clear from reading both that the grace of the sevenfold Spirit was reflected in the judges themselves of the ancient Jews and that the mysteries of the heavenly sacraments were revealed through the Holy Spirit, whom Moses was not unaware of as eternal, accordingly at the beginning of the world—rather, before the beginning —he joined Him with God, whom he knew to be eternal before the beginning of the world. For, if anyone notices carefully, he will recognize in the beginning the Father and the Son and the Spirit. For of the Father it is written: 'In the beginning God created heaven and earth.' Of the Spirit it is said: 'The Spirit was moved over the waters.'[1] And in the beginning of creation the figure of baptism is well indicated,

---

1 Gen. 1.1,2.

through which the creature had to be cleansed. It is also read of the Son that it is He who made a separation of the light and the darkness; for there is one God the Father who speaks, and one Lord Jesus who acts.

(2)   But, again, lest you think that there was either arrogant power on the part of Him who spoke or base compliance on the part of Him who acted, the Father confesses the Son as equal to Himself in the oneness of the work, saying: 'Let us make man to our image and likeness.'[2] For what else do image and working and common likeness signify than the oneness of the same majesty?

(3)   Yet, that you may recognize more fully the equality of the Father and of the Son, just as the Father spoke and the Son did, so, too, the Father works and the Son speaks. The Father works, as it is written: 'My Father worketh until now.'[3] You have it said to the Son: 'Say the word, and he shall be healed.'[4] And the Son says to the Father: 'I will that where I am, they also may be with me.'[5] The Father did what the Son said.

(4)   But Abraham was not ignorant of the Holy Spirit. And thereupon he saw three, and adored one,[6] because there is one God, one Lord, and one Spirit. And so there is oneness of honor, because there is oneness of power.

(5)   And what shall I say of each one? Samson, born by the divine promise, had the Spirit with him, for so we read: 'The Lord blessed him, and the Spirit of the Lord began to be with him in the camp.'[7] And thus foreseeing the future

---

2 Gen. 1.26.
3 John 5.17.
4 Cf. Matt. 8.8.
5 Cf. John 17.24.
6 Gen. 18.2-3.
7 Judges 13.25.

mystery, he demanded a wife from the foreigners, which his father and mother did not know, as it is written, because it is from the Lord. And rightly was he held stronger than the rest, for the Spirit of the Lord directed him, under whose guidance, he alone now put to flight the peoples of the foreigners, now tore the lion asunder with his hands, inaccessible to its bite, invincible in his strength.[8] Would that he had been as careful to preserve grace as he was strong to overcome the beast!

(6) Perhaps this was not only a marvel of courage, but also a mystery of wisdom, an oracle of prophecy. For it does not seem to be without meaning that when he was on his way to the sacrament of marriage, a roaring lion met him, whom he tore apart with his hands, in whose body, as he was on the point of gaining the desired wedlock, he finds a swarm of bees, and from whose mouth he took honey, which he gave to his father and mother to eat.[9] The people of the Gentiles, who believed, had honey; the people who before belonged to savagery is now of Christ.

(7) The riddle is not without mystery, which he proposed to his companions, saying: 'Out of the eater came forth meat, and out of the strong came forth sweetness.'[10] Then it was mysterious to the point that its solution was sought within three days, which could not have been solved except through the faith of the Church on the seventh day, when the time of Law had been completed, after the passion of the Lord. For thus you have it, that the Apostles also did not understand, 'because Jesus was not yet glorified.'[11]

---

8 Cf. Judges 14.1-5ff.
9 Cf. Judges 14.8ff.
10 Cf. Judges 14.14.
11 John 7.39.

(8) They say: 'What is sweeter than honey? and what is stronger than a lion?' To this he replied: 'If you had not ploughed with my heifer, you had not found out my riddle.'[12] O divine mystery! O manifest sacrament! We have evaded the slayer; we have overcome the powerful! There now is the food of life, where before was the hunger of a miserable life. Dangers are turned into safety, bitterness into sweetness. Grace has come forth from the offence; power from weakness, life from death.

(9) Yet there are those who on the other hand believe that the wedlock could not have been established except by the slaying of the lion of the tribe of Judas, and that so in His body, that is, the Church, bees were found, who store up the honey of wisdom, because after the Lord's passion the Apostles believed more. So Samson, as a Jew, kills this lion, but in it he found honey, as in the figure of the heritage to be redeemed, that a remnant might be saved according to the election of grace.[13]

(10) Scripture says: 'And the Spirit of the Lord came upon him; and he went down to Ascalon, and slew there thirty men.'[14] For he was unable not to possess the victory, who comprehended the mysteries. So in the garments they receive the reward of wisdom, the badge of intercourse, who resolve and answer the riddle.

(11) Here, again, other mysteries arise, in that his wife is carried away, and so foxes set fire to the sheaves of aliens.[15] For those who contend against the divine sacraments are usually deceived by their own cunning. So again Scripture

12 Judges 14.18.
13 Cf. Rom. 11.5.
14 Judges 14.19.
15 Cf. Judges 15.1ff.

says in the Canticle of Canticles: 'Catch us the little foxes that destroy the vines, that our vineyards may flourish.'[16] Well did he say 'little,' because the larger could not destroy the vineyards, although to the strong even the Devil is little.

(12) He, then (to make a summary of the story, for the consideration of the whole passage must be reserved for its own time), was unconquered as long as he possessed spiritual grace, as was the people of God chosen by the Lord, that Nazarene in the Law. So Samson was unconquered, and so invincible that he struck a thousand men with the jawbone of an ass,[17] so full of heavenly grace that when thirsty he even found water in the jawbone of an ass, whether you compare this to a miracle, or turn it to a mystery, since in the humility of the people of the Gentiles there was both rest and triumph, according as it is written: 'If anyone strike thee on the cheek, turn to him the other also.'[18] For by this endurance of injuries, which the sacrament of baptism teaches, we triumph over some stings of anger, that, when we have met death, we may obtain the rest of the resurrection.

(13) Was it that Samson, then, who broke the ropes intertwined with thongs, who broke new cords like weak threads? Was it that Samson who did not feel the bonds of his hair fastened by a fixed beam, so long as he possessed spiritual grace? He, I say, after the Spirit of God departed from him, greatly changed from that Samson who returned clothed in the spoils of the foreigners, fallen from his strength on the knees of a woman, caressed and deceived, shorn of his consecrated hair.[19]

---

16 Cf. Cant. 2.15.
17 Cf. Judges 15.15.
18 Cf. Matt. 5.39.
19 Cf. Judges 16.7-19.

(14) So did the hairs of his head possess such importance that, while these remained, his strength remained unconquered, but when the head was shorn, all the strength of the man was suddenly lost? We should not think that the hairs of the body possess such strength. There is the hair of religion and faith; the hair of the Nazarene perfect in the Law, consecrated in parsimony and abstinence, with which she, in type the Church, who had poured oil over the feet of the Lord, wiped the feet of the heavenly word;[20] for then she knew Christ also according to the flesh. Manifestly, that is the hair of which it is said: 'Thy hair is as flocks of goats'; growing from that head of which it is said: 'The head of every man is Christ' and elsewhere: 'His head is as the finest gold; his locks as black pine-trees.'[21] The good ships of Tharsis are of pine, which float upon the floods of the world, and show the safe oarage of salvation.

(15) And so also in the Gospel our Lord, pointing out that certain hairs of the head are visible and perceptible, says: 'But the very hairs of your head are all numbered,'[22] pointing out manifestly the deeds of spiritual virtue, for God has no care for our hair. And yet it is not absurd to believe that, since in accord with His divine majesty nothing can be hidden from Him.

(16) But what does it profit me, if God Himself knows all my hairs? That redounds and is of benefit to me if He, the ever-watchful witness of good deeds, grants the reward of eternal glory. Finally, Samson himself, declaring that these hairs are not corporeal but perceptible, says: 'If my head

---

20 Cf. John 12.3.
21 Cant. 4.1; 1 Cor. 11.3; cf. Cant. 5.11.
22 Matt. 10.30.

be shaven, my strength shall depart from me.'[23] This concerns
the mystery. Now let us consider the order of the passage.

Chapter 1

(17) Above you have it that 'the Lord blessed him, and
the Spirit of the Lord began to be with him.' Below it says:
'And the Spirit of the Lord came upon him.' Likewise it
says: 'If my head be shaven, my strength shall depart from
me.' After he was shaven, see what Scripture says: 'The Lord,'
it says, 'was departed from him.'[1]

(18) You see, then, that He who was with him, Himself
departed from him. The same, then, is the Lord, who is the
Spirit of the Lord; that is, He called the Spirit of the Lord,
Lord, just as also the Apostle says: 'Now the Lord is a spirit;
and where the Spirit of the Lord is, there is liberty.'[2] You have
then, the Lord called also the Holy Spirit; for the Holy Spirit
and the Son are not one Person, but one Substance.

(19) In this place, also, he mentioned Power and signified
the Spirit. For just as the Father is Power, so, too, is the
Son Power, and is the Holy Spirit Power.[3] Of the Son you
have read that 'Christ is the power of God, and the wisdom
of God.'[4] We read also that the Father is Power, as it is
written: 'You shall see the Son of man sitting on the right
hand of the power of God.'[5] Here, surely, He called the Father

---

23 Judges 16.17.

---

1 Judges 13.24-25; 14.6; 16.17,20.
2 2 Cor. 3.17.
3 Cf. 1 John 5.17.
4 1 Cor. 1.24.
5 Matt. 26.64.

Power, on whose right hand the Son sits, as you have it: 'The Lord said to my Lord: Sit thou at my right hand.'[6] The Lord Himself also named the Holy Spirit Power when He said: 'You shall receive the power, when the Ghost comes upon you.'[7]

Chapter 2

(20) For the Spirit Himself is power, for you have read: 'The Spirit of counsel, and of fortitude [power].'[1] And as the Son is the Angel of great counsel, so also is the Spirit of counsel, that you may know that the counsel of the Father and of the Son and of the Holy Spirit is one—the counsel not on some doubtful matters, but on foreknown and established matters.

(21) But that the Spirit is the Arbiter of divine Counsel, learn also from this. For when we taught above[2] that the Arbiter of baptism is the Holy Spirit, and have read that baptism is the counsel of God, as you have it: 'But the Pharisees despised the counsel of God against themselves, being not baptized by him,'[3] it is very clear that, since there can be no baptism without the Spirit, there can also be no counsel of God without the Spirit.

(22) And that we may know more fully that the Spirit is Power, we should know that He was promised, when the Lord said: 'I will pour out my spirit upon all flesh.'[4] He

6 Ps. 109.1.
7 Cf. Acts 1.8.

1 Isa. 11.2.
2 See Book 1, ch. 6.
3 Cf. Luke 7.30.
4 Joel 2.28.

then who was promised us is Himself Power, just as also in the Gospel the same Son of God declared when He said: 'And I send the promise of my Father upon you; but stay you in the city, till you are clothed with power from on high.'[5]

(23) And the Evangelist so far points out that the Holy Spirit is power, so that St. Luke also related that He descended with great power, when he says: 'And suddenly there came a sound from heaven, as though the Spirit were borne with great power.'[6]

(24) But lest you again think that this is to be referred to sensible and corporeal things, learn that the Spirit so descended just as Christ is to descend, as you have it: 'They shall see the Son of man coming in the clouds of heaven with great power and majesty.'[7]

(25) For how is not the power one and the might the same, when the work of the Father and of the Son and of the Holy Spirit is one, the judgment one, the temple one, the vivification one, the sanctification one, the kingdom also one?

Chapter 3

(26) For let them say in whom they think there is an unlikeness of the divine work. Since just as life is to know the Father and the Son, as the Lord himself declared when He said: 'This is life everlasting; that they may know thee, the only true God, and Jesus Christ, whom thou hast sent,'[1] so also is life to know the Holy Spirit. For the Lord says: 'If

---

5 Luke 24.49.
6 Cf. Acts 2.2.
7 Matt. 24.30.

---

1 John 17.3.

you love me, keep my commandments; and I will ask the Father, and he shall give you another Paraclete, that he may abide with you for ever, the Spirit of truth, whom the world cannot receive; because it seeth him not, nor knoweth him; but you know him, because he abides with you, and he is in you.'[2]

(27) The world, then, did not have eternal life, because it had not received the Spirit; moreover, where the Spirit is, there is eternal life, for the Spirit himself is He who effects eternal life. Therefore, I wonder why the Arians raise the question as to the only true God. For just as it is eternal life to know the only true God, so it is eternal life to know Jesus Christ, so it is eternal life to know the Holy Spirit, whom the world does not see as it sees the Father, does not know as it knows the Son. Moreover, he who is not of this world has eternal life, and the Spirit, who is the light of eternal life, abides with him for ever.

(28) So, if the knowledge of the only true God confers this which the knowledge of the Son and of the Spirit confers, why do you separate the Son and the Spirit from the honor of the true God, when you do not separate them from the magnitude of the benefit? For either you must believe that this greatest boon is of the only true Godhead, and as you will confess the only true Godhead of the Father, so you will confess it of the Son and of the Spirit, or if you should say that he, too, can confer eternal life who is not true God, you will fall into the position of seeming to derogate rather from the Father, whose work you do not think to be the chief work of the only true Godhead, but to be compared to the works of a creature.

---

2 Cf. John 14.15-17.

Chapter 4

(29) Moreover, what wonder is it if the Spirit works life, who gives life as the Father does, who gives life as the Son does?[1] Moreover, who would deny that to give life is of the Eternal Majesty? For it is written: 'Enliven thy servant.'[2] So he is enlivened who is a servant, that is, man, who did not have life before, but received the privilege of having it.

(30) Therefore, let us see whether the Spirit is enlivened, or Himself enlivens. But it is written: 'The letter killeth, but the Spirit giveth life.'[3] So the Spirit giveth life.

(31) But that you may understand that the quickening of the Father and of the Son and of the Holy Spirit is not divided, learn that there is a oneness of quickening also, since God himself quickens through the Spirit; for Paul said: 'He that raised up Jesus Christ from the dead shall quicken also your mortal bodies, because of his Spirit dwelling in you.'[4]

Chapter 5

(32) Who indeed can doubt that the Holy Spirit quickens all things, since He, too, just as the Father and the Son, is the Creator of all things, and God, the omnipotent Father, is understood to have done nothing without the Holy Spirit; for even in the beginning of the creation the Spirit moved over the waters?[1]

---

1 Cf. John 5.21.
2 Cf. Ps. 118.17.
3 2 Cor. 3.6.
4 Rom. 8.11.

---

1 Cf. Gen. 1.1.

(33) So, when the Spirit moved over the waters, there was no grace in creation, but after the creation of this world also received the operation of the Spirit, it gained all the beauty of that grace with which the world is illumined. Finally, the Prophet declared that the grace of the universe cannot abide without the Holy Spirit, when he said: 'Thou shalt take away their breath, and they shall fail, and shall return to their dust. Send forth thy spirit, and they shall be created, and thou shalt renew the face of the earth.'[2] Not only then did he teach that all creation cannot stand without the Spirit, but also that the Spirit is the Creator of the whole creation.

(34) And who will deny that the work of the Holy Spirit is the creation of the earth, whose work it is that it is renewed? For if they should desire to deny that it was created through the Spirit, since they cannot deny that it must be renewed through the Spirit, then those who desire to separate the Persons will maintain that the operation of the Holy Spirit is better than that of the Father and of the Son, which is far from the truth; for there is no doubt that the renewed earth is better than the created earth. Or, if at first the Father and the Son made the earth without the operation of the Holy Spirit, but afterwards the operation of the Holy Spirit was joined to this, that which was made will seem to have needed the aid of that which was added. God forbid that anyone should think this, that the divine operation be believed to have a variety of authors, which Manichaeus introduced.[3]

(35) Or, indeed, do we think that the substance of the

---

2 Cf. Ps. 103.29,30.

3 Manes or Manichaeus, the author of Manichaeism, professed to have effected the true synthesis of all the religious systems then known. It actually consisted of Zoroastrian dualism, Babylonian folklore, Buddhist ethics, and some small and superficial addition of Christian elements. The theory of two eternal principles, good and evil, is predominant. See article on Manichaeism in *Cath. Encycl.*

earth exists without the work of the Spirit, without whose
work the vault of the heavens does not subsist? For it is
written: 'By the word of the Lord, the heavens were established; and all the power of them by the spirit of his mouth.'[4]
Notice what he says. He says that all the power of the heavens
is to be referred to the Spirit. For how was He who was moving, before the earth was made, resting when the earth was
being made?

(36) Gentile writers, following ours through shadows, as
it were, because they could not take in the truth of the Spirit,
have indicated in their verses that the Spirit within nourishes
the heaven and the earth, as well as the spheres of the glitter-
ing moon and stars.[5] Thus they do not deny that the power
of creatures stands firm through the Spirit; do we who read
deny this? But you think that a spirit produced from air is
indicated. If they have declared a spirit made of air as the
author of all, do we doubt that the Spirit of God is the creator
of all?

(37) But why do I delay with unrelated matters? Let
them accept the evident proof that there can be nothing which
the Spirit is denied to have made, nor can it be denied
regarding the Angels, the Archangels, the Thrones, and
Dominions, that they subsist by His operation, since the Lord
Himself according to the flesh, whom the angels serve, was
begotten when the Spirit came upon the Virgin, just as according to Matthew the angel said to Joseph: 'Joseph, son
of David, fear not to take unto thee Mary thy wife; for that
which is conceived in her is of the Holy Ghost.' And according
to Luke, he said to Mary: 'The Holy Ghost shall come upon
thee.'[6]

---

4 Ps. 32.6.
5 Cf. Vergil, *Aeneid* 6.724.
6 Matt. 1.20; Luke 1.35.

(38) So the birth from the Virgin is the work of the Spirit. The fruit of the womb is the work of the Spirit, according to what is written: 'Blessed art thou among women; and blessed is the fruit of thy womb.'[7] The flower of the root is the work of the Spirit, that flower, I say, of which it was well prophesied: 'There shall come forth a rod out of the root of Jesse, and a flower shall rise up out of his root.'[8] The root of the patriarch Jesse is the family of the Jews; Mary is the rod; Christ is the flower of Mary, who sprouted forth from a virginal womb to spread the good odor of faith throughout the whole world, as he himself said: 'I am the flower of the field, and the lily of the valley.'[9]

(39) The flower, even when cut, keeps its odor, and when bruised increases it, and when torn does not lose it; so, too, the Lord Jesus on that gibbet of the cross neither failed when bruised, nor fainted when torn; and when cut by the pricking of the lance, made more beautiful by the sacred color of the outpoured blood, He grew young again, Himself not knowing how to die and exhaling among the dead the gift of eternal life. On this flower, then, of the royal rod the Holy Spirit rested.

(40) A good rod, as some think, is the flesh of the Lord, which raised itself from the root of the earth to the regions above and carried about the world the sweet-smelling fruits of the holy religion, the mysteries of the divine generation, and pouring out grace upon the altars of heaven.

(41) So we cannot doubt that the Spirit is Creator, whom we know as the Author of the Lord's Incarnation. For who will doubt when in the beginning of the Gospel you have it,

---

7 Luke 1.42.
8 Isa. 11.1.
9 Cant. 2.1.

that the generation of Christ was thus: 'When Mary his Mother was espoused to Joseph, before they came together, she was found with child of the Holy Ghost'?[10]

(42) Although most manuscripts have *de Spiritu,* nevertheless, the Greek from which the Latins translated, said: ἐκ πνεύματος ἁγίου, that is, *ex Spiritu Sancto.* For what is from someone is either of his substance or of his power. Of his substance as the Son, who says: 'I came out of the mouth of the most High,'[11] as the Spirit who proceeds from the Father, of whom the Son says: 'He shall glorify me; because he shall receive of mine.'[12] Of the power, moreover, according to this: 'One God, the Father, of whom are all things.'[13]

(43) How, then, did Mary have Him of the Holy Spirit in her womb? If as of her substance, then was the Spirit turned into flesh and bones? Surely not. If the Virgin conceived as of His operation and power, who will deny the Spirit as Creator?

(44) What of the fact that Job also clearly indicated the Spirit as his Creator, when he said: 'The divine Spirit, who made me.'[14] Surely in one small verse he showed Him to be both divine and Creator. If, then, the Spirit is Creator, He certainly is not a creature, for the Apostle separated creature and Creator, when he said: 'They served the creature rather than the Creator.'[15]

(45) At the same time he warns that the Creator is to be served by condemning those who serve the creature, when we owe service to the Creator. And since he knew the Spirit as Creator, he taught that He should be served saying: 'Beware

---

10 Matt. 1.18.
11 Eccli. 24.5.
12 John 16.14.
13 1 Cor. 8.6.
14 Cf. Job 33.4.
15 Rom. 1.25.

of dogs, beware of evil-workers, beware of the concision. For we are the circumcision, who serve the Spirit of God.'[16]

(46) But if someone objects because of the disagreement in the Latin manuscripts, some of which heretics have falsified, let him examine the Greek manuscripts, and notice that it is written there: οἱ πνεύματι Θεοῦ λατρεύοντες, which is translated in Latin: 'Who serve the Spirit of God.'

(47) So, when the same Apostle says that the Spirit should be served who asserts that not the creature but the Creator is to be served, surely he shows clearly that the Holy Spirit is Creator, and is to be venerated with the honor of the eternal Godhead, because it is written: 'The Lord thy God thou shalt adore and him only shalt thou serve.'[17]

Chapter 6

(48) And it does not escape me that heretics have been accustomed to object that the Holy Spirit seems to have been created on this account, because many of them advance as an argument to establish their impiety what Amos said about the blowing of the wind, as the very words of the Prophet declare. For you have these words: 'Behold I am He that established the thunders, and createth the wind [spirit], and declareth His Christ to men, that maketh the light and mist, and walketh upon the high places of the earth; the Lord the God of hosts is his name.'[1]

(49) If they make an argument out of this, that he said

16 Cf. Phil. 3.2,3.
17 Matt. 4.10.

1 *Spiritus*, meaning 'wind' or 'spirit,' is also used for the Holy Spirit. Throughout several chapters here St. Ambrose battles the heretics who would confuse the meaning of Scripture.

'spirit' was created, Esdras taught us that spirit is created, saying in the fourth book: 'And again on the second day you made the spirit of the firmament';[2] yet, to stick to the point, manifestly from these words which Amos spoke, does not the order of the words clearly prove that the Prophet spoke of the creation of this world?

(50) Then he begins thus: 'I am He that established the thunders, and createth the wind [spirit].'[3] Let the very order of the words teach us; for, if he had wished to speak of the Holy Spirit, surely he would not have placed the thunders first. For the thunders are not more ancient than the Holy Spirit; although they are impious, yet they dare not say this. Then, when we see that something is added about the light and mist, is it not manifest that what is said is to be understood of the creation of the world? For we know from daily experience and example that, when the storms of this world take place, thunders come first, blasts of wind follow, the sky grows dark with clouds, and the light comes forth again from the darkness. For the blasts of the winds are also called 'spirits,' as it is written: 'Fire and brimstone and storms of winds.'[4]

(51) And that you might know that he called this 'spirit' he says: 'He that establisheth the thunders, and createth the wind [spirit],' because these are often created when they take place, but the Holy Spirit is eternal, and, if anyone dares to say that He is created, yet he cannot say that He is created daily, like the breeze of the winds. Then Wisdom herself, when speaking with reference to the assumed body, says: 'The Lord created me.'[5] Although He was prophesying of things to come, yet, because the coming of our Lord and Saviour was predes-

---

2 Cf. Amos. 4.13.
3 Cf. 4 Esd. 6.41, following the Latin version of MIGNE.
4 Ps. 10.7.
5 Cf. Prov. 8.22.

tined, it is not said 'creates' but 'created me,' that it might not be believed that the body of Jesus was to be begotten frequently, of the Virgin Mary but once.

(52) So, as to that which the Prophet declared as the daily working of God in the firmament of thunder and in the creation of the wind, it is impious for us to consider any such thing of the Holy Spirit, whom the impious themselves cannot deny to exist before the ages. Therefore, with pious assertion we testify both that He always is and always abides. For He who before the world moved over the waters cannot seem to have begun after the world; or, if not, it is proper to believe that many Holy Spirits exist, who are begotten as it were by daily generation. God forbid that anyone contaminate himself by such impiety as to say that the Holy Spirit is created frequently or is ever created. For I do not understand why He seems to be created frequently, unless, perchance, they believe that He both dies frequently and is created frequently. But how can the Spirit of life die? So, if He cannot die, there is no reason for the necessity of His being created frequently.

(53) But those who think otherwise fall into that sacrilege of not distinguishing the Holy Spirit, who think that the Word which went forth returns to the Father, that the Spirit which went forth flows back into God, so that there is a restitution and a kind of alternation of one changing himself often into various forms, whereas the distinction between the Father and the Son and the Holy Spirit is ever abiding and retains the Oneness of its power.

(54) Yet if anyone thinks that the words of the Prophet should be diverted to an interpretation of the Holy Spirit, because he says: 'declaring His Christ to men,'[6] he will more

---

6 Cf. Amos 4.13.

easily divert the words to the mystery of the Lord's Incarnation. For if it troubles you that he said spirit, and so you think that this should not be diverted to the assumption of human nature, read the Scriptures further, and you will find that it agrees very well with reference to Christ, of whom it is well fitting that he established thunders by His coming, namely, the force and sound of the heavenly Scriptures, by a kind of thunder of which, as it were, our minds are struck with astonishment, so that we learn to fear and offer reverence to the heavenly pronouncements.

(55) Finally, in the Gospel the brothers of the Lord were called Sons of Thunder, and when the voice of the Father was uttered saying to the Son: 'I have glorified it, and will glorify it again,' the Jews said: 'It thundered on Him.'[7] For although they could not receive the grace of truth, yet they confessed unwillingly, and unwittingly spoke a mystery, whereby a great testimony of the Father to the Son resulted. In the Book of Job also Scripture says: 'Who knows when He will make the power of His thunder.'[8] Surely, if the words pertained to these thunders of heavenly disturbances, he would have said not that force would be, but was made.

(56) So he referred the thunders to the words of the Lord, whose sound went out into all the land; moreover, we understand spirit in this place as soul, which He took endowed with reason and perfect, because Scripture frequently designates the soul of man by the word spirit as you have it: 'Who formeth the spirit of man in him.'[9] Thus also the Lord, signifying His soul by the word Spirit, said: 'Into thy hands I commend my spirit.'[10]

---

7 Cf. John 12.28.
8 Cf. Job. 26.14 (Septuagint).
9 Zach. 12.1.
10 Luke 23.46.

(51)   And that you might know that he made mention of the descent of the Lord Jesus, he added that He announced His Christ to men,[11] for He proclaimed Him in baptism, saying: 'You are my beloved Son, in whom I am well pleased.' He proclaimed Him on the mount, saying: 'This is my most beloved Son; hear ye him.' He proclaimed Him in His passion, when the sun withdrew, and the sea and the earth trembled. He proclaimed Him in the centurion, who said: 'This was truly the Son of God.'[12]

(58)   So we ought to refer this entire passage either to the simple understanding of that spirit which is drawn in by living or to the mystery of the Lord's Incarnation, for, if He had said here that the Holy Spirit was created, surely Scripture could have declared the same elsewhere, also, just as we often read about the Son of God, that according to the flesh He was both made and created.[13]

(59)   Yet it is fitting that we consider His majesty in the very fact that He took on flesh for us, that we may see the divine power in the very assumption of the body. For as we read that the Father created the sacrament of the Lord's Incarnation, the Spirit also created it. So, too, we read that Christ himself also created His own body, for the Father created it according to what is written: 'The Lord created me,' and elsewhere: 'God sent His Son, made of a woman, made under the law.'[14] And the Spirit created that whole mystery, according to what we read, namely: 'Mary was found with child of the Holy Ghost.'[15]

(60)   You have it that the Father created, that the Spirit

---

11 Cf. Amos 4.13.
12 Cf. Matt. 3.17; Mark 9.6; cf. Matt. 14.33.
13 Cf. Rom. 1.3.
14 Cf. Prov. 8.23; Gal. 4.4.
15 Matt. 1.18.

also created; accept that the Son of God also created, when Solomon says: 'Wisdom has built herself a house.'[16] Therefore, how can the Holy Spirit, who created the sacrament of the Lord's Incarnation, which is above all creations, be a creature?

(61) We have shown above,[17] generally, that the Holy Spirit is our Creator according to the flesh in the outer man; now let us show that He is our Creator also according to the sacrament of grace. And just as the Father creates, so the Son also creates, so the Holy Spirit also creates, as we read in the words of Paul: 'For it is the gift of God, not of works, that no man may glory. For we are his workmanship, created in Christ Jesus in good works.'[18]

Chapter 7

(62) Therefore, the Father creates in good works; the Son also creates, because it is written: 'But as many as received him, to them he gave power to be made the sons of God, to them that believe in His name; who are born, not of blood, nor of the will of the flesh, nor of the will of man but of God.'[1]

(63) Similarly, the Lord himself testifies that we are reborn of the Spirit according to grace, when He says: 'That which is born of the flesh, is flesh, because it is born of the flesh; and that which is born of the Spirit, is spirit, because God is spirit. Wonder not that I said to thee, you must be

---

16 Prov. 9.1.
17 Ch. 5.
18 Eph. 2.8-10.

1 John 1.12,13.

born again. The Spirit breatheth where he will; and thou hearest his voice; but thou knewest not whence he cometh, nor whither he goeth; so is everyone that is born of the Spirit.'[2]

(64) Therefore, it is clear that the Holy Spirit is also the author of spiritual generation, because we are created according to God, to be the sons of God. So, when He has assumed us into His kingdom through the adoption of holy regeneration, do we deny Him what is His? He has made us heirs of supernal regeneration, do we claim the heritage and reject the Author? But the benefit cannot remain when the Author is excluded; neither is the author without the gift, nor the gift without the author. If you claim the grace, believe the power; if you reject the power, do not ask for the grace. He who has denied the Spirit has at the same time denied the gift, also. For if the Author is cheap, how are His gifts precious? Why do we ourselves grudge our gifts, diminish our hopes, repudiate our dignity, deny our Comforter?

(65) But we cannot deny Him. For God forbid that we deny what is the greatest, since the Apostle says: 'Now you, brethren, as Isaac was, are the children of the promise. But as then he, who was born according to the flesh, persecuted him, who was according to the Spirit.'[3] Again, surely from what is said above he is understood who is born according to the Spirit. He, then, who is born according to the Spirit is born according to God. Now, we are born again when we are renewed in our inward affections and lay aside the old age of the outer man. And so the Apostle says again: 'And be ye renewed in the spirit of your mind, and put on the new man, who, according to God, is created in truth, and justice, and

2 Cf. John 3.6-8.
3 Cf. Gal. 4.28,29.

holiness.'[4] Let them hear how Scripture has signified the unity of the divine operation. He who is renewed in the spirit of his mind has put on the new man, who is created according to God.

(66) That more pre-eminent regeneration, then, is the work of the Holy Spirit; and the Spirit is the author of this new man, who is created according to the image of God, who surely no one will doubt to be better than this exterior man of ours, since the Apostle has indicated that the one is heavenly, the other earthly, when he says: 'Such as is the earthly, such also are they that are heavenly.'[5]

(67) Since, then, spiritual grace makes man heavenly, we ought also to note with reason that it can create man earthly, although we are lacking examples. For holy Job says elsewhere: 'The Lord liveth, who so judges me; and the Almighty, who hath brought my soul to bitterness; but the divine Spirit who is in my nostrils.'[6] Surely he did not here signify the Spirit as the vital breath and the corporal breathing passages, but he signifies here the nostrils of his inner man, with which he gathered in the odor of eternal life, and drew in the grace of the heavenly ointment by a twofold sense, as it were.

(68) For there are spiritual nostrils, as we read, which the spouse of the Word has, to whom it is said: 'The odor of thy nostrils,' and elsewhere: 'The Lord smelled a sweet savour.'[7] There are then, as it were, members of the interior man, whose hands are considered to be in action, ears in hearing, feet in a kind of progress in a good work. And so

4 Cf. Eph. 4.23,24.
5 1 Cor. 15.48.
6 Cf. Job. 27.2,3.
7 Cf. Cant. 7.8; Gen. 8.21.

from functions we gather, as it were, figures of the members, for it is not fitting that we consider anything in the interior man in the manner of fleshly things.

(69) There are some who think that God was formed in a bodily manner, when they read either of His hand or finger. They do not notice that these are written not on account of the form of the body, because in the divinity those are neither members nor parts but are expressed because of the unity of the Godhead, that we may believe that it is impossible for either the Son or the Holy Spirit to be separated from God the Father, since the fullness of the Godhead dwells as it were corporeally in the substance of the Trinity. Thus, then, is the Son called the right hand of the Father, as it is written: 'The right hand of the Lord hath wrought strength; the right hand of the Lord hath exalted me.'[8]

Chapter 8

(70) But what wonder is it if senseless men raise questions about words, when they do so also about syllables? For there are those who think that distinction should be made here, in that they say that God should be spoken of *in* the Spirit, not *with* the Spirit; and who think that the importance of the Godhead is to be considered from a syllable or from a kind of custom, arguing that if they think that God is to be praised *in* the Spirit, they seem to indicate an office of the Holy Spirit; but if they say that either power or glory is God's with the Spirit they seem to designate a kind of association and communion of the Father, the Son, and the Holy Spirit.

(71) But who will separate what cannot be separated?

8 Ps. 117.16.

Who will divide an association which Christ shows to be indivisible? He said: 'Go ye, therefore, and baptize all nations in the name of the Father, and of the Son, and of the Holy Ghost.'[1] Did He change here either a word or a syllable regarding the Father or the Son or the Holy Spirit? Certainly not. But He says: 'In the name of the Father, and of the Son, and of the Holy Ghost.' He speaks the same of the Spirit as of the Father and of Himself. Therefore, no office of the Holy Spirit is considered but rather a sharing of honor or of work, when 'in the Spirit' is said.

(72) Consider also here that this injury is diverted from your opinion to the Father and the Son, because the latter did not say: *'With* the name of the Father and of the Son, and of the Holy Spirit,' but *'in* the name,' and yet no office but the power of the Trinity is expressed by this syllable.

(73) Finally, that you may know that a syllable does not injure faith, but faith commands a syllable, Paul also speaks in Christ. Thus Christ is not less because Paul has spoken in Christ, as you have it: 'In the sight of God we speak in Christ.'[2] Just as then the Apostle says that we speak in Christ, so is it that we speak in the Spirit, as the Apostle himself said: 'No man says the Lord Jesus, except in the Holy Spirit.'[3] So in this passage no subjection of the Holy Spirit, but a connection of grace, is indicated.

(74) And that you may know that there is no distinction dependent on a syllable, he also says elsewhere: 'And these indeed you were; but you are washed, but you are sanctified, but you are justified in the name of Jesus Christ, and in the Spirit of our God.'[4] How many examples of this can I bring

1 Cf. Matt. 28.19.
2 2 Cor. 2.17.
3 Cf. 1 Cor. 12.3.
4 Cf. 1 Cor. 6.11.

forward! For it is written: 'For you are all one in Christ
Jesus'; and elsewhere: 'To them that are sanctified in Christ
Jesus'; and again: 'That we might be made the justice of
God in him'; and in another place: 'To fall from the chastity,
which is in Christ Jesus.'[5]

(75) But what am I doing? For while I say that similar
words are written of the Son as of the Spirit, I go on rather
to this: that not because it was written of the Son, does it
seem to have been written devoutly of the Spirit, but because
the same thing is written of the Spirit, they oppose that there
is disparagement of the Son because of the Spirit. For they
say: 'Is it written of God the Father?'

(76) But let them learn that it is said also of God the
Father: 'In the Lord I will praise the word'; and elsewhere:
'In God we shall do mightily'; and: 'In thee will be my
remembrance always'; and: 'In thy name we shall rejoice';
again elsewhere: 'That his works may be made manifest,
because they are done in God.'[6] And Paul says: 'In God, who
created all things'; and again: 'Paul and Silvanus, and Timothy, to the church of the Thessalonians in God our Father,
and the Lord Jesus Christ.'[7] And in the Gospel: 'I am in the
Father, and the Father in me'; and: 'The Father who abideth
in me.'[8] It is written also: 'He that glorieth, let him glory
in the Lord'; and elsewhere: 'But our life is hidden with
Christ in God.'[9] Did he ascribe more here to the Son than
to the Father, that he said that we are with Christ in God?
Or does our state avail more than the grace of the Spirit, that

5 Gal. 3.28; 1 Cor. 1.2.; 2 Cor. 5.21, 11.3.
6 Cf. Ps. 55.5; 59.14; cf. Ps. 70.16; 88.17; John 3.21.
7 Eph. 3.9; 1 Thess. 1.1.
8 John 14.10.
9 2 Cor. 10.17; cf. Col. 3.3.

we can be with Christ, and the Holy Spirit cannot so be? And when Christ wills to be with us, as He himself said: 'Father, I will that where I am, they also whom thou hast given me may be with me,'[10] will He disdain to be with the Spirit? It is written also: 'You being gathered together and my spirit, with the power of our Lord Jesus.'[11] Therefore, do we come together with the power of the Lord, and do we dare to say that the Lord Jesus does not will to come together with the Spirit, who does not disdain to come together with us?

(77) So the Apostle thinks there is no difference whether you use this or that particle, for both are conjunctive particles. Moreover, conjunction does not effect disjunction, for if it separated, it would not be called conjunction.

(78) What, then, moves you to say that to God the Father or His Christ there is glory, life, strength, greatness, power *in* the Holy Spirit, and you will not say *with* the Holy Spirit? Is it because you fear to seem to associate the spirit with the Father and the Son? But hear that it is also written of the Spirit: 'For the law of the spirit of life in Christ Jesus.'[12] And elsewhere God the Father says: 'And they will worship thee, and shall make supplication in thee.'[13] God the Father says that we ought to pray in Christ; and do you think that there is any disparagement of the Spirit, if the glory of Christ is said to be in Him?

(79) Hear that what you fear to confess of the Spirit the Apostle did not fear to claim regarding himself for himself, for he says: 'To be dissolved and to be with Christ being by much the better.'[14] Do you deny, then, that the Spirit, through

10 John 17.24.
11 1 Cor. 5.4.
12 Rom. 8.2.
13 Cf. Isa. 45.14.
14 Phil. 1.23.

whom the Apostle merited to be with Christ, is with Him with whom the Apostle is?

(80) What is the reason, then, that you prefer to say that the glory of God or of Christ is *in* the Spirit rather than with the Spirit? Is it because, if you say in the Spirit, the Spirit is declared to be less than Christ? Although this is refutable, your making the Lord greater or less, yet, since it is read: 'For Christ was made sin for us, that we might be made the justice of God in him,'[15] He is found the most prominent, in whom we are the lowest. So, too, you have it elsewhere: 'In him all things consist,'[16] that is, in His power. The things that consist in Him cannot be compared to Him, because they obtain the substance to consist from His power.

(81) Do you wish then that God so rule in the Spirit that the power of the Spirit, as a kind of source of substance, grants to God the beginning of His ruling? But this is impious. And so that our ancestors might say that the power of the Father and of the Son and the Holy Spirit was one, they declared that the glory of Christ was with the Spirit, in order to set forth their connection as inseparable.

(82) For how is the Holy Spirit separated from the Son, when 'the Spirit himself giveth testimony to our spirit, that we are the sons of God. And if sons, heirs also; heirs indeed of God, and joint heirs with Christ'?[17] Who is so mad that he disjoins the eternal conjunction of the Spirit and Christ, when the Spirit, through whom we are made coheirs of Christ, brings together even the separated parts.

(83) He says: 'Yet if we suffer with him, that we may be also glorified with him.'[18] If, then, we shall be glorified

---

15 Cf. 2 Cor. 5.21.
16 Col. 1.17.
17 Rom. 8.16,17.
18 Rom. 8.17.

with Christ through the Spirit, how do we reject the Spirit Himself also being glorified with Christ? Do we dissociate the life of Christ and the life of the Holy Spirit, when the Spirit says that we shall live together with the Son of God? For the Apostle says: 'Now if we be dead with Christ we believe that we shall live also together with Christ';[19] then elsewhere: 'For if we suffer with Him,' He says, 'we shall also live with Him; not only shall we live with Him, but we shall also be glorified with Him; not only shall we be glorified with Him, but we shall also reign with Him.'[20]

(84) There is, then, in these particles no sense of division, for each particle is conjunctive. Lastly, we often find in Scriptures one inserted and the other understood, as it is written:[21] 'I will go into thy house in whole burnt offerings,' that is, with whole burnt-offerings; and elsewhere he says: 'He brought them out in silver and gold,' that is, with silver and gold. Also in another place he says: 'Thou wilt not go out with us in our armies,'[22] for what is really meant: with our armies. Since, then, even in the use of words there can be no misrepresentation, and misrepresentation of the Godhead should not be deduced from words, it is necessary that there be belief with the heart unto justice, and that from the belief of the heart there be made confession in the mouth unto salvation.[23] But those who do not believe with the heart, spread misrepresentation with their words.

---

19 Rom. 6.8.
20 Cf. 2 Tim. 2.11,12.
21 Cf. Ps. 65.13; 104.37.
22 Cf. Ps. 43.10.
23 Cf. Rom. 10.10.

Chapter 9

(85) Then similar, too, is that passage which they say indicates a difference, because it is written: 'Yet to us there is but one God, the Father, of whom are all things, and we unto him; and one Lord Jesus Christ, through whom are all things, and we through him.'[1] For when 'of Him' is said they wish that matter be indicated, when 'through Him' is said, that a kind of instrument of the work or ministry is proclaimed; but when 'in Him' is said, that either a place or time is signified in which all things that have been made are seen.

(86) Thus, then, they desire to prove a certain difference of substance, wishing, as it were, to separate the instrument from the proper worker or author, and, as it were, the time or place from the instrument. Is, then, the Son alien from the Father according to nature because the instrument is alien from the proper worker or author? Or is the Son alien from the Spirit because either the place or time is separated from the kind of instrument?

(87) Compare, now, our assertions. They wish that matter be of God as of the nature of God, so that, if you say that a chest is made of wood, a statue of stone, thus matter has come forth from God, and the same matter has been made through the Son as through a kind of instrument; so that they declare the Son to be not so much the operator as the instrument of the work, and all things thus to be made in the spirit, as in some place or time; they attribute each thing to an individual, and deny that they are all in common.

(88) But we show that all things are so of God the Father that God the Father has suffered no loss because all things

---

1 1 Cor. 8.6.

are either through Him or in Him, and all things are not of Him as of matter; also, that all things are so through the Lord the Son that He is not deprived of this, that all things are of the Son and all things are in Him; and that all things are so in the Spirit that we teach that all things are through the Spirit and all things are of the Spirit.

(89) For these particles, just as those of which we have spoken above, signify each other. For the Apostle did not speak as follows: All things are of God; all things are through the Son, so as to signify a separable substance of the Father and of the Son, but to teach that with a distinction that cannot be confused the Father is one and the Son another. Those particles, then, are not, as it were, opposed to each other, but are, as it were, associated and in harmony, so that they often even suit one, just as it is written: 'For of him, and through him, and in him are all things.'[2]

(90) But if you should really consider whence the passage is taken, you would not doubt that it was said of the Son. For the Apostle says according to the prophecy of Isaias: 'Who hath known the mind of the Lord, or who hath been his counsellor?' And he added: 'For of him, and through him, and in him are all things,' which Isaias said of the Artificer of all, as you have it. 'Who hath measured the water with his hand, and the heaven with his palm, and the whole earth with his closed hand? Who hath weighed the mountains in scales and the hills in a balance? Who hath known the mind of the Lord, or who hath been his counsellor?'[3]

(91) And the Apostle added: 'For of him, and through him, and in him are all things.' What is 'of Him'? That the nature of all things is of His will, and He is the author of all

---

2 Rom. 11.36.
3 Cf. Isa. 40.13,12.

things that come into existence. 'Through Him' means what? That establishment and continuance are seen to have been bestowed on all things through Him. 'In Him' means what? That all things by a certain wonderful desire and ineffable love look upon the Author of their lives and the Minister of their graces and functions, according to what is written: 'The eyes of all hope in thee,' and: 'Thou openest thy hand, and fillest every living creature with thy good pleasure.'[4]

(92) If you speak also regarding the Father, then 'of him' because of Him was the operative Wisdom, which of His own and the Father's will gave being to all things which were not; 'through Him,' because through His Wisdom all things were made; 'in Him,' because He is the source of the vivifying substance, in whom we live and are and move.

(93) Of the Spirit, also, so that, having been formed through Him, established through Him, strengthened in Him, we receive the gift of eternal life.

(94) Since, then, these words seem to befit either the Father or the Son or the Holy Spirit, it is certain that nothing derogatory is declared in them, when we say that many things are of the Son and many things through the Father, as you have it said of the Son: 'That we may in all things grow up in him who is the head, Christ, from whom,' he says, 'the whole body, compacted and fitly jointed together, through what every joint supplieth, according to the operation, in the measure of every part, maketh increase of the body, unto the edifying of itself in charity.'[5] And again, he says to the Colossians about those who have not knowledge of the only begotten Son of God: 'because they do not hold the head, from which all the body, by joints and bands being supplied with nourish-

4 Cf. Ps. 144.15.
5 Cf. Eph. 4.15,16.

ment and compacted, groweth unto the increase of God.' For we have said above that Christ is the Head of the Church.[6] And elsewhere you have it: 'Of his fulness we all have received'; and the Lord Himself has said: 'He shall receive of mine, and will declare it to you.'[7] And before He said: 'I know that virtue is gone out from me.'[8]

(95) Similarly, that you may recognize the unity, it is also said of the Spirit: 'For he that soweth in the Spirit, of the Spirit shall reap life everlasting.'[9] And John says: 'From this we know that he is in us, because he hath given us of his Spirit.'[10] And the Angel says: 'For that which shall be born of her, is of the Holy Ghost.'[11] And the Lord says: 'That which is born of the spirit, is spirit.'[12]

(96) Therefore, as we read that all things are of the Father, so, too, we read that all things can be said to be of the Son, through whom are all things, and we are taught by proof that all things are of the Spirit, in whom are all things.

(97) Now let us consider whether we can teach that something is through the Father. But it is written: 'Paul, called to be a servant of Jesus Christ, through the will of God'; and elsewhere: 'Therefore now he is no more a servant, but a son. And if a son, an heir also through God'; and elsewhere: 'As Christ is risen from the dead through the glory of the Father.'[13] And elsewhere God the Father says to the Son: 'Behold proselytes shall come to thee through me.'[14]

---

6 Cf. Col. 2.19; 1.18.
7 John 1.16; 16.14.
8 Luke 8.46.
9 Gal. 6.8.
10 Cf. 1 John 4.13.
11 Cf. Matt. 1.20.
12 John 3.6.
13 Cf. 1 Cor. 1.1; Gal. 4.7; cf. Rom. 6.4.
14 Cf. Isa. 54.15.

(98) You will find many other passages, if you search for things done through the Father. Is the Father any less on this account, because we read that many things are in the Son and of the Son, and find in heavenly Scriptures that many things are made or given through the Father?

(99) But we also read that many things were made similarly through the Spirit, as you have it: 'But to us God hath revealed through his Spirit; and elsewhere: 'Keep that which is committed to thy trust through the Holy Spirit'; and to the Ephesians: 'to be strengthened with power through his Spirit'; and to the Corinthians: 'To one indeed, through the Spirit, is given the word of wisdom'; and elsewhere: 'But if through the spirit you mortify the deeds of the flesh, you shall live'; and before this: 'He that raised up Jesus Christ from the dead shall quicken also your mortal bodies through his Spirit dwelling in you.'[15]

(100) But perhaps one may say: 'Show me a specific quotation that all things are of the Son, or all things are of the Spirit. But I reply that they, too, show me that there is a quotation that all things are through the Father. But since we have proved that these statements befit either the Father or the Son or the Holy Spirit, and that no distinction of divine power can arise from such particles, there is no doubt but that all things are of Him through whom are all things; and that all things are through Him of whom are all things; and that we should understand that all things are through Him or of Him in whom all things are. For every creature is of the will and through the operation and in the power of the Trinity, as it is written: 'Let us make man to our image and likeness'; and elsewhere: 'By the word of the Lord, the heavens were

---

15 1 Cor. 2.10; cf. 1 Tim. 6.20; Eph. 3.16; 1 Cor. 12.8; cf. Rom. 8.13,11.

established and all the power of them by the spirit of his mouth.'[16]

Chapter 10

(101) Not only is there one operation everywhere on the part of the Father and the Son and the Holy Spirit, but also one and the same will, one calling, and one giving of commands, which may be seen in the great and saving mystery of the Church. For just as the Father called the Gentiles to the Church, saying: 'I shall call her my people, who was not my people, and her beloved, who was not beloved,' and elsewhere: 'My house shall be called the house of prayer for all nations,'[1] so, too, does the Lord Jesus say that Paul has been chosen to call forth and gather the Church, as you have it said by the Lord Jesus to Ananias: 'Go, for this man is a vessel of election to me, to carry my name before the Gentiles.'[2]

(102) So, just as God the Father called the Church, so Christ also called; and as Christ called, so the Spirit also called, saying: 'Separate me Saul and Barnabas, for the work to which I have called them. Then they fasting,' he said, 'and praying, and imposing their hands upon them, sent them away. But they being sent by the Holy Ghost, went to Saleucia.'[3] So Paul received the apostolate at the command not only of Christ, but also of the Holy Spirit, and he hastened to the gathering of the Gentiles.

(103) And not only Paul, but also Peter, as we read in

---

16 Gen. 1.26; Ps. 32.6.

---

1 Cf. Osee 2.24; Isa. 56.7.
2 Acts 9.15.
3 Cf. Acts 13.2-4.

the Acts of the Apostles. For when in prayer he had seen the heavens opened, and a kind of vessel tied at the four corners, in which were all manner of four-footed animals and wild beasts and fowls of the air, 'there came a voice to him: Arise, Peter, kill and eat. And Peter said: Far be it from me Lord; I have never eaten any common and unclean thing. And the voice spoke to him again: That which God hath purified, do not thou call common. And this was done thrice; and presently the vessel was taken up into heaven.' So when Peter considered this silently by himself, and the servants of Cornelius appointed by the Angel had come to him, the Spirit said to him: 'Behold men seek thee. Arise therefore, go down, and go with them doubting nothing; for I have sent them.'[4]

(104) How clearly did the Holy Spirit express His own power? First of all, because He breathed upon him as he prayed, and was present to him as he entreated; then because Peter, when called, replied: 'Lord,' and thus clearly merited a second pronouncement, because he confessed the Lord. But Scripture declares who this Lord is, for He surely whom he had answered spoke to him when he replied. Moreover, what follows shows the Spirit made manifest, for He who fashioned the mystery revealed the mystery.

(105) And also notice this, that the figure of the mystery repeated three times expressed the operation of the Trinity. And so in mysteries a threefold question is put, and a threefold confirmation is repeated, and no one can be cleansed except by a threefold confession.[5] Thus Peter also in the Gospel[6] is questioned three times as to whether he loves the Lord, in order that by his threefold response the bonds, which

---

4 Cf. Acts 10.11-16; 19,20.
5 Cf. *On the Sacraments* 2.7.
6 Cf. John 21.15.

he had contracted by denying the Lord and with which he tied himself, might be loosed.

(106) Then, because the angel is sent to Cornelius,[7] the Holy Spirit addresses Peter: 'My eyes were upon the faithful of the earth.'[8] Nor is it without significance that, when He had said in the earlier passages: 'That which God hath purified, do not thou call common,'[9] the Holy Spirit suddenly came upon the Gentiles to purify them, whereby it is shown that the operation of the Spirit is a divine operation. Peter, moreover, when sent by the Spirit, did not await the command of God the Father, but even confessed that oracle as of the Spirit Himself, and testified to the grace as of the Spirit Himself, saying: 'If then God gave to them the same grace as to us also, who was I that I could oppose God?'[10]

(107) So it is the Holy Spirit who has cleansed us from that Gentile contamination. For in those kinds of four-footed animals and wild beasts and fowl of the air there was a figure of man's condition which seems to have put on bestial cruelty in the manner of wild animals, unless it becomes gentle by the sanctification of the Spirit. Good then is the grace which changes the madness of beasts for the simplicity of the Spirit: 'For we ourselves also were some time unwise, incredulous, erring, slaves to diverse desires of pleasures; but now through the renovation of the Spirit we begin to be heirs of Christ and co-heirs with the angels.'[11]

(108) And so the holy Prophet David, seeing in the Spirit that from wild animals we will become like the dwellers in

---

7 Cf. Acts 10.3.
8 Ps. 100.6.
9 Acts 10.15.
10 Acts 11.17.
11 Cf. Titus 3.3-6.

heaven, says: 'Rebuke the wild beasts of the wood,'[12] clearly
signifying not the wood broken by the paths of wild animals
or terrifying with the roaring of beasts, but that wood of which
it is written: 'We have found it in the fields of the wood,'[13]
in which, as the Prophet said: 'The just shall flourish like the
palm-tree, and shall be multiplied like the cedar which is in
Libanus.'[14] That wood which was shaken in the tops of its
trees mentioned in prophecy, and ushered forth the nourishment of the heavenly Word. That wood which Paul indeed
entered as a ravening wolf, but came out as a shepherd, for
'their sound hath gone forth into all the earth.'[15]

(109)   We, then, were wild animals, and so the Lord says:
'Beware of false prophets who come to you in the clothing
of sheep, but inwardly they are ravenous wolves.'[16] But now
through the Holy Spirit the madness of lions, the spots of
leopards, the craftiness of foxes, the rapacity of wolves have
passed away from our affections. Great, then, is the grace
which changed the earth to heaven, so that the conversation
of us who before wandered like wild beasts in the wood may
be, as the Apostle said, in heaven.[17]

(110)   But not only in this place but also elsewhere has
the Apostle Peter pointed out that the Church was built by
the Holy Spirit. For you have it that he said: 'And God who
knoweth the hearts of men gave them testimony, giving to
them the Holy Ghost as well as to us. And made no difference
between us and them, purifying their hearts by faith.'[18] In
this the following is to be observed: that just as Christ is the

---

12 Ps. 67.32.
13 Ps. 131.6.
14 Cf. Ps. 92.13.
15 Ps. 18.5.
16 Matt. 7.15.
17 Cf. Phil. 3.20.
18 Cf. Acts 15.8,9.

cornerstone, who has put together the unity of both peoples, so, too, the Holy Spirit has not separated but joined the hearts of both peoples.

(111) So you should not, like a Jew, scorn the Son, whom the prophets proclaimed; you would scorn also the Holy Spirit, you would scorn Isaias, you would scorn Jeremias, whom he who was chosen by the Lord brought forth out of the dungeon of the Jewish abode with rags and cords.[19] For despising the word of prophecy, the people of the Jews had plunged him into a dungeon. And no one of the Jews was found to bring the Prophet forth, except an Ethiopian, Abdemeleck, as Scripture testifies.

(112) In this account there is a very beautiful figure, for we, namely, sinners of the Gentiles, formerly black with sins, and once fruitless, have brought forth from the depth the words of prophecy which the Jews had thrust, as it were, into the mire of their minds and of their flesh. And so it is written: "Ethiopia shall stretch out her hands to God.'[20] In this a figure of Holy Church is signified, which says in the Canticle of Canticles: 'I am black but beautiful, O ye daughters of Jerusalem';[21] black through sin, beautiful through grace; black through normal condition, beautiful through redemption; or surely black by the dust of their exercise. So she is black, while there is fighting; she is beautiful, while she is crowned with the decorations of her victory.

(113) And well is the Prophet raised with cords, for the faithful writer said: 'The lines are fallen unto me in goodly places.'[22] And well is it said 'with rags,' for the Lord himself,

---

19 Cf. Jer. 38.10,11.
20 Ps. 67.32.
21 Cant. 1.4.
22 Ps. 15.6.

when those who had first been invited to the wedding made excuses, sent to the ends of the highways, that as many as might be found might be invited to the wedding.[23] So with these rags He raised the words of prophecy from the mire.

Chapter 11

(114) Therefore, you also will be Abdemelech, that is, chosen by the Lord, if you shall raise the Word of God from the depth of Gentile ignorance, if you believe that He is not deceived, that the Son of God is not passed by, is not ignorant of what is to be, that the Holy Spirit also is not deceived, of whom the Lord says: 'But when he, the spirit of truth, shall come, he shall lead you into all truth.'[1] He who says 'all' passes by nothing, not day, not hour, not things of the past, not things of the future.

(115) And that you may know that He both knows all things, and proclaims things of the future, and is of one knowledge with the Father and the Son, hear what the truth of God says of Him: 'For he shall not speak of himself; but what things soever he shall hear, he shall speak; and the things that are to come, he will show you.'[2]

(116) So that you may notice that He knows all things, when the Son said: 'But of that day or hour no man knoweth, not even the angels in heaven,'[3] He excepted the Holy Spirit. But, if the Holy Spirit was excepted from ignorance, how was the Son of God not excepted?

---

23 Cf. Matt. 22.9,10.

1 Cf. John 16.13.
2 John 16.13.
3 Mark 13.32.

(117)   But you say that He numbered the Son of God also with the angels. Indeed, He did number the Son, but He did not number also the Spirit. Therefore, either confess that the Holy Spirit is greater than the Son of God, so that you speak now not only as an Arian but also as a Photinian,[4] or acknowledge to what you ought to refer, that He said that the Son knew not. For He who was created could, as a human being, have been numbered with creatures.

(118)   But if you are willing to learn that the Son of God knows all things, and has foreknowledge of all things that are to be, those things which you think are unknown to the Son, the Holy Spirit received from the Son. Moreover, He received through unity of substance just as the Son received from the Father. He says: 'He shall glorify me; because he shall receive of mine, and will declare it to you. All things whatsoever the Father hath, are mine. Therefore, I said, that he shall receive of mine, and will declare it to you.'[5] What then is more evident than this unity? The things that the Father has are the Son's; what the Son has the Spirit also received.

(119-120)   Accept, then, that the Son knows the day of judgment. It is written in Zacharias: 'And the Lord my God shall come, and all the saints with him. In that day there shall be no light, but cold and frost; and there shall be one day, and that day is known to the Lord.'[6] This day then was known to the Lord, who will come with His saints, to enlighten us by His second coming.

(121)   But let us pursue what we began with reference

---

4 It is difficult to say just what Photinus taught, since all his works are lost. It seems that St. Ambrose considered him worse than Arius, since he maintained that our Lord was mere man. Cf. *Cath. Encycl.* s.v.

5 John 16.14,15.

6 Cf. Zach. 14.5-7.

to the Spirit. For you have in that passage which we presented that the Son said of the Spirit: 'He shall glorify me.' So the Spirit glorifies the Son, just as the Father also glorifies Him, but the Son of God also glorifies the Spirit, as we have said above. Thus, He is not weak who brings about mutual glory through the unity of eternal light, nor is He inferior to the Holy Spirit of whom this is true, that He is glorified by the Spirit.

(122) Therefore, you too shall be chosen, if you believe that the Spirit said this which the Father said, and which the Son said. So Paul was chosen, because he so believed, and so taught: 'The eye hath not seen, nor ear heard, neither hath it entered into the heart of man, what things God hath prepared for them that love him; but to us God hath revealed them through his Spirit,'[7] as it is written. And so He is called the Spirit of revelation, as you read: 'For God giveth to those who thus prepare themselves the Spirit of wisdom and revelation under recognition of him.'[8]

(123) So there is unity of knowledge, when, as the Father reveals, who gives the Spirit of revelation, so the Son also reveals, for it is written: 'No one knoweth the Son but the Father; neither doth any one know the Father, but the Son, and he to whom the Son will reveal him.'[9] He said more about the Son, not because He has more than the Father, but lest He be believed to have less. And not unworthily is the Father so revealed by the Son, because the Son knows the Father, just as the Father knows the Son.

(124) Learn now that the Spirit also knows God the Father; for it is written: 'Just as no man knoweth the things

7 1 Cor. 2.9-11.
8 Cf. Isa. 64.4.
9 Matt. 11.27.

that are of man but the spirit which is in him, so the things
also that are of God no man knoweth but the Spirit of God.'[10]
'No man,' he says, 'knoweth but the Spirit of God.' The Son
of God is not excluded, is He? Certainly not, since neither is
the Holy Spirit excluded, when it is said: 'No one knoweth
the Father, but the Son.'

(125) Therefore, the Father and the Son and the Holy
Spirit are of one nature and knowledge. And the Spirit is not
to be numbered with all things which have been made through
the Son, since He knows God the Father, whom, as it is
written,[11] who can know but the Son? But the Holy Spirit also
knows. What then? When the totality of created things is
mentioned, the Holy Spirit is not included.

(126) Now I would wish them to answer what is in man
which knows the things that are of men. Surely a reasonable
thing which surpasses the other powers of the soul, and by
which the highest nature of man is estimated. What, then, is
the Spirit, who knows the profound things of God, through
whom Omnipotent God is revealed? Is He inferior in fullness
of the Godhead, who is proved by this example to be of the
same substance with the Father? Or is He ignorant of something, who knows the counsels of God and His mysteries
concealed from the beginning? What is it that He does not
know, who knows all things that are of God? 'For the Spirit
searcheth even the profound things of God.'[12]

(127) And lest you think that He searches unknown
things, and so searches that He may learn that of which He
is ignorant, it is said first that God revealed to us through His
Spirit; at the same time that you might learn that the Spirit

10 Cf. 1 Cor. 2.11.
11 Cf. Matt. 11.27.
12 1 Cor. 2.10.

knows what things are revealed to us through the Spirit Himself, it is said later: 'For who of men knoweth what things are of man, but the spirit of man who is in him; so too no one knoweth the things that are of God, but the Spirit of God.'[13] Therefore, if the spirit of a man knows what things are of a man, and knows them before he searcheth them, can there be something of God which the Spirit does not know? Of Him the Apostle said not idly: 'No man knoweth the things that are of God but the Spirit of God, not that He knows by searching but knows by nature; not that the knowledge of divine things in Him is an accident, but is His natural knowledge.

(128) But if it disturbs you that He said 'searcheth,' learn that this also was written of God, because He is the searcher of the mind and reins. For He Himself said: 'I am He who searcheth the heart and the reins.'[14] Also of the Son of God you have it in the Epistle to the Hebrews: 'Who is the searcher of the mind and thoughts.'[15] Therefore, it is clear that no one who is inferior searches the internal things of a superior, for to know the hidden things is of divine power alone. So, similarly, is the Holy Spirit a searcher as the Father; similarly, also, is the Son, by the proper understanding of which expression this is set forth: that there seems properly to be nothing which He does not know, whom nothing escapes.

(129) Finally, he was chosen by Christ, and instructed by the Spirit. For, as he himself testifies, having obtained knowledge of the divine secret through the Spirit, he shows both that the Spirit knows God, and the Spirit has revealed to us the things that are of God, as the Son also has revealed them.

13 Cf. Matt. 11.27.
14 Cf. Jer. 17.10.
15 Heb. 4.12.

And he added: 'Now we have received not the spirit of this world, but the Spirit that is of God, that we may know the things that are given us from God, which things also we speak, not in the learned words of human wisdom but in the manifestation of the Spirit and in the power of God.'[16]

Chapter 12

(130) It is has been proved, then, that, just as God has revealed to us the things that are His, so, too, the Son and so also the Spirit has revealed the things that are God's. For from one Spirit through one Son into one Father does our knowledge proceed; and from one Father through one Son into one Holy Spirit is goodness and sanctification and the imperial right of eternal power handed down. Where, then, there is the manifestation of the Spirit, there is the power of God; nor can there be any distinction where there is one work. And so, what the Son says the Father also says; and what the Father says the Son also says, and what the Father and the Son say the Holy Spirit also says.

(131) Therefore, the Son of God also has said of the Spirit: 'For he shall not speak of himself,'[1] that is, not without the mutual participation of myself and the Father, for the Spirit is not divided and separated, but what He hears He speaks, that is, He hears through the unity of substance, and through the property of knowledge. For not by some openings in the body does He receive hearing, and by certain bodily measures does the voice resound, or does He hear that which

---

16 Cf. 1 Cor. 2.12,13.

1 John 16.13.

He does not know, because in human affairs hearing often produces knowledge, and yet neither in men themselves is there always bodily speech or bodily hearing, 'for he that speaketh in tongues, speaketh not to men, but to God, for no man heareth. But by the Spirit he speaketh mysteries.'[2]

(132) Therefore, if among men there is not always bodily hearing, do you require in God the sounds of human weakness and certain organs of bodily hearing, when He is said to hear so that He may be believed to know? For we know that which we have heard, and we hear first, that we may be able to know, but in God, who knows all things before they take place, knowledge precedes hearing. So, in order that we may say that the Son is not ignorant of what the Father wishes, we say that He has heard, but there is no sound in God, nor are there the syllables which usually signify the indication of the will; but the oneness of will is indeed understood in the hidden ways of God, but in us is signified by signs.

(133) What, then, does it mean: 'He shall not speak from Himself'? This is, He does not speak without Me, because He will speak the truth, He breathes wisdom. He does not speak without the Father, because He is the Spirit of God; He hears not from Himself, because all things are of God.

(134) The Son received all things from the Father, because He Himself said: 'All things are delivered to me by my Father.'[3] All things of the Father the Son has, for again He says: 'All things whatsoever the Father has, are mine.' And the things that He Himself received through unity of nature, the Spirit also received from Him through the same unity, as the Lord Jesus Himself declares, speaking of His Spirit: 'Therefore I said, that he shall receive of mine, and will

2 Cf. 1 Cor. 14.2.
3 Matt. 11.27.

declare it to you.'[4] What, then, the Spirit says is the Son's; what the Son has given is the Father's. So neither the Son nor the Spirit says anything from Himself, because the Trinity says nothing outside Itself.

(135) But, if you contend that this points to the weakness of the Holy Spirit and to a certain likeness to bodily lowliness, you will also point to the injury of the Son, for the Son said also of Himself: 'As I hear, so I judge' and 'The Son cannot do anything of himself, but what he seeth the Father do.'[5] For, if that is true, as true it is, which the Son said: 'All things whatsoever the Father hath, are mine,'[6] and according to divinity the Son is one with the Father, one through natural substance, not one according to Sabellian[7] falsehood, what is one by the property of the substance, cannot be separated, and so the Son cannot do anything except what He has heard from the Father, because the Word of God persists forever,[8] and never is the Father separated from the operation of the Son, and that which the Son operates He knows that the Father wills, and what the Father wills the Son knows how to operate.

(136) Finally, that you might not think that there is some difference of work either in time or in order between the Father and the Son, but might believe the oneness of the same operation, He said: 'And the works which I do He himself doeth.' And again, that you might not believe that there is some difference in the distinction of work, but might judge

---

4 John 16.15.
5 John 5.30,19.
6 John 16.15.
7 The Sabellians denied the orthodox teaching of the Trinity, teaching that God is one Person only, manifesting Himself in three characters. Cf. *Cath. Encyl. s.v.*
8 Cf. Ps. 118.89.

that the Father and the Son wish the same, do the same, and have the same power, Wisdom said to you about the Father: 'For what things soever he doeth, these the Son also doeth in like manner.'[9] So the action of anyone is not prior or second, but the same result of one operation. And thus the Son is said to be able to do nothing by Himself, because His operation cannot be separated from the Father. In like manner, the operation of the Holy Spirit also is not separated. Therefore, the things also which He says He is said to hear from the Father.

(137) What if I teach that the Father also hears the Son, just as the Son also hears the Father? For you have it written in the Gospel that the Son says: 'Father, I give thee thanks that thou hast heard me.' How did the Father hear the Son, when in the earlier passage about Lazarus He said nothing to the Father? And that you might not think that the Son was once heard by the Father He added: 'And I know that thou hearest me always.'[10] Thus the hearing is not of subject obedience but of eternal oneness.

(138) So in like manner, also, the Spirit is said both to hear from the Father and to glorify the Son. To glorify on this account, because the Holy Spirit taught us that the Son of God is the image of the invisible God,[11] and the splendor of His glory, and the figure of His substance,[12] for the Spirit spoke also in the Patriarchs and the Prophets, and finally the Apostles then began to be more perfect after they had received the Holy Spirit. Thus there is no separation of the divine power and grace, for, although 'there are diversities of graces,

9 Cf. John 5.17,19.
10 John 11.41,42.
11 Cf. Col. 1.15.
12 Cf. Heb. 1.3.

yet it is the same Spirit; and there are diversities of ministries, yet the same Lord; and there are diversities of operations, yet the same God who worketh all in all.'[13] There are diversities of offices, not separations of the Trinity.

(139) Finally, it is 'the same God who worketh all in all, that you may know that there is no difference of operation between God the Father and the Holy Spirit, when those things which the Spirit works, God the Father also works, 'who worketh all in all.' For, although the Father worketh all in all, yet 'to one through the Spirit is given the word of wisdom; and to another, the word of knowledge according to the same Spirit; to another, faith in the same Spirit; to another, the grace of healing in one Spirit; to another, the working of miracles; to another, prophecy; to another, the discerning of spirits; to another, divers kinds of tongues; to another, interpretation of speeches. But all these things one and same Spirit worketh, dividing to everyone according as he will.'[14]

(140) Thus, there is no doubt but that the things which the Father worketh the Spirit also worketh. Not according to a command does He work, as one who hears corporeally, but according to His will, who is free in His own will, not the servant of another's power. For He does not obey as if ordered, but as a giver He is the director of His own gifts.

(141) Meanwhile, now see whether you say that the Spirit works all things that the Father also works; yet you cannot deny that the Father works what the Holy Spirit works; otherwise the Father does not work all things if He does not work those things that the Spirit also works. But, if those things which the Spirit works the Father also works, since the Spirit divides His works according to His will, you must say that

---

13 1 Cor. 12.4-6.
14 1 Cor. 12.8-11.

what the Spirit divides He either divides according to His own will against the will of the Father, or, if you say that the Father wills the same as the Holy Spirit wills, you must confess the unity of the divine will and operation even though unwilling, and if not with the heart, at least with the mouth.

(142) But if the Holy Spirit is both of one will and operation with God the Father, He is also of one substance, since the creator is known from his works. So He says: 'It is the same Spirit, the same Lord, the same God.'[15] And if you say Spirit, He is the same; and if you say Lord, He is the same; and if you say God, He is the same. Not the same so that He Himself is Father, Himself Son, Himself Spirit,[16] but because both the Father and the Son are of the same Power. Accordingly, He is the same through substance and power, because there is in the Godhead neither the confusion of the Sabellians nor the division of the Arians nor any earthly or corporeal change.

Chapter 13

(143) Holy Emperor, accept another strong example on the subject, and one known to you. He says: 'God also spoke to the Fathers by the Prophets in many ways and in divers manners.'[1] And the Wisdom of God said: 'I will send prophets and apostles.'[2] And 'To one,' as it is written, 'through the Spirit is given the word of wisdom; and to another, the word of knowledge according to the same Spirit; to another, faith

---

15 Cf. 1 Cor. 12.5.
16 That is, one and the self-same Person.

---

1 Cf. Heb. 1.1.
2 Cf. Luke 11.49.

in the same Spirit; to another, the grace of healing in one
Spirit; to another, the working of miracles; to another,
prophecy.'[3] Therefore, according to the Apostle, prophecy is
not only through the Father and the Son, but also through
the Holy Spirit; and on this account the office is one, the grace
is one. You have it, then, that the Spirit also is the author of
prophecies.

(144)   The Apostles also have said: 'It hath seemed good
to the Holy Ghost and to us.'[4] And when they say, 'seemed
good,' they point out not only the worker of grace, but also
the Author of the execution of what was commanded. For
just as we read about God: 'It pleased God,' so also, when
it is said: 'It hath seemed good to the Holy Ghost,' the Master
of His own power is expressed.

(145)   And how is He not the Master, who says the things
which He wills, and commands the things that He wills, just
as the Father commands and the Son commands? For just
as Paul heard the voice saying to him: 'I am Jesus, whom
thou dost persecute,'[5] so, too, the Spirit forbade Paul and
Silas to go into Bethynia. And just as the Father spoke through
the Prophets, so, too, Agabus says concerning the Spirit:
'These things saith the Holy Ghost: The man whose girdle
this is, thus shall the Jews bind him in Jerusalem.'[6] And just
as Wisdom sent the Apostles, saying: 'Go ye into the whole
world, and preach the Gospel,' so, too, the Holy Spirit says:
'Separate me Saul and Barnabas, for the work to which I
have taken them.'[7] Thus being sent ahead by the Holy Spirit,
as Scripture points out later, they had no distinction among

---

3 1 Cor. 12.8-10.
4 Acts 15.28.
5 Acts 9.5.
6 Acts 21.11.
7 Mark 16.15; Acts 13.2.

the rest of the Apostles, as if they were sent in one way by God the Father, in another way by the Spirit.[8]

(146) Finally, when Paul was sent by the Spirit, he was both the vessel of election of Christ, and recalls that God wrought in him, saying: 'For he who wrought in Peter to the apostleship of the circumcision wrought in me also among the Gentiles.'[9] Since, then, the same wrought in Paul as wrought in Peter, this surely is indicated when the Spirit wrought in Paul, namely, that the Holy Spirit wrought in Peter. But Peter himself testifies that God the Father also wrought in Him, as we have it in the Acts of the Apostles, that Peter arose and said to them: 'My brethren, you know that in former days God made choice among us, that the Gentiles by my mouth should hear the word of the gospel.'[10] Behold, then, in Peter God wrought the grace of preaching. Since indeed he was chosen and taken up through Christ, will anyone dare to deny the working of Christ in him, when the Lord himself says: 'Feed my lambs'?[11]

(147) The operation of the Father and the Son and the Holy Spirit, then, is one, unless you, perchance, who deny the oneness of the same work with respect to the Apostles, think this: that on this account the Father wrought and the Spirit wrought in Peter, in whom the Son had wrought, as if the operation of the Son did not at all suffice him for grace; and that on this account, as if, when the strengths of the Father and the Son and the Holy Spirit were joined and brought together, the operation became manifold, lest the operation of Christ alone waver in establishing Peter.

(148) And not only is one operation of the Father, Son,

---

8 Cf. Acts 13.4.
9 Gal. 2.8.
10 Acts 15.7.
11 John 21.15.

and Holy Ghost found in Peter, but the oneness of the divine operation is revealed also in all the Apostles, also a kind of authority over heavenly dispensations. For the divine operation consists of command; it does not consist of ministry, for, when God operates, He does not work something out by labor or skill, but 'He spoke, and they were made.'[12] He said: 'Be light made. And light was made';[13] for in the commandment of God is the effecting of the operation.

(149) So, if we are willing to notice, we can easily find on the testimony of the Scriptures that this, as it were, royal power was ascribed also to the Holy Spirit, and it will be revealed that all the Apostles not only were disciples of Christ but also were ministers of the Father, Son, and Holy Spirit, just as the teacher of the Gentiles teaches when he says: 'God, indeed, hath set some in the church, first apostles, secondly prophets, thirdly teachers, after that miracles, the grace of healings, helps, governments, divers kinds of tongues.'[14]

(150) Behold, God established apostles, established prophets and teachers, gave the grace of healings, which you have above, was given through the Holy Spirit, gave divers kinds of tongues. But yet not all are apostles, not all prophets, not all teachers. Not all, he says, have the grace of healings, and not all speak with tongues.[15] For not all divine gifts can be in each man individually; each one receives according to his capacity that which he either desires or deserves. But the power of the Trinity which is bountiful with all graces is not like this weakness.

(151) Finally, God established apostles. Those whom God established in the Church, Christ chose and ordained as

12 Ps. 32.9.
13 Gen. 1.3.
14 Cf. 1 Cor. 12.28.
15 Cf. 1 Cor. 12.30.

apostles, and He ordered them into the world saying: 'Go ye into the whole world, and preach the gospel to every creature, He that believeth, and is baptized, shall be saved; but he that believeth not, shall be condemned. And these signs shall follow them that believe: In my name they shall cast out devils; they shall speak with new tongues; they shall take up serpents; and if they shall drink any deadly thing, it shall not hurt them; they shall lay their hands upon the sick, and they shall recover.'[16] Behold, the Father established the teachers; Christ also established them in the churches; and just as the Father gives the grace of healings, so the Son also gives it; just as the Father gives the gifts of tongues, so the Son also has bestowed it.

(152) Similarly, with regard to the Holy Spirit above we have accepted that He bestows the same kinds of graces. 'For,' he says, 'to another is given the grace of healings through the Spirit, to another divers kinds of tongues, to another prophecy.'[17] So the Spirit gives the same things as the Father gives, as the Son also gives. Let us now receive more expressly what we touched upon above, that the Holy Spirit also enjoins the same duty as the Father and the Son, and appoints the same, for Paul said: 'Take heed to yourselves, and to all the flock over which the Holy Ghost hath placed you bishops to rule the church of God.'[18]

(153) Therefore, oneness of authority, oneness of establishment, oneness of bestowing. For, if you separate establishment and power, what cause was there for God the Father establishing and the Holy Spirit establishing those whom Christ had established as apostles, unless, perchance, as if

16 Mark 16.15-18.
17 Cf. 1 Cor. 12.9,10.
18 Acts 20.28.

sharing a possession or a right they, like men, feared prejudice, and so the operation was divided, and the authority
distributed?

(154) These things among men themselves are narrow
and of little consequence, who for the most part, even if they
do not agree in operation, agree in will. Thus, a certain person,
when asked what a friend was, said: 'A second self.' If, then,
man so defines a friend as to say that he was a second self,
namely, through oneness of love and friendship, how much
more ought we to consider the oneness of majesty in the Father
and Son and Holy Spirit, when by the same operation and
divinity either oneness or surely that which is more, ταὐτότης,
as it is called in Greek, is expressed? For ταὐτό signifies 'the
same,' because the Father and the Son and the Spirit have
the same, so that to will the same and to have the same power
is not from the affection of the will, but is in the substance
of the Trinity.

(155) This is the inheritance of apostolic faith and devotion, which may be observed also in the Acts of the Apostles.
So Paul and Barnabas obeyed the orders of the Holy Spirit.
And all the Apostles obeyed, and at once ordained those
whom the Spirit had ordered to be separated: 'Separate me
Saul and Barnabas.'[19] Do you see the authority of Him com-
manding? Behold the merits of those serving.

(156) Paul believed, and because he believed, he cast
aside the zeal of a persecutor, and brought back a crown of
justice. He believed who used to lay waste the churches, but,
converted to the faith, he preached in the Spirit what the
Spirit commanded. The Spirit anointed His champion, and,
having shaken off the dust of irreligion, presented him as the
insuperable conqueror of the unbelievers at various gatherings

19 Acts 13.2.

of the irreligious and trained him by various sufferings for the prize of his high calling in Jesus Christ.[20]

(157) Barnabas also believed, and, because he believed, he obeyed. And so, being chosen by the authority of the Holy Spirit, which redounded for him unto every mark of honor, he was not unworthy of so great an association. For one grace shone on those whom one Spirit had chosen.

(158) Neither was Paul inferior to Peter, although the latter was the foundation of the Church, and the former, a wise builder, knowing how to establish firm the footsteps of nations who believed; nor was Paul, I say, unworthy of the association of the Apostles, since he is also easily to be compared to the first, and is second to none. For he who does not know that he is inferior makes himself equal.

---

20 Cf. Acts 9.20ff.

THE HOLY SPIRIT

Book Three

Chapter 1

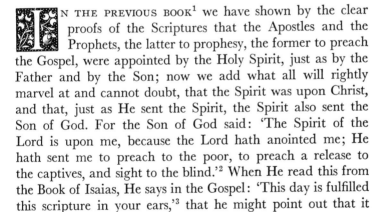N THE PREVIOUS BOOK[1] we have shown by the clear proofs of the Scriptures that the Apostles and the Prophets, the latter to prophesy, the former to preach the Gospel, were appointed by the Holy Spirit, just as by the Father and by the Son; now we add what all will rightly marvel at and cannot doubt, that the Spirit was upon Christ, and that, just as He sent the Spirit, the Spirit also sent the Son of God. For the Son of God said: 'The Spirit of the Lord is upon me, because the Lord hath anointed me; He hath sent me to preach to the poor, to preach a release to the captives, and sight to the blind.'[2] When He read this from the Book of Isaias, He says in the Gospel: 'This day is fulfilled this scripture in your ears,'[3] that he might point out that it was said of Himself.

1 Book II.12.
2 Cf. Isa. 61.1.
3 Luke 4.21.

(2) Therefore, can we wonder if the Spirit sent both the Prophets and the Apostles, when Christ said: 'The Spirit of the Lord is upon me'?[4] And well did He say 'upon me,' because He was speaking as the Son of Man. For as the Son of Man He was both anointed and sent to preach the Gospel.

(3) But if no credence is given the Son, let them hear the Father also saying that the Spirit of the Lord is upon Christ. For He says to John: 'He upon whom thou shalt see the Spirit descending, and remaining on ·him, he it is that baptizeth with the Holy Ghost.' God the Father said this to John; and John heard and saw and believed. He heard from God; he saw in the Lord; he believed that it was the Spirit who was descending from heaven. For not a dove, but like a dove He descended, for thus it is written: 'I saw the Spirit coming down as a dove from heaven.'[5]

(4) Just as John said that he had seen, so too did Mark write. Luke,[6] however, added that the Holy Spirit descended in a bodily appearance like a dove. You should not think that this was an incarnation, but an appearance. But He put forth the appearance on this account, that through the appearance he might believe, who did not see the Spirit, and through the appearance He might declare that He had a share with the Father and the Son of the one honor in the authority, of the one operation in the mystery, of the one gift in the bath, unless, perchance, we believe Him, in whom the Lord was baptized, weak for the servant to be baptized in Him.

(5) Well did he say: 'Remaining on him,' because with reference to the Prophets the Spirit, as often as He wished, inspired a word or acted, but always remained in Christ.

---

4 Luke 4.18.
5 John 1.33,32.
6 Luke 3.22.

(6) Let it not again disturb you that he said 'upon Him,' for he was speaking of the Son of Man, because He was baptized as the Son of Man. For according to Godhead the Spirit is not upon Christ but in Christ, because, just as the Father is in the Son, and the Son in the Father, so the Spirit of God and the Spirit of Christ is both in the Father and in the Son, for He is the Spirit of His mouth. For He who is of God abides in God, as it is written: 'Now we have received not the spirit of this world, but the spirit that is of God.[7] And He abides in Christ, who has received from Christ; and He is in Christ, for again it is written: 'He shall receive of mine'; and elsewhere: 'For the law of the spirit of life, in Christ Jesus, hath delivered me from the law of sin and of death.'[8] He is not, then, over Christ according to the Godhead of Christ, because the Trinity is not over Itself, but over all things; It is not over Itself, but in Itself.

(7) Who, then, will doubt that the Spirit sent the Prophets and the Apostles, when the Son of God says: 'The Spirit of the Lord is upon me'?[9] And elsewhere: 'I am the first, and I am forever; and my hand hath founded the earth, and my right hand hath established the heavens; I shall call them, and they shall stand together, and they shall all assemble themselves, and shall hear. Who hath declared these things to them? Loving you, I have done your pleasure against Babylon, that the seed of the Chaldaean may be taken away. I have spoken, I have called, I have brought him, and I have made his way prosperous. Come ye near unto me, and hear this: I have not spoken in secret from the beginning; when those things were done, I was there; and now the Lord God

7 1 Cor. 2.12.
8 John 16.14; Rom. 8.2.
9 Luke 4.18.

hath sent me, and His Spirit.'[10] Who is He who says: 'The Lord God hath sent me', but He who came from the Father, to make sinners safe? And as you hear: 'And the Spirit sent Him,' lest, when you read that the Son sends the Spirit, you might believe that the Spirit is of inferior power.

(8) So both the Father and the Spirit sent the Son; also, the Father and the Son sent the Spirit. The Father sent Him because it is written: 'But the Paraclete, the Holy Ghost, whom the Father will send in my name.'[11] The Son sent Him, because He said: 'But when the Paraclete shall come, whom I will send you from the Father, the Spirit of truth.'[12] If, then, the Son and the Spirit send each other, as the Father sends, there is no affront of subjection, but a community of power.

Chapter 2

(9) Not only did the Father send the Son, but He also gave Him, just as the Son Himself gave Himself. For we read: 'Grace be to you from God the Father and from our Lord Jesus Christ, who gave himself for our sins.'[1] If they think that He was subject in this, that He was sent, they cannot deny that it was of grace that He was given. Moreover, He was given by the Father, as Isaias said: 'A child is born to us; and a son is given to us';[2] moreover, He was given, I dare say, also by the Spirit, who sent by the Spirit. For, since the Prophet has not defined by whom He was given, he shows that He was

10 Cf. Isa. 48.12-16.
11 John 14.26.
12 John 15.26.

1 Cf. Gal. 1.3,4.
2 Isa. 9.6.
5 Cf. Isa. 42.5-7.

given by grace of the Trinity; but since the Son himself gave Himself, surely He himself could not have been subject to Himself according to His Godhead. Therefore, that He was given could not have been a matter of subjection in the Godhead.

(10) But the Holy Spirit also was given, because it is read: 'I will ask the Father, and he shall give you another Paraclete.'[3] And the Apostle says: 'He therefore that despiseth these things, despiseth not man, but God; who also hath given his Holy Spirit in us.'[4] Isaias also shows[5] that both the Spirit and the Son were given; he says: 'Thus saith the Lord God that made the heavens, and fashioned them; that established the earth and the things which are in it; that giveth breath to the people upon it, and spirit to them that tread thereon.' And to the Son: 'I am the Lord God, who have called thee in justice, and will hold thine hand, and will strengthen thee; and I have given thee for a covenant of my people, for a light of the Gentiles, to open the eyes of the blind, to bring forth those that are bound from their fetters.' Since, then, the Son was both sent and given, and the Spirit also was sent and given, surely they have oneness of Godhead who have oneness of action.

Chapter 3

(11) Therefore, also, the Spirit is even called the finger of God, because there is an indivisible and inseparable communion between the Father, the Son, and the Holy Spirit. For just as Scripture called the Son of God the right hand

---

3 John 14.16.
4 1 Thess. 4.8.

of God, as it is read: 'Thy right hand, O Lord, is made glorious in power; thy right hand, O Lord, hath crushed the enemy,' so the Holy Spirit is called the finger of God, as the Lord himself says: 'But if I, in the finger of God, cast out devils.'[1] For in another book of the Gospel in the same place He called this finger the Spirit of God, as you have it: 'But if I by the Spirit of God cast out devils.[2]

(12) What, then, could have been said more precisely to point out the unity of the Godhead or of the operation, which unity is according to the Godhead of the Father, or of the Son, or of the Holy Spirit, than that we may understand that the fullness of the eternal Godhead, much more than this body of ours, seems to be divided, if anyone separates the unity of substance and multiplies Its powers, when the eternity of the same Godhead is one?

(13) For it is often convenient to consider from our own words the things that are above us, and, since we cannot see them, we may draw inferences from those things which we can see. 'For the invisible things of him,' says the Apostle, 'from the creation of the world, are clearly seen, being understood by the things that are made.'[3] And he adds: 'His eternal power also and divinity.' Of these things one seems to be said of the Son, another of the Holy Spirit, so that, just as the Son is called the eternal power of the Father, so too the Spirit, because He is divine, may be believed to be His eternal Godhead. For the Son, too, because He lives forever, is eternal life. This finger of God, then, is both eternal and divine. For what is there proper to God, which is not eternal and divine.

(13[2]) By this finger, as we read, God wrote on the

1 Cf. Exod. 15.6; Luke 11.20.
2 Matt. 12.28.
3 Rom. 1.20.

stone tablets which Moses received.[4] For not with a finger of flesh did God make the forms and elements of those letters which we read; by His Spirit He gave the law. And so the Apostle said: 'For the Law is spiritual, which indeed is written not with ink, but with the Spirit of the living God; not in tables of stone, but in fleshly tables of the heart.'[5] For, if the letter of the Apostle is written in the Spirit, what stands in the way of our being obliged to believe that the Law of God was written not in ink but in the Spirit of God, which surely does not stain the secrets of our heart and mind but illuminates them?

(14) Moreover, the Law was written in tablets of stone,[6] because it was written in a type, but at first the tablets were broken and cast out of Moses' hands, because the Jews fell away from the works of the Prophets. And well were the tablets broken, the writing not destroyed. And do you beware lest your tablet be broken, lest your mind and soul be divided. Is Christ divided? He is not divided, but is one with the Father. And let no one separate you from Him. If faith fails, the tablet of your heart is broken. The stability of your soul is lessened, if you do not believe the unity of the Godhead in the Trinity. Your faith is written, and your sin is written, as Jeremias said: 'Thy sin, O Judas, is written with a pen of iron and with the point of a diamond. And it is written,' he says, 'on thy breast and on thy heart.'[7] So sin is there where grace is; but sin is written by a pen, grace is indicated by the Spirit.

(15) The Lord Jesus also, with head bowed, wrote mys-

---

4 Cf. Exod. 31.18.
5 Cf. 2 Cor. 3.3.
6 Cf. Exod. 32.19.
7 Cf. Jer. 17.1.

tically with this finger on the ground,[8] when the adulteress was presented to Him by the Jews, signifying by a figure that, when we judge of the sins of another, we should be mindful of our own sin.

(16) And lest again, because God wrote the Law by His Spirit, we might believe something, as it were, inferior about the ministry of the Spirit, or might think from a consideration of our body that the Spirit is a kind of small part of God, the Apostle says elsewhere[9] that he is speaking, not in the words of human wisdom, but in words taught by the Spirit, and is comparing spiritual things with spiritual; furthermore, that man as animal does not perceive the things that are of the Spirit of God. For he knew that he who compared divine things with things of the flesh was to be reckoned among the animals not among spiritual men. 'For it is foolishness to him,' he says. And so, because he knew that these would be the questions of men as animals, having foreknowledge of the future, he says: 'For who hath known the mind of the Lord, that he may instruct him? But we have the mind of Christ.'

Chapter 4

(17) But if anyone still clings to the doubts of the flesh and vacillates with examples of the body, let him consider that he cannot think well of the Son who can think badly of the Spirit. For if, then, they think that the Spirit is a kind of small part of God, because He is called the finger of God, these same people surely also say that a small part of God is in the Son, since He is called the right hand of God.

---

8 Cf. John 8.6.
9 Cf. 1 Cor. 2.13-16.

(18) But the Son is called both the right hand and the power of God. So, if we weigh our words, there can be no perfection without power, and thus let them beware lest they think, what is impious to say, that the Father, half-perfect in His substance, received perfection through the Son, and let them cease to deny that the Son is co-eternal with the Father. For when did the power of God not exist? But, if they think that at some time the power of God did not exist, they will say that at some time fullness did not exist in God the Father, to whom they think power was at one time lacking.

(19) But, as I said, these things have been written that we may refer them to the unity of the Godhead, and that we may believe what the Apostle said, that the fullness of the God-head dwells bodily in Christ, and dwells in the Father, and dwells in the Holy Spirit, and that, just as there is oneness of Godhead, so, too, there is oneness of operation.

(20) This also can be gathered from the Song of Moses, for, when he had led the people of the Jews through the sea, he confessed the operation of God the Father, the Son, and the Holy Spirit, saying: 'Thy right hand, O Lord, is magnified in strength; thy right hand, O Lord, hath slain the enemy.'[1] You have it that he confessed both the Son and the Father, whose right hand He is. And below, not to pass over the Holy Spirit, He added: 'You sent thy Spirit, and the sea covered them, and the water was divided by the Spirit of thy anger.'[2] By this the oneness of the Godhead is signified, not the in-equality of the Trinity.

(21) You see, then, that the Holy Spirit also co-operated with the Father and the Son, so that, just as if with the freezing of the waves in the middle of the sea, a kind of wall

1 Col. 2.9.
2 Exod. 15.6,10.

of water arose for the passage of the Jews, and again, when
poured back through the Spirit, overwhelmed the people of
the Egyptians. From this source, also, many think that a
column of cloud preceded the people of the Jews by day, and
a column of fire by night, in order that the grace of the Spirit
might protect His people.[3]

(22) Moreover, this operation of God, which the whole
world rightly admires, the Apostle also declared did not take
place without the work of the Holy Spirit, saying that in that
figure the truth of a spiritual mystery preceded, for thus you
have it: 'For our fathers were all under the cloud, and all
passed through the sea; and all in Moses were baptized, in
the cloud, and in the sea; and they all ate the same spiritual
food. And all drank the same spiritual drink.'[4]

(23) For how could the type of the sacrament have been
without the operation of the Holy Spirit, whose entire truth
is in the Spirit? This, too, the Apostle taught, when he said:
'But you are washed, but you are sanctified, but you are
justified, in the name of our Lord Jesus Christ, and in the
Spirit of our God.'[5]

(24) You see then both that the Father operates in the
Son and the Son operates in the Spirit. And therefore, according to the order of the Scriptures, do not doubt that there was
in the figure that which Truth itself declared to be in the
truth. For who will deny His operation in the Font, in which
we feel His operation and grace?

(25) For just as the Father sanctifies, so the Son also
sanctifies, and the Holy Spirit sanctifies. The Father sanctifies,
according as it is written: 'May the God of peace sanctify

3 Cf. Exod. 14.22; 13.21.
4 1 Cor. 10.1-4.
5 1 Cor. 6.11.

you, that your spirit, and soul, and body be preserved entire and blameless in the day of our Lord Jesus Christ. And elsewhere the Son says: 'Father, sanctify them in truth.'[6]

(26) But of the Son the same Apostle said: 'Who is made to us wisdom from God, and justice, and sanctification, and redemption.'[7] Do you see that He was made sanctification? But He was so made for us, not that He might change what He was, but that He might sanctify us in the flesh.

(27) The Apostle teaches that the Holy Spirit also sanctifies. For he speaks as follows: 'We ought to give thanks to God always for you, brethren, beloved of God, for that God hath chosen you first-fruits unto salvation, in sanctification of the Spirit, and belief of the truth.'[8]

(28) Therefore, the Father sanctifies, the Son also sanctifies, and the Holy Spirit sanctifies, but the sanctification is one, because the baptism is one,[9] and the grace of the sacrament is one.

Chapter 5

(29) But what wonder is it, if He Himself in no need of sanctification, but abounding in it, sanctifies each one, when, as I have said, we have learned that His majesty is so great that the Holy Spirit seems as inseparable from God the Father as a finger from the body?

(30) But if anyone thinks that this should be referred to a diminution, not to a unity of power, he surely will fall into such madness as to seem to fashion the Father, Son, and Holy

6 Cf. 1 Thess. 5.23; John 17.17.
7 1 Cor. 1.30.
8 2 Thess. 2.12.
9 Cf. Eph. 4.5.

Spirit into one form of body, as it were, and to make certain distinctions of its members.

(31) But let them learn, as I have often said, that not inequality but unity of power is pointed out by this testimony, since what are works of God, the same are works of the hands, and the same, also, we shall read, are the works of fingers. For it is written: 'The heavens show forth the glory of God, and that firmament declareth the work of his hands,' and elsewhere: 'In the beginning, O Lord, thou foundest the earth, and the heavens are works of thy hands.'[1] The same things then are works of the hands as are works of God. Therefore, there is no distinction of operation according to the nature of the members of the body, but oneness of power.

(32) But what are works of the hands, the same are works of the fingers, for it is equally written: 'For I will behold thy heavens, the works of thy fingers; the moon and the stars which thou hast founded.'[2] What, then, are the fingers declared to have done less than the hands, when the fingers have done the same as the hands, as it is written: 'For thou hast given me, O Lord, a delight in thy doings, and in the works of thy hands I shall rejoice.'[3]

(33) And yet, since we read that the Son is the hand (for it is written: 'Hath not my hand made all these things?' and elsewhere: 'I will set thee in a hole of the rock, and protect thee with my hand. I have placed my hand under the covering of the rock,'[4] which refers to the mystery of the Incarnation, because the eternal power of God took on the covering

---

1 Ps. 18.2; 101.26.
2 Ps. 8.4.
3 Ps. 91.5.
4 Cf. Isa. 66.2; Exod. 33.22.

of a body), surely it is clear that Scripture spoke of the hand both of the Son of God and of the Holy Spirit.

(34) And again, since we read that the Spirit is the finger of God,[5] on this account we think that fingers are mentioned to signfy the Son and the Spirit. Finally, that he may mention that he possesses the sanctification of both the Son and the Spirit, a certain holy man says: 'Thy hands have made me and fashioned me.'[6]

Chapter 6

(35) For why do we reject similarity of words, when we assert the oneness of power, when the oneness of power is to such a point that the Spirit also rebukes, just as the Father rebukes, and the Son rebukes? For thus is it written: 'O Lord, rebuke me not in thy indignation, nor chastise me in thy wrath.'[1] Then in Psalm 49, the Lord speaks thus: 'I will reprove thee, and set thy sins before thy face.'[2] Thus, too, regarding the Holy Spirit, the Son said: 'But when I go, I will send the Paraclete to you. And when he shall come, he will convince the world of sin, and of justice, and of judgment.'[3]

(36) But, whither is the madness of faithless men leading us, so that we seem to be proving, as if a matter of doubt, the fact that the Holy Spirit rebukes, when the judges themselves cannot judge except through the Spirit? Finally, that famous judgment of Solomon, when, in the midst of the difficulties of those in contention, as one woman, having smoth-

---

5 Cf. Luke 11.20.
6 Job. 10.8.

1 Ps. 6.1.
2 Cf. Ps. 49.21.
3 Cf. John 16.7,8.

ered the child which she herself had conceived, wished to claim that of another, and the other woman protected her own son, he both detected the deceit in the very hidden thoughts and the goodness in the mother's vitals, was so admirable surely through the gift of the Holy Spirit.[4] For no other sword would have penetrated the hidden feeling of the women, except that of the Holy Spirit, of which the Lord says: 'I came not to send peace, but the sword,'[5] because the interior mind can be penetrated not by steel but by the Spirit; 'For the Spirit of understanding is holy, one, manifold, subtle, active,' and below, 'overseeing all things.'[6]

(37) Behold what the prophet says, that He oversees all things. And so Solomon also oversaw, so that he ordered a sword to be brought to him, because, although he pretended that he wished to divide the son, he bore in mind that the true mother would consider the welfare of her son more than her own solace, and would prefer kindness to the law, not the laws to kindness, but that she who feigned the feelings of a mother, blinded by her anxiety to conquer, would consider the son's destruction of little account, in whom she had no knowledge of giving forth love. So that spiritual man who judged all things (for 'the spiritual man judgeth all things'[7]) sought in the feelings the nature which was hidden in words, and questioned the love, to bring forth the truth. So the mother conquered by the feeling of love, which is the fruit of the Spirit.

(38) He judges in a Prophet, for the word of wisdom is given through the Spirit;[8] how then is it denied that the Holy

---

4 Cf. 3 Kings 3.16-28.
5 Matt. 10.34.
6 Cf. Wis. 7.22,23.
7 1 Cor. 2.15.
8 Cf. 1 Cor. 12.8.

Spirit can rebuke the world regarding judgment, who takes away the doubt in judgment, and grants the issue?

(39-40) Daniel, also, unless he had received the Spirit of God, never could have apprehended the lustful adultery, the deceitful lie. For when Susanna, attacked by the conspiracies of the elders, saw the minds of the people moved by consideration for the elders, and destitute of all help, alone among men conscious of her chastity, prayed for God as her judge, he says: 'The Lord heard her voice, when she was led to be put to death; and the Lord raised up the holy spirit of a young boy, whose name was Daniel.'[9] And so, according to the grace of the Holy Spirit which he had received, he discovered the changing testimonies of the faithless, for it was nothing other than the operation of the divine power that his voice should bring forth those whose feelings lay hidden.

(41) Perceive, then, the sacred and heavenly miracle of the Holy Spirit. She who preferred to be chaste within herself than before the people, she who preferred to undergo danger to her innocence rather than to her modesty, when she was accused, kept silent, when she was condemned said nothing, content with the judgment of her conscience, who preserved respect for her modesty even in dangers, lest they should seem to have extorted petulance who had been unable to extort her chastity, when she called upon the Lord, merited the Spirit, who revealed the hidden conscience of the elders.

(42) Let the chaste learn not to fear calumny. For she who preferred chastity to life did not suffer the loss of life and brought back the glory of chastity. Thus, too, Abraham, when once ordered to go to foreign lands, held back neither

9 Cf. Dan. 13.44,45.

by the danger to his wife's chastity nor by the fear of awaiting death, preserved both his life and his wife's chastity. So no one has ever repented his faith in God, and chastity increased the devotion in Sarah, and devotion chastity.[10]

(43) And lest anyone, perchance, think that, when the Scripture says: 'God roused the Holy Spirit of a young youth,' it supposes that the Spirit in him was of a man, not the Holy Spirit, let him read further on and he will find that Daniel received the Holy Spirit, and thus prophesied. Finally, also, the king preferred him because he had spiritual grace. For thus he speaks: 'But thou art able, Daniel, for the Holy Spirit of God is in thee.' And below Scripture says: 'And Daniel was preferred to them, because a greater spirit of God was in him.'[11] But the Spirit of Moses also was divided among those who were to judge.[12]

Chapter 7

(44) But what shall we say of the rest? We have learned that the Lord Jesus not only judges in the Spirit but also punishes. For He would not punish Antichrist, unless He first judged of his merits, 'whom,' as we read, 'the Lord Jesus shall kill with the spirit of his mouth.'[1] Here grace was not acquired, but remains an undivided unity, because neither can Christ be without the Spirit, nor the Spirit without Christ. For the unity of divine nature cannot be separated.

(45) And since that instance comes forth, that the Lord

10 Cf. Gen. 20.1ff.
11 Cf. Dan. 5.14; 6.3.
12 Cf. Num. 11.25.

1 2 Thess. 2.8.

Jesus shall kill with the Spirit of his mouth, the Spirit is to be, as it were, a sword.[2] Finally, also, in the Gospel, the Lord Jesus himself says: 'I came not to send peace, but the sword.'[3] For He came that He might give the Spirit, and so in His mouth was a two-edged sword;[4] in truth, spiritual grace. Thus the Spirit is the sword of the Word.

(46) And that you may know that there is no inequality, but unity of nature, the Word also is the sword of the Holy Spirit, for it is written: 'Taking the shield of faith, wherewith you may be able to extinguish all the fiery darts of the wicked one, and take unto you the helmet of salvation, and the sword of the Spirit, which is the word of God.'[5]

(47) Since, then, the sword of the word is the Holy Spirit, and the sword of the Holy Spirit is the Word of God, surely unity of power is in them.

Chapter 8

(48) One may consider this unity also in other passages of the Scriptures. For, while Ezechiel says to the people of the Jews: 'Thou hast provoked me in all these things, saith the Lord,' Paul says to the new people in his Epistle: 'Grieve not the Holy Spirit of God, whereby you are sealed.'[1] Again, while Isaias says of the Jews themselves: 'But they believed not, but provoked the Holy Spirit to wrath,' David says of God: 'And they provoked the Most High to wrath in the

---

2 Cf. Eph. 6.17.
3 Matt. 10.34.
4 Cf. Apoc. 19.15.
5 Eph. 6.16,17.

---

1 Cf. Ezech. 16.43; Eph. 4.30.

place without water, and they tempted God in their hearts.'[2]

(49) Learn, also, that, while the Scripture said elsewhere that the Spirit was tempted, and that even God was tempted, the same Scripture says that Christ also was tempted, for you have the Apostle saying to the Corinthians: 'Neither let us tempt Christ; as some of them tempted, and perished by serpents.'[3] Just was the punishment, that the adversaries might feel the venom, who did not venerate the Author.

(50) And when the brazen serpent was set up,[4] well did the Lord order the wounds of the injured to be healed, for the brazen serpent is a representation of the Cross. For, although Christ was set up in His flesh, yet in Him was the Apostle also crucified to the world, and the world was crucified to him, for he says: 'The world is crucified to me, and I to the world.'[5] So the world was crucified in its allurements, and thus not the true but the brazen serpent was set up, because in the truth of the body indeed, but without the truth of sin did the Lord take on the appearance of a sinner, that through the deceit of human weakness by imitating the serpent, throwing off the slough of the flesh, He might destroy the cunning of the true serpent. Thus through the cross of the Lord, which came to our aid in the vengeance of temptation, I, who accept the medicine of the Trinity, recognize the offence against the Trinity in the faithless.

(51) Therefore, when you have in the book of Moses[6] that the Lord being tempted sent serpents among the people of the Jews, either you must confess the unity in the divine majesty of the Father and the Son and the Holy Spirit, or

---

2 Cf. Isa. 63.10; Ps. 77.17,18.
3 1 Cor. 10.9.
4 Cf. Num. 21.9.
5 Gal. 6.14.
6 Cf. Num. 21.6.

certainly, when apostolic Scripture says that the Spirit was tempted, surely it pointed out the Spirit by the name of the Lord. Moreover, the Apostle, writing to the Hebrews, says that the Holy Spirit was tempted, for you have the following: 'Wherefore, as the Holy Ghost saith: Today, if you shall hear his voice, harden not your hearts, as in the provocation, in the day of temptation in the desert, where your fathers tempted me, proved, and saw my works. Forty years was I near to this generation, and I said: They always err in heart; and they have not known my ways, as I have sworn in my wrath: If they shall enter into my rest.'[7]

(52) Therefore, according to the Apostle the Spirit was tempted. If He was tempted, He surely was directing the people of the Jews into the land of promise, as it is written: 'For He led them out through the deep, as a horse in the wilderness, and they labored not, and like the castle through the plain. The Spirit descended from the Lord, and directed them.'[8] He Himself certainly ministered the calm rain of heavenly nourishment; He Himself with fertile shower made rich the daily harvest which the earth had not brought forth and the farmer had not sown.

(53) Now let us look at these matters one by one. God had promised the Jews rest, and the Spirit says that this rest is His.[9] God the Father recalls that He was tempted by the unbelievers; the Spirit also says that He was tempted by the same; for there is one temptation whereby the one Godhead of the Trinity is tempted by the sacrilegious. God condemns the people of Israel, so that they cannot come into the land flowing with milk and honey,[10] that is, to the rest of the

7 Cf. Heb. 3.7-11.
8 Cf. Isa. 63.13,14.
9 Cf. Exod. 16.12.
10 Cf. Num. 14.8.

resurrection; the Spirit, too, condemns them with the same judgment, saying: 'If they shall enter into my rest.'[11] It is, then, the judgment of one will, the excellence of one power.

Chapter 9

(54) Perhaps, however, some one might have said that this passage cannot be cited with reference to the nature of the Holy Spirit, had not the Apostle Peter also taught us that the Spirit, too, can be tempted by our sins, for thus you have it said to the wife of Ananias: 'Why have you agreed together to tempt the Spirit of the Lord?'[1] For the Spirit of the Lord is Himself the Spirit of God, for there is one Holy Spirit, as the Apostle Paul also taught, saying:[2] 'But you are not in the flesh, but in the spirit, if so be that the Spirit of God dwell in you. Now if any man have not the Spirit of Christ, he is none of his.' He first presented the Spirit of God, and immediately added that the Same is the Spirit of Christ. And when he had spoken of the Spirit, that we might understand that where the Holy Spirit is, there is Christ, he added: 'And if Christ be in you.'

(55) Then, as we here understand that where the Spirit is, there, too, is Christ, so also he shows that where Christ is, there also is the Holy Spirit. For, when he had said: 'Do you seek a proof of Christ who speaketh in me,' he says elsewhere: 'And I think that I also have the Spirit of God.'[3] Indivisible, then, is the unity, because where, on the testimony of Scrip-

---

11 Cf. Ps. 94.11.

1 Acts 5.9.
2 Rom. 8.9.10.
3 2 Cor. 13.3; 1 Cor. 7.40.

ture, either the Father, or Christ, or the Spirit, is signified, there is all the fullness of the Trinity.

(56) But Peter, too, in that passage which we set forth, mentioned the Holy Spirit first, and then called Him the Spirit of the Lord, for thus you have it: 'Ananias, why hath Satan filled thine heart to lie to the Holy Spirit, to deal with fraud over the price of the field? Whilst it remained, did it not remain to thee, and being sold, was it not in thy power? Why hast thou conceived this wickedness in thy heart? Thou hast not lied to men, but to God.' And below he says to the wife: 'Why have you agreed together to tempt the Spirit of the Lord?'[4]

(57) First, we understand that he called the Holy Spirit the Spirit of the Lord. Then, when he first mentioned the Holy Spirit, and added: 'Thou hast not lied to men but to God,' you must understand either the oneness of the Godhead in the Holy Spirit, for when the Spirit is tempted, God is deceived, or, if you try to exclude the oneness of the Godhead, according to the words of Scripture, you yourself certainly believe the Spirit to be God.

(58) For, if we understand that the expression is used both of the Spirit and of the Father, surely in God the Father and in the Holy Spirit we observe the oneness of truth and knowledge, for the lie is detected alike by the Holy Spirit and by God the Father. But, if we receive both truths concerning the Spirit, why, faithless man, do you try to deny what you read? So, either confess the oneness of the Godhead of the Father and of the Son and of the Holy Spirit, or the Godhead of the Holy Spirit. Whichever you say, you have said both in God, for both the unity affirms the Godhead and the Godhead the unity.

4 Cf. Acts 5.3,4,9.

Chapter 10

(59) Not only does the Scripture in this place clearly bear witness to the θεότης of the Holy Spirit, that is the Godhead, but the Lord himself also said in the Gospel: 'For the Spirit is God.'[1] This passage, O Arians, you testify to be so expressly regarding the Spirit that you remove it from your texts, and would that you had taken it from your texts and not also from those of the Church.[2] For at the time when Auxentius[3] of impious infidelity had seized the Church of Milan with his arms and forces, or the Church of Sirmium[4] was attacked by Valens and Ursatius, when their priests[5] wavered in faith, this falsehood and sacrilege of yours was detected in the ecclestistical texts. And perhaps you did this also in the East.

(60) And you have been able indeed to blot out letters, but you have not been able to do away with faith. That erasure betrayed you more, that erasure condemned you more; for you could not obliterate the truth, but that erasure rubbed out your names from the book of life. Why was 'For the Spirit is God' done away with, if it did not pertain to the Spirit? For, if you wish it expressed of God the Father, then you also deny God the Father, you who

---

1 Cf. John 3.6.
2 Probably a false charge, since the words have no Greek authority, and are obviously a later comment.
3 Auxentius of Milan, a native of Cappadocia, was ordained to the priesthood in 343 by Gregory, the violent opponent of St. Athanasius and the intruded Bishop of Alexandria. After the banishment of Dionysius of Milan in 355, Auxentius was made bishop of that see through Arian intrigue. In spite of the efforts of the principal Western bishops, he held this post until his death in 374.
4 The reference here is undoubtedly to the synods of Sirmium. These synods were concerned chiefly with attempts to persuade orthodox bishops to accept unorthodox views and to make the unorthodox appear orthodox. They were very harmful to the Church. Cf. *Cath. Encycl., s.v.*
5 That is, bishops.

think that it ought to be blotted out. Select which you wish; in each case the snare of your impiety will bind you, if you confess to be heathen by denying either the Father or the Spirit to be God. So your confession is maintained, whereby you blotted out the Word of God, while you fear the original.

(61) You have, indeed, blotted it out in your breasts and minds, but the Word of God is not blotted out, the Holy Spirit is not blotted out, but He turns away from impious minds; not grace, but iniquity is blotted out, for it is written: 'I am, I am he that blot out thy iniquities,'[6] Finally, Moses, petitioning for the people, says: 'Blot me out of thy book, if you spare not this people.'[7] Yet he was not blotted out, for he had no iniquity, but poured forth grace.

(62) Thus you are convicted by your own confession that you cannot say that it was done with wisdom, but with shrewdness. For with shrewdness you know that you are convicted by the testimony of that passage, and that your arguments cannot meet that testimony. For how otherwise can an understanding of that passage be derived, when the entire context of the passage is about the Spirit?

(63) Nicodemus asks about regeneration, and the Lord replies: 'Amen, amen I say to thee, unless a man be born again of water and the Holy Ghost, he cannot enter into the kingdom of God.'[8] And to show that there is one generation according to the flesh, another according to the Spirit, He added: 'That which is born of the flesh, is flesh, because it is born of the flesh; and that which is born of the Spirit, is Spirit, because the Spirit is God.'[9] Proceed then through the entire

---

6 Isa. 43.25.
7 Cf. Exod. 32.32.
8 John 3.5.
9 Cf. John 3.6. This is St. Ambrose's reading of the passage as referred to above in Chapter 59.

context, and you will find that the Lord has excluded your impiety by the fulness of His assertion. He says: 'Wonder not that I said to thee, you must be born again. The spirit breatheth where he will; and thou hearest his voice; but thou knowest not whence he cometh, nor whither he goeth; so is every one that is born of the Spirit.'[10]

(64) Who is he who is born of the Spirit, and who is made Spirit, if not he who is who is renewed in the Spirit of his mind? Surely this is he who is regenerated through water and the Holy Spirit, for through the laver of regeneration and renewing of the Holy Spirit we receive the hope of eternal life.[11] And elsewhere the Apostle Peter says: 'You shall be baptized with the Holy Ghost.'[12] But who is he who is baptized by the Holy Ghost, if not he who is born again through water and the Holy Ghost? Therefore, of the Holy Spirit the Lord said: 'Amen, amen I say to thee, unless a man be reborn again of water and the Spirit, he cannot enter into the kingdom of God.' And so He declared that we were born of Him in the latter case, through whom He said that we were born in the former. This is the statement of the Lord. I rely on what is written, not on argument.

(65) Yet I ask why, if there is no doubt that we are born again through the Holy Spirit, there is doubt that we are born of the Holy Spirit, since the Lord Jesus himself was both born and born again of the Holy Spirit? If you confess that He was born of the Holy Spirit,[13] since you cannot deny it, but you deny that He was reborn,[14] it is with great folly that

10 John 3.7,8.
11 Cf. Eph. 4.33.
12 Acts 11.16.
13 Cf. Matt. 1.20.
14 Cf. Matt. 3.16.

you confess what is peculiar to God, and deny what is common to men. And thus that is well said to you which was said to the Jews: 'If I have spoken to you earthly things, and you believe not, how will you believe, if I shall speak to you heavenly things?'[15]

(66) Yet we find each passage so written in Greek, that He said not *through* the Spirit, but *of* the Spirit. Thus, then, we have it: Ἀμὴν ἀμὴν λέγω σοι, ἐὰν μή τις γεννήθη ἐξ ὕδατος καὶ πνεύματος, that is, 'of water and the Spirit.' So, since there should be no doubt that 'that which is born of the Holy Spirit' is written of the Holy Spirit, there is no doubt but that the Holy Spirit also is God, according to that which is written: 'The Spirit is God.'

(67) Elsewhere, also, the same Evangelist, that he might disclose that he wrote this of the Holy Spirit, says: 'Christ Jesus came by water and the Spirit, not only in water but through water and blood. And the Spirit bears testimony that Christ is the truth. For there are three witnesses: the Spirit, the water, and the blood; and these three are one.'[16]

(68) Hear how they are witnesses: The Spirit renews the mind, the water is beneficial for the laver, the blood looks to the price. For the Spirit made us sons of God by adoption, the water of the sacred Font washed us, the blood of the Lord redeemed us. Thus we obtain one invisible and one visible testimony in the spiritual sacrament, 'for the Spirit giveth testimony to our spirit.'[17] Although there is the fullness of the sacrament in each, yet there is a distinction of office; so, where there is a distinction of office, surely there is no equality of witness.

---

15 John 3.12.
16 Cf. 1 John 5.6,7.
17 Rom. 8.16.

Chapter 11

(69) But perhaps attention may be turned to the fact that in the later part of that very book the Lord again spoke of God as Spirit, but had in mind God the Father. For thus you have it in the Gospel: 'Now is when the true adorers shall adore the Father in Spirit and in truth. For the Father also seeketh such to adore him. God is Spirit, and those that adore him must adore Him in Spirit and in truth.'[1] For by this passage you not only wish to deny the divinity of the Holy Spirit, but you also divert God's being worshiped in the Spirit, as it were, to the subjection of the Spirit.

(70) To this point I shall reply briefly that the Spirit is often presented as grace of the Spirit, as the Apostle also said: 'For the Spirit himself asketh for us with unspeakable groanings,'[2] that is the grace of the Spirit, unless, perchance, you were able to hear the groanings of the Holy Spirit. So here also God is adored, not in the malice of the heart, but in the grace of the Spirit. 'For wisdom does not enter into a malicious soul';[3] because 'no man can say the Lord Jesus but in the Holy Ghost.' And straightway he adds: 'Now there are diversities of graces.'[4]

(71) Now this does not pertain to the fullness nor to a portion of the Spirit, because neither does the human mind grasp His fulness, nor is He divided into any portions of Himself, but He pours out the gift of the grace of the Spirit, in which God is adored, as He is also adored in truth, for no one adores him except he who draws in the truth of His God-

1 Cf. John 4.23,24.
2 Rom. 8.26.
3 Cf. Wis. 1.4.
4 1 Cor. 12.3.4.

head with pious affection. Certainly he does not, as it were, apprehend Christ personally, nor the Holy Spirit personally.

(72) Or if you think that this seems to have been said personally of the Spirit and of Christ, then God is similarly adored in truth, just as He is adored in the Spirit. So either there is a like subjection, which God forbid that you believe, and the Son is not adored, or, which is true, there is a like grace of unity, and the Spirit is adored.

(73) Let us then gather here and put an end to the impious questions of the Arians. For, if they say that the Spirit is not to be adored on this account, because God is adored in the Spirit, let them say that Truth is not to be adored on this account, because God is adored in truth. For, although there are many truths, for it is written: 'Truths are decayed from among the children of men,' yet they have been granted by Divine Truth, which is Christ, who says: 'I am the way, and the truth and the life.'[5] So, if in this passage they understand truth according to usage, let them also understand the grace of the Spirit, and there is no stumbling, or, if they accept Christ as the Truth, let them deny that he should be adored.

(74) But they are refuted by the deeds of the pious and by the sequence of the Scriptures. For Mary adored Christ, and so is chosen as the messenger of the resurrection to the Apostles,[6] loosening the hereditary debt and the great offence of womankind. For the Lord worked this in a mystery, that where sin had abounded, grace also might abound.[7] And worthily is a woman chosen [as a messenger] to men, that she

5 Ps. 11.1; John 14.6.
6 Cf. John 20.17,18.
7 Cf. Rom. 5.20.

who had first announced sin to man, might be the first to announce the grace of the Lord.

(75) The Apostles also adored,[8] and so, because they bore the proof of the faith, they received the *magisterium* of the faith. The angels, too, adored, of whom it is written: 'And let all his angels adore him.'[9]

(76) Moreover, they adore not only His Godhead, but also His footstool, as it is written: 'Adore his footstool, for it is holy.'[10] Or, if they deny that in Christ also the mysteries of the Incarnation are to be adored, in which we note, as it were certain express traces of the Godhead and certain ways of the heavenly Word, let them read that the Apostles also adored Him when He arose in the glory of His flesh.[11]

(77) Therefore, if it detracts nothing from Christ, that God is adored in Christ, because Christ also is adored,[12] surely it also detracts nothing from the Spirit, that God is adored in the Spirit, because the Spirit also is adored, as the Apostle said: 'We serve the Spirit of God.'[13] For he who serves also adores, as it has been said above: 'Thou shalt adore the Lord thy God, and shalt serve him only.'[14]

(78) But lest, perchance, someone seem to pass over the example set forth above, let us consider in what way that which the Prophet says, 'Adore his footstool,' seems to point to the mystery of the Lord's incarnation, for we should not estimate the footstool according to the custom of men. For neither is God corporeal nor is He not beyond measure, that

---

8 Cf. Matt. 28.17.
9 Cf. Heb. 1.6.
10 Ps. 98.5.
11 Cf. Matt. 28.17.
12 St. Ambrose is in this section refuting Apollinarianism, which separated the two natures of Christ, and taught that He should be worshiped only in His divine nature. Cf. *Cath. Encycl,. s.v.*
13 Cf. Phil. 3.3.
14 Cf. Deut. 6.13.

we should think of a footstool placed as a support for His feet. And we read that nothing but God is to be adored, because it is written: 'Thou shalt adore the Lord thy God, and shalt serve him only.' How, then, could the Prophet, raised under the Law and taught in the Law, have instructed contrary to the Law? So the question is not an ordinary one, and for this reason let us consider more carefully what the footstool is. For we read elsewhere: 'Heaven is my throne and the earth my footstool.'[15] But the earth is not to be adored by us, because it is a creature of God.

(79) Let us observe, however, whether the Prophet says that that earth is to be adored which the Lord Jesus took on in the assuming of flesh. Thus, by footstool is understood earth, but by earth the flesh of Christ, which we adore today in the mysteries, and which the Apostles, as we said above, adore in the Lord Jesus; for neither is Christ divided but He is one,[16] nor, when He is adored as the Son of God, is He denied to have been born from the Virgin. Since, then, the mystery of the Incarnation is to be adored, and the Incarnation is the work of the Spirit, as it is written: 'The Holy Ghost shall come upon thee, and the power of the most High shall overshadow thee; and the Holy which shall be born of thee, shall be called the Son of God,'[17] without doubt the Holy Spirit also is to be adored, when He is adored who was born according to the flesh of the Holy Spirit.

(80) And lest anyone divert this to the Virgin Mary, Mary was the temple of God, not the God of the temple. And thus He alone is to be adored who was operating in the temple.

(81) That God is adored in the Spirit does not stand in

---

15 Isa. 66.1.
16 Cf. 1 Cor. 1.13.
17 Cf. Luke 1.35.

the way of our argument, because the Spirit, too, is adored. Although, if we consider the words themselves, what else should we understand in the Father and Son and Holy Spirit but the unity of the same power? For what is 'must adore him in spirit and in truth,'[18] if, however, you do not refer this to the grace of the Spirit, nor to the true faith of conscience, but, as we have said, if you accept it personally (if on the other hand this word is worthy to express the Divine Majesty) of Christ and of the Spirit?

(82) What, then, is 'the Father is adored in Christ,' if not that the Father is in Christ, and the Father speaks in Christ, and the Father remains in Christ? Surely not as a body in a body, for God is not a body; nor as one confused in one confused; but as the true in the true, God in God, light in light, as eternal Father in co-eternal Son. So, not the insertion of a body is understood, but the unity of power. So, through the unity of power Christ is adored in the Father, when God the Father is adored in Christ. Thus, similarly, through the unity of the same power the Spirit is also adored in God, when God is adored in the Spirit.

(83) Let us examine the force of this word and expression still more carefully, and let us gather its proper meaning from other sources. It is said: 'Thou hast made all things in wisdom.'[19] What, then, do we understand here, that Wisdom is without a share in what was made? But 'all things were made by him.'[20] And David says: 'By the word of the Lord, the heavens were established.'[21] Therefore, he himself who calls the Son of God the author even of heavenly things thus surely said that all things were made in the Son, that in

18 John 4.24.
19 Ps. 103.24.
20 John 1.3.
21 Ps. 32.6.

the renewal of His works He might least of all separate the Son from the Father, but might join Him with the Father.

(84) Paul, too, says: 'For in him were all things created in heaven and on earth, visible and invisible.'[22] When He says 'in Him,' did He deny that they were made through Him? Surely he did not deny but declared this. Finally, he said in another place also: 'One Lord Jesus, by whom are all things.'[23] When, then, he says 'through Him,' did he deny that all things were made in Him, through Whom he says that all things are? These words, 'in Him' and 'with Him,' have this force, that by these is understood one and like, not contrary. This he also made manifest in later passages, when he said: 'All things were created by him and in him,' for, as we have said above,[24] Scripture bears witness that these three phrases—'with Him,' and 'through Him,' and 'in Him' —are one in Christ. For you have it that all things were made through Him and in Him.

(85) Learn, also, that the Father was with Him, and He with the Father, when all things were being made. Wisdom says: 'When he prepared the heavens, I was present, when he was making the fountains of waters.'[25] And in the Old Testament the Father, by saying: 'Let us make,'[26] showed that the Son was to be adored with Him, as the maker of all things. So just as those things are said to have been created in the Son, of which the Son is accepted as the creator, so too, when God is said to be adored in truth by the proper meaning of the word itself, expressed frequently in the same manner, it should be understood that the Son also is adored. Thus

22 Col. 1.16.
23 1 Cor. 8.6.
24 Book 2.8-9.
25 Cf. Prov. 7.27.
26 Gen. 1.26.

similarly, the Spirit also is adored, because God is adored in the Spirit. Therefore, the Father is also adored with the Son and with the Spirit, because the Trinity is adored.

Chapter 12

(86) But does anyone deny that the Godhead of the eternal Trinity is to be adored, when the Scriptures also set forth the inexplicable majesty of the divine Trinity, as the Apostle says elsewhere: 'For God who commanded the light to shine out of darkness, hath shined in our hearts, to give the light of the knowledge of the glory of God, in the face of Christ Jesus'?[1]

(87) Surely, the Apostles saw this glory, when the Lord Jesus on the mount shone in the light of His Godhead. He said: 'The apostles saw it, and fell upon their face.'[2] Do you not think that they, even when they fell, adored, although they could not endure the brightness of the divine light with bodily eyes, and the splendor of eternal light dulled the sharpness of mortal sight? Or what else did they say at that time on seeing His glory but: 'Come, let us adore and fall down before him'?[3] For 'God hath shined in our hearts to give the light of the knowledge of the glory of God in the face of Christ Jesus.'[4]

(88) Who is it, then, who shined that we might know God in the face of Christ Jesus? For he said: 'God shined,' that the glory of God might be known in the face of Jesus Christ. Who else do we think but the Spirit who was made

---

1 2 Cor. 4.6.
2 Cf. Matt. 17.6.
3 Cf. Ps. 94.6.
4 2 Cor. 4.6.

manifest? Or who else is it but the Holy Spirit, to whom the power of the Godhead is referred? For those who exclude the Spirit must introduce another to receive with the Father and Son the glory of the Godhead.

(89) Therefore, let us repeat the same words: 'It is God who hath shined to give the light of glory of God in the face of Jesus Christ.' You have Christ clearly expressed. Whose glory is said to give light but that of the Spirit? So he expressed God himself, because he spoke of the Glory of God; if of the Father, it remains that 'He who commanded the light to shine out of darkness, and hath shined in our hearts,' be understood to be the Holy Spirit, for we cannot venerate any other with the Father and the Son. If, then, you understand the Spirit and the Apostle spoke of Him as God, then you, who deny it, must also confess the Godhead of the Spirit.

(90) But how shamelessly you deny it, when you have read that the Holy Spirit has a temple! For it is written: 'You are the temple of God, and the Spirit of God dwelleth in you.'[5] God, then, has a temple; a creature has no true temple. But the Spirit who dwells in us has a temple. For it is written: 'Your members are a temple of the Holy Spirit.'[6]

(91) But He dwells in the temple not as a priest nor as a minister, but as God, for the Lord Jesus Himself said: 'I will dwell in them, and I will walk among them, and I will be their God, and they will be my people.'[7] And David says: 'The Lord is in his holy temple.'[8] Thus, the Spirit dwells in His holy temple, just as the Father dwells and the Son dwells, who says: 'I and the Father will come, and will make an abode with him.'[9]

5 1 Cor. 3.16.
6 Cf. 1 Cor. 6.15.
7 Cf. Lev. 26.12.
8 Ps. 10.5.
9 Cf. John 14.23.

(91A) So we observe that the Father and the Son and the Holy Spirit abide in one and the same through the one-ness of the same nature. Thus He is of divine power, who dwells in the temple, for just as we are the temple of the Father and the Son, so also are we of the Holy Spirit. There are not many temples but one temple, for the temple is of one power.

(92) Moreover, the Father abides in us through the Spirit, whom He has given us. How, then, can different natures abide together? Of course, they cannot. But the Holy Spirit abides with the Father and the Son. Therefore, the Apostle also joined the communication of the Holy Spirit with the grace of Jesus Christ and the charity of God, saying: 'The grace of our Lord Jesus Christ, and the charity of God, and the communication of the Holy Ghost be with you all.'[10]

Chapter 13

(92A) But whom do you fear? Is it that which you are accustomed to rail at lest you make three Gods? God forbid, for where one Godhead is understood, one God is mentioned. For neither do we speak of two Gods, when we speak of the Son as God. For if, when you confess the Godhead of the Spirit, you think that three Gods are spoken of, so, too, when you speak of the Godhead of the Son, because you cannot deny it, you introduce two Gods. You must, then, according to your opinion, if you think that God is the name of one person, not of one nature, either speak of two Gods or deny the Son as God.

10 2 Cor. 13.13.

(93) But let us excuse you of ignorance, although we do not excuse you of blame. For according to our opinion, because there is one God, one Godhead and oneness of power are understood. As we say that there is one God, while confessing the Father by the true name of Godhead and not denying the Son, so, too, we do not exclude the Holy Spirit from the oneness of the Godhead, and we do not assert three Gods, but deny this, because not oneness but division of power makes plurality. For how does oneness of Godhead admit of plurality, since plurality belongs to numbers, but the divine nature does not admit of numbers?

Chapter 14

(94) Therefore, God is one, the majesty of the eternal Trinity being preserved, as it is set forth in the example set before us. And yet not in that place alone do we see the Trinity expressed in the name of the Godhead, but both in many places, as we have said above, and especially in those letters which the Apostle wrote to the Thessalonians, did he very clearly declare the Godhead and the sovereignty of the Father and the Son and the Holy Spirit. For thus it reads: 'And may the Lord multiply you, and make you abound in charity towards one another, and towards all men, as we do also towards you, to confirm your hearts without blame, in holiness before God and our Father, at the coming of our Lord Jesus Christ.'[1]

(95) Who, then, is the Lord who multiplies us, and makes us abound before God and our Father at the coming of the Lord Jesus? He has said the Father, and has said the Son.

---

1 1 Thess. 3.12,13.

Whom, then, has he joined with the Father and the Son but
the Spirit? Who is the Lord who confirms our hearts in holiness? For holiness is a grace of the Spirit, as he also said
further on: 'In holiness of the Spirit, and belief of the truth.'[2]

(96) Who, then, do you think is here called the Lord but
the Spirit? Has not God the Father been able to teach you,
who says: 'He upon whom thou shalt see the Spirit descending
and remaining on him, he it is that baptizeth with the Holy
Ghost'?[3] For the Spirit descended in the likeness of a dove,[4]
that He might bear witness to His wisdom and fulfill the
sacrament of the spiritual laver, and show Himself of one
operation with the Father and the Son.

(97) And lest you judge that something fell from the
Apostle through imprudence, and that knowingly and with
prudence and inspired by the Holy Spirit he signified Him
as the Lord, whom he felt to be God, he also repeated this
same thought in the second epistle to the Thessalonians, saying: 'And the Lord direct your hearts in the charity of God,
and in the patience of Christ.'[5] If love belongs to God, and
patience to Christ, it should be shown who is the Lord who
directs, if we deny direction on the part of the Holy Spirit.

(98) But we cannot deny it, since of Him the Lord said:
'I have yet many things to say to you, but you cannot bear
them now. But when he, the spirit of truth, shall come, he
will lead you into all truth.'[6] And David says of Him: 'Thy
good spirit shall lead me into the right way.'[7]

(99) Behold what the voice of the Lord has re-echoed

2 2 Thess. 2.12.
3 John 1.33.
4 Cf. Luke 3.22.
5 2 Thess. 3.5.
6 Cf. John 16.12,13.
7 Cf. Ps. 142.10.

with regard to the Holy Spirit. The Son of God came, and because He had not yet poured forth the Spirit, He declared that we were living as little children without the Spirit. He said that the Spirit was to come, who out of little children would make us stronger men, that is, by an increase of spiritual age. He established this for the following reason, not that He might place the power of the Spirit first, but that He might show that fulness of power is in the knowledge of the Trinity.

(100) It is necessary, then, either that you speak of some fourth person, of whom you should be conscious besides the Spirit, or certainly that you do not judge that anyone else other than the Spirit is designated as Lord.

(101) But if you demand a clear statement of the words by which the Scripture has called the Spirit Lord, this cannot have escaped you, for it is written: 'Now the Lord is a Spirit.'[8] And the sequence of the whole passage shows that this certainly was said of the Holy Spirit. And so let us consider the declaration of the Apostle: 'As often as Moses is read,' he says, 'the veil is upon their heart. But when they shall be converted to the Lord, the veil shall be taken away. Now the Lord is a Spirit, and where the Spirit of the Lord is, there is liberty.'[9]

(102) So not only did he speak of the Spirit as Lord but he also added: 'And where the Spirit of the Lord is, there is liberty. But we all, beholding the glory of the Lord with face uncovered, are transformed into the same image from glory to glory, as by the Spirit of the Lord,'[10] that is, we, who have been before converted to the Lord, so that by spiritual under-

---

8 2 Cor. 3.17.
9 Cf. 2 Cor. 3.15-17.
10 2 Cor. 3.18.

standing we see the glory of the Lord in a kind of mirror of the Scriptures, now are transformed from this glory, which converted us to the Lord, to the heavenly glory. So, since the Lord is He to whom we are converted, but the Lord is that Spirit by whom we are transformed, who are converted to the Lord, surely the Lord is designated as the Holy Spirit, for He who receives those converted is He who transforms. For how would He have transformed those whom He had not received?

(103) Although, why do we seek the expression of words, where we perceive the expression of unity? For, although you distinguish the Lord and the Spirit, yet you cannot deny that where the Lord is, there, too, is the Spirit, and he who has been converted to the Lord will have been converted to the Spirit. If you misrepresent the letter, you do not harm the unity. If you wish to separate the unity, you confess the Spirit Himself as the Lord of power.

Chapter 15

(104) But perhaps again you say: 'If I call the Spirit Lord, I shall declare three Lords.' When you call the Son Lord, do you then either deny the Son or confess two Lords? God forbid, for the Son Himself said: 'Do not serve two lords.'[1] But certainly He did not deny either Himself or the Father as Lord, for He called the Father Lord, as you read: 'I give thanks to thee, O Father, Lord of heaven and earth.'[2] And He spoke of Himself as Lord, as we read in the Gospel: 'You call me Master and Lord, and you say well, for so I am.'[3] But He did not speak of two Lords; rather, He

---

1 Cf. Matt. 6.24.
2 Matt. 11.25.
3 John 13.13.

shows that He did not speak of two Lords, when He warns: 'Do not serve two lords.' For there are not two Lords, where the lordship is one, for the Father is in the Son, and the Son in the Father, and so there is one Lord.

(105) Thus, too, did the Law teach: 'Hear, O Israel, the Lord thy God is one Lord,'[4] that is, unchangeable, always persisting in unity of power, always the same; He is not changed by an addition or diminution. Therefore, Moses spoke of Him as one, and yet likewise said that the Lord poured down rain from the Lord.[5] The Apostle also says: 'The Lord grant to him to find mercy of the Lord.'[6] The Lord rains down from the Lord; the Lord grants mercy from the Lord; the Lord is not divided when He rains down from the Lord, nor is He separated when He grants mercy from the Lord, but in each passage the oneness of the lordship is expressed.

(106) In the Psalms, too, you have: 'The Lord said to my Lord.'[7] So he did not deny the Father as His Lord, because he said that the Son was His Lord, but on this account he spoke of the Son as his Lord, that you might not believe Him to have been the Son but the Lord of the Prophet, which the Lord himself made clear in the Gospel when He said: 'For if David in the Spirit calls him Lord, how is he his Son?'[8] In the Spirit David calls Him Lord; the Spirit does not so call Him. Of if from this they misrepresent that the Spirit spoke of Him as Lord, necessarily with like sacrilege they seem to declare the Son of God also the Son of the Holy Spirit.

---

4 Cf. Deut. 6.4.
5 Cf. Gen. 19.24.
6 2 Tim. 1.18.
7 Ps. 109.1.
8 Cf. Matt. 22.43.

(107) So, just as we do not say that there are two Lords when we designate both the Father and the Son, so we do not speak of three Lords when we confess the Spirit as Lord. For just as it is a sacrilege to speak of three Lords and Gods, so this too is a complete sacrilege to speak of two Lords or Gods, because there is one God, one Lord, one Holy Spirit, and He who is God, is Lord, and He who is Lord, is God, because both in the Lordship is the Godhead, and in the Godhead is the Lordship.

(108) Finally, you have read of the Father as both Lord and God: 'O Lord my God, I shall cry to thee, hear thou me.'[9] You have the Son as both Lord and God, as you have read in the Gospel, because, when Thomas had touched the side of Christ, he said: 'My Lord, and my God.'[10] Therefore, as the Father is God, and the Son Lord, so is both the Son God and the Father Lord. The holy designation is interchanged, the divine nature is not interchanged, but the esteem remains unchangeable. For they are not contributions of bounty but acceptable gifts of natural love, for both unity has its special property, and the special property has unity.

Chapter 16

(109) So the Father is holy, the Son is holy, and the Spirit is holy, but they are not three Holies, because there is one Holy God, there is one Lord. For the true holiness is one, as the true Godhead is one, as that natural[1] true holiness is one.

---

9 Ps. 29.2.
10 John 20.28.

---

1 That is, belonging to the divine nature.

(110) Thus, all these things which we believe to be holy proclaim that sole holiness. Cherubim and Seraphim praise Him with indefatigable voices and say: 'Holy, holy, holy, the Lord God of Sabaoth.'[2] Not once do they say it, lest you believe in but one; not twice do they say it, lest you exclude the Spirit; they do not say holies, lest you think there is plurality, but they repeat three times, and say the same word, that even in a hymn you may understand the distinction [of Persons] in the Trinity, and the oneness of the Godhead; when they say this, they proclaim God.

(111) We also find nothing more precious with which we can proclaim God than to call Him holy. Anything else is inferior to God, is inferior to the Lord. From this, then, consider also whether anything ought to be detracted from the Holy Spirit, whose name is praise of God. For thus is the Father praised, thus is the Son also praised, just as the Spirit, too, is named and praised. The Seraphim praise, the entire chorus of the blessed praise, so that they call God holy, the Son holy, the Spirit holy.

(112) How, then, does He not possess everything that is God's, who is named by priests together with the Father and the Son in baptism, and is invoked in oblations, is proclaimed by the Seraphim in heaven with the Father and the Son, dwells in the saints with the Father and the Son, is poured forth among the just, is infused within the Prophets. For this reason in divine Scripture every prophet is called θεόπνευστος, because God infuses [inspires] what the Spirit has spoken.[3]

(113) Or if they do not wish that the Holy Spirit possess all things that are God's or have all His powers, let them say what He does not possess or what power He does not have.

2 Cf. Isa. 6.3.
3 Cf. 2 Tim. 3.16.

For, as the Son possesses all things, and the Father does not begrudge giving all things to the Son according to His nature, who gave what is greater than all, as the Scripture testifies, saying: 'That which my Father hath given me, is greater than all,'[4] so, too, the Spirit has of Christ what is greater than all, for justice knows not envy.

(114) Thus, if we note carefully, here, too, we comprehend the oneness of divine power. He says: 'That which my Father hath given me is greater than all; and no one can snatch them out of the hand of my Father. I and the Father are one.'[5] For if we have rightly shown above[6] that the Holy Spirit of the Father is the hand of God, the same is surely the hand of the Father, which is the hand of the Son, since the same is the Spirit, which is the Spirit of the Son. Therefore, whoever of us has received eternal life in this name of the Trinity, just as he is not snatched from the Father, so he is not snatched from the Son, so he is not snatched also from the Spirit.

(115) But from the very fact that the Father is said to have given to the Son, and the Spirit to have received from the Son, for it is written: 'He shall glorify me, because he shall receive of mine, and will declare it to you'[7] (which He seems to have said rather regarding the office of dispensation than of the right of divine power, for whom the Son redeemed, the Spirit also received to sanctify them), from these very words, I say, from which they devise their misrepresentation, the oneness of the Godhead is perceived, not the need of bounty.

---

4 John 10.29.
5 John 10.29,30.
6 Book 3.3.
7 John 16.14.

(116) The Father gave by begetting, not by adoption; He gave, as it were, that which was in the very right of the divine Nature, not what was lacking, as it were, by favor of His generosity. And so, because the Son so acquires peoples as the Father does, the Son revivifies as the Father does, He has expressed His equality with the Father in the oneness of power, saying: 'I and the Father are one.' For, when He says: 'I and the Father,' equality is revealed; when He says: 'are one,' oneness is declared. Equality excludes confusion; oneness separation; equality distinguishes between the Father and the Son; oneness does not separate the Father and the Son.

(117) Therefore, when He says: 'I and the Father,' He rejects the Sabellian, for He has called Himself one Person and the Father another; He rejects the Photinian, for He has joined Himself with God the Father. With the former words He rejects those, for He says: 'I and the Father'; with the latter words the Arians, for He says: 'We are one,' yet both with the former and with the latter He silences the madness of the Sabellians, because He said: 'We are one [substance],' not 'We are one [Person].' He silences the madness of the Arians, because He said: 'I and the Father,' not 'the Father and I.' This surely was not a part of arrogance, but of dutifulness and prescience, lest we make an error in our thinking from the order of the words. For oneness knows not order, equality knows no gradation; nor can it fall upon the Son of God that the Teacher himself of dutifulness should offend against dutifulness through arrogance.

Chapter 17

(118) So it is of profit to notice in what place the Lord discussed these matters, for His pronouncements are frequently appraised by the kind of places in which He tarried. When about to fast, He was lead by the Spirit, as we read,[1] into the desert, that He might evade the temptations of the Devil. For, although to have lived temperately in an abundance of riches is to be praised, yet the allurement of temptation is more frequently to be found in the midst of wealth and pleasures. Then the tempter, in order to tempt, promises riches, and the Lord, in order to overcome, supports hunger. Nor do I deny that temperance can exist in the midst of wealth, but, although he who navigates the sea frequently escapes, yet he is more subject to danger than he who will not navigate.

(119) Let us look at other matters. When about to promise the kingdom of heaven, Jesus went up into a mountain.[2] Elsewhere He leads the disciples through corn-fields,[3] when He is about to sow in their hearts a crop of heavenly precepts, that a plentiful harvest of souls might ripen. When about to consummate the duties of the flesh which He had assumed, having now seen perfection in the disciples, whom He had established in the root of His words, He enters a garden,[4] that He might plant slips of olive trees in the house of the Lord, that He might water the just flourishing like a palm-tree,[5] and the fertile vine with the stream of His blood.

(120) In this passage, also, He was walking in the Solomon's porch on the day of dedication, as we read,[6] that is,

---

1 Cf. Matt. 4.1.
2 Cf. Matt. 5.1.
3 Cf. Matt. 12.1.
4 Cf. John 18.1.
5 Cf. Ps. 127.3.
6 Cf. John 10.22,23.

He was walking in the breast of the wise and peaceable, to dedicate His affection to Himself. What that porch is, the Prophet teaches, saying: 'I walked in the innocence of my heart in the midst of your house.'[7] We have, then, in ourselves the house of God; we have the walls; we have also the porches; we have, too, the courts, for it is written: 'Let thy waters flow into thy courts.'[8] Open, then, this porch of thy heart to the Word of God, for He says to you: 'Open thy mouth wide, and I will fill it.'[9]

(121) So let us, then, hear what the Word of God says, walking in the breast of the wise and peaceful: 'I and the Father are one.'[10] He will not say this in the breast of the disturber and the foolish, because 'the sensual man perceiveth not the things that are of the Spirit of God; for it is foolishness to him.'[11] The narrow breasts of the irreligious do not take in the magnitude of the faith. Then the Jews, on hearing: 'I and the Father are one, took up stones to stone him.'[12]

(122) He who cannot give heed to this is a Jew; he who cannot hear this stones Christ with rougher rocks than any stone of his treachery and, if you believe me, wounds Christ. For, although He cannot feel a wound: 'For now we know Christ according to the flesh no longer,'[13] yet He who rejoices in the pious affection of the Church is stoned by the impiety of the Arians.

(123) 'The law of thy mouth, O Lord, is good to me, I keep thy commandment.'[14] You yourself have said that you are

---

7 Cf. Ps. 100.2.
8 Cf. Prov. 5.16.
9 Ps. 80.11.
10 John 10.30.
11 1 Cor. 2.14.
12 Cf. John 10.31.
13 Cf. 2 Cor. 5.16.
14 Cf. Ps. 118.72,73.

one with the Father. Because Peter believed this, he received
the keys of the kingdom of heaven,[15] and without anxiety
for himself forgave sins. Because Judas did not believe this,
he strangled himself with the halter of his own wickedness.[16]
Oh, the hard stones of unbelieving words! Oh, the hideous
halter of the betrayer, but the still more hideous purchase
money of the Jews! Oh, the wicked silver with which either
the just is bought or sold for slaughter! Joseph was sold,[17]
Jesus Christ was bought;[18] the one for slavery, the other for
death. O detestable inheritance, O fatal sale, which either
sold a brother to violence or offers the Lord, the Redeemer
of the salvation of all, to death for a price.

(124) So the Jews did violence to two things, more pre-
eminent than all, to faith and duty, and in both to Christ
the Author of faith and duty. For both in the patriarch
Joseph was a type of Christ, and in the truth of His body was
Christ, 'who thought it no robbery himself to be equal to God,
but took the form of a servant,'[19] namely, because of our fall,
taking on slavery and not avoiding suffering.

(125) In one place, the sale is for twenty pieces of gold;
in the other, for thirty. For could His true price be comprehended whose worth cannot be limited? There is an error in
the price, because there is an error in the study. The sale
is for twenty pieces of gold in the Old Testament, for thirty
in the Gospel, for the Truth is more precious than the type,
grace more generous than training, the presence richer than
the Law, because the Law promised the coming, the coming
fulfilled the Law.

(126) The Ismaelites bought for twenty pieces of gold;

15 Cf. Matt. 16.19.
16 Cf. Matt. 27.5.
17 Cf. Gen. 37.28.
18 Cf. Matt. 26.15.
19 Cf. Phil. 2.6,7.

the Jews, for thirty. No moderate figure here! The faithless are more generous for iniquity than the faithful for salvation. Yet it is fitting to consider the quality of each contract. Twenty pieces of gold is the price for slavery; thirty pieces of gold, for the cross. For, although the mysteries of the Incarnation and of the Passion are in like manner to be regarded with admiration, yet the fulfilment of the faith is in the mystery of the Passion. I do not indeed consider the giving birth by the Virgin of less importance, but I accept more gratefully the mystery of the sacred Body. What is more merciful than that He donated His injuries to me? Yet it is more complete that He contributed so much to us that He, who was not destined to die, because He was God, died by our death, that we might live by His Spirit.

(127) Finally, not indifferently did Judas Iscariot value that ointment at 300 pence,[20] which surely seems to point out the cross by the statement of the price itself. Therefore, the Lord also says: 'For she in pouring this ointment upon my body hath done it for my burial.'[21] Why, then, did Judas value this rather dearly? Because remission of sins is of more value to sinners, and the indulgence seems more precious. Finally, you have it written: 'Because to whom much is forgiven, he loveth more.'[22] Therefore, the sinners themselves also confess the grace of the Lord's passion, which they have lost, and they bear testimony to Christ, who have persecuted Christ.

(128) Or because 'wisdom will not enter into a malicious soul,'[23] the disposition of the betrayer said this, and valued the passion of our Lord's body at a dearer price, that he might

---

20 Cf. John 12.5.
21 Matt. 26.12.
22 Cf. Luke 7.47.
23 Wis. 1.4.

withdraw all from the faith by the enormity of the price. Therefore, the Lord offered Himself at no price, lest the necessity of poverty withdraw anyone from Christ. The patriarchs sold Him for a cheap price that all might buy. Isaias said: 'You that have no money, go, buy, and drink; eat without money,'[24] that he might gain him who had no money. O traitor Judas, you value the ointment of His Passion at 300 pence, and you sell His Passion at thirty pence.'[25] Rich in valuing, cheap in wickedness!

(129) Thus, not all buy Christ at the same price. Photinus, who buys Him for death, buys Him at one price; the Arian, who buys Him for injury, at another; the Catholic, who buys Him to glorify Him, at another. But he buys Him without money, according to what is written: 'Let him who has no money buy without price.'[26]

(130) 'Not everyone,' He says, 'that saith to me Lord, Lord, shall enter into the kingdom of heaven.'[27] Although many call themselves Christians, they usurp the name and do not have the reward. Both Cain offered sacrifices[28] and Judas received the kiss,[29] but He heard him say: 'Judas, dost thou betray the Son of man, with a kiss?' that is, you fulfill wickedness with a pledge of love, and you sow hatreds with the instrument of peace, and you inflict death with the function of love.

(131) So, let not the Arians flatter themselves by the name which they have usurped, because they say that they are Christians. The Lord will reply to them: 'You put forth My name, and you deny My substance; but I do not recognize

---

24 Cf. Isa. 55.1.
25 Cf. Matt. 26.15.
26 Cf. Isa. 55.1.
27 Matt. 7.21.
28 Cf. Gen. 4.3.
29 Luke 22.48.

My name where my eternal Godhead is not. My name is not that which is divided from the Father, is separated from the Spirit; I do not recognize My name where I do not recognize My doctrine; I do not recognize My name where I do not recognize My Spirit.' For he does not know that he is comparing the Spirit of the Father with the servants whom He created. We have already said much on this subject.[30]

Chapter 18

(132) But in summary, to gather together at the end more clearly what has been said here and there, the manifest glory of God is proved not only by other arguments, but also by these four in addition to the others. For God is known from the following: either because He is without sin, or because He forgives sin, or because He is not a creature, but is the Creator, or because He is adored, but does not adore.

(133) Thus, no one is without sin except the one God, because there is no one without sin except the one God.[1] Also, no one forgives sins except the one God, for it is likewise written: 'Who can forgive sins, but God alone?'[2] Also, one cannot be the Creator of all things, except one who is not a creature; moreover, he who is not a creature is without doubt God, for it is written: 'They served the creature rather than the Creator, who is blessed for ever.'[3] God also does not adore, but is adored, for it is written: 'Thou shalt adore the Lord, thy God, and shalt serve him only.'[4]

30 Cf. Book 1.1.

1 Cf. Matt. 19.17.
2 Luke 5.21.
3 Rom. 1.25.
4 Cf. Deut. 6.13.

(134) Let us consider, then, whether the Holy Spirit has something of these marks which offer proof of His Godhead. Let us first, then, treat of the fact that no one is without sin except the one God, and demand that they show that the Holy Spirit has sin.

(135) But they cannot show this, and they seek the authority, that we show by a text, that the Holy Spirit has not sinned, as it is read of the Son, that He has not committed sin.[5] And let them learn that we teach this by the authority of the Scriptures, for it is written: 'For in Wisdom is the Spirit of understanding, holy, one, manifold, subtle, active, eloquent, undefiled.'[6] The Scripture calls Him undefiled; did it lie about the Son, that you should believe that it lied about the Spirit? For the Prophet said of Wisdom in the same place that nothing defiled enters into her. She herself is undefiled, and undefiled is her Spirit. Therefore, if the Spirit has no sin, He is God.

(136) But how can He be guilty of sin who Himself forgives sin? So, He has not committed sin, and, because He is without sin, He is not a creature. For every creature is subject to the capability of sin, but only the eternal Godhead is free from sin and undefiled.

(137) Now let us see whether the Spirit forgives sins. But here there can be no doubt, since the Lord himself has said: 'Receive ye the Holy Ghost, whose sins you shall forgive, they shall be forgiven.'[7] Behold that sins are forgiven through the Holy Spirit. But men exhibit their ministry for the forgiveness of sin, they do not exercise the right of some power. For not in their own name but in that of the Father and the Son and the Holy Spirit do they forgive sins. They ask, the God-

---

5 Cf. 1 Peter 2.22.
6 Cf. Wis. 7.22.
7 Cf. John 20.22,23.

head forgives; the obedience is of man, but the munificence is of the Power above.

(138) Also, that sins are forgiven through baptism is not doubtful, but in baptism is the operation of the Father and the Son and the Holy Spirit. If, then, the Spirit forgives sin, since it is written: 'Who can forgive sins, but God only?'[8] surely He who cannot be separated from the oneness of the name of the Nature, cannot also be severed from the power of God. Moreover, if He is not severed from the power of God, how is He severed from the name of God?

(139) Let us now see whether He is a creature or the Creator. But, since we have proven very clearly above[9] that He is the Creator, for it is written: 'The Spirit of God who made me,'[10] and since it has been declared that the face of the earth is renewed through the Spirit,[11] and all things become exhausted without the Spirit, it is apparent that the Spirit is the Creator. But who will doubt this, when, as we have shown above, not even the generation of the Lord assumed from the Virgin, which is more distinguished than all creatures, is without the operation of the Spirit?

(140) Therefore, the Spirit is not a creature, but is the Creator, but He who is the Creator is certainly not a creature. And since He is not a creature, without doubt He is the creator, who with the Father and the Son produces all things. But if He is the Creator, surely the Apostle by saying to the condemnation of the Gentiles: 'That they served the creature rather than the Creator, who is blessed for ever,'[12] and by persuading them also, as we have shown above,[13] that the

---

8 Mark 2.7.
9 Book 2.5-6.
10 Cf. Job 33.4.
11 Cf. Ps. 103.30.
12 Cf. Rom. 1.25.
13 Book 2.5-6.

Holy Spirit is to be served, both showed Him to be the Creator, and, because He is the Creator, has proved that He ought to be called God. This, too, he expresses in his letter which was written to the Hebrews, saying: 'For he who created all things is God.'[14] Therefore, either let them say what it is that is created without the Father and the Son and the Spirit, or let them confess that the Spirit also is of the one Godhead with the Father and the Son.

(141) He also showed that He whom he called Lord and God is to be adored. For He who is God and Lord of the universe is surely to be adored by all, for it is written thus: 'Thou shalt adore the Lord thy God, and thou shalt serve him only.'[15]

(142) Or let them say where they have read that the Spirit adores. For it is written of the Son of God: 'Let all His angels adore Him.'[16] It is not read: Let the Spirit adore. For how can He adore who is not among servants and ministers, but with the Father and the Son He has the services of the just under Him, for it is written: 'We serve the Spirit of God.'[17] So, we must adore Him whom the Apostle has shown must be served by us. Moreover, whom we serve, Him also we adore, according to what has been written, to repeat the same words again and again: 'Thou shalt adore the Lord thy God, and thou shalt serve him only.'

(143) Although the Apostle did not even pass over this, he said that the Spirit also should be adored. For, since we have shown that the Spirit is in prophecy, and since no one can doubt this, that prophecy is given through the Spirit, surely when He is adored who is in the Prophets, the same

14 Heb. 3.4.
15 Cf. Deut. 6.13.
16 Cf. Heb. 1.6.
17 Cf. Phil. 3.3.

Spirit is adored. Accordingly, you find it so: 'If, therefore, the whole church come together into one place, and all speak with tongues, and here come in unlearned persons or unbelievers, will not they say that you are made? But if all prophesy, and there come in one that believeth not, or one unlearned, he is convinced of all, he is judged of all. The secrets of his heart are made manifest; and so, falling down on his face, he will adore God, affirming that God is among you indeed.'[18] It is God, then, who is adored, God who abides and who speaks in the Prophets; moreover, the Spirit abides and speaks; therefore, the Spirit also is adored.

Chapter 19

(144) Thus, just as the Father and the Son are one, because the Son has all things that the Father has,[1] so, too, the Spirit is one with the Father and the Son, because He too knows all the things of God.[2] For He did not obtain it by force, lest there be injury to him who lost it; He did not seize it, lest harm be to him, from whom it seemed to have been snatched. For neither did He seize it because of need, nor did He obtain it by force through the excellence of greater power, but He possesses it through oneness of power. Therefore, if He works all these things, all of which the one and the same Spirit works,[3] how is He not God who has all things that God has?

(145) Or, let us consider what God has that the Holy

---

18 1 Cor. 14.23-25.

1 Cf. John 16.15.
2 Cf. 1 Cor. 2.16.
3 Cf. 1 Cor. 12.11.

Spirit does not have. God the Father has Godhead; the Son also has it, in whom dwells the fulness of the Godhead; and the Spirit has it, because it is written: 'The Spirit of God, who is in my nostrils.'[4]

(146) God is able to search the hearts and reins, for it is written: 'The searcher of hearts and reins is God.'[5] The Son, too, is so able, who said: 'Why do you think evil in your hearts?'[6] For Jesus knew their thoughts. The Spirit also is so able, who makes manifest to the Prophets also the hidden things of others, just as we have said above,[7] 'for the secrets of his heart are made manifest.' And why do we wonder if he searches the secrets of men, 'who searcheth even the profound things of God'?[8]

(147) God has the power of being true, for it is written: 'But God is true, and every man a liar.'[9] And elsewhere it is written: 'Faithful God, who lieth not.'[10] Does the Spirit lie, who is the Spirit of Truth,[11] rather whom we have shown to have been called the Truth, for John called Him also the Truth, as he did the Son? And in the psalm, David says: 'Send forth thy light and thy truth; they have conducted me, and brought me unto thy holy hill, and into thy tabernacles.'[12] If you consider the Son here is light, then the Spirit is Truth; or if you consider the Son is Truth, then the Spirit is light.

(148) God has a name above every name, and He has given a name to the Son, as we read that in the name of

---

4 Cf. Job. 27.3.
5 Ps. 7.10.
6 Matt. 9.4.
7 Book 2.13.
8 Cf. 1 Cor. 2.10.
9 Rom. 3.4.
10 Cf. Titus 1.2.
11 Cf. John 16.13.
12 Ps. 42.3.

Jesus all should genuflect.[13] Let us consider whether the Spirit has this name. But it is also written: 'Go ye, baptize the nations in the name of the Father, and of the Son, and of the Holy Ghost.'[14] So, He has a name above every name. So, what the Father and the Son have, the Spirit also has through the oneness of the name of His nature.

(149) God has the power to raise up the dead. For, 'as the Father raiseth up the dead, and giveth life; so the Son also giveth life to whom he will.'[15] Moreover, the Spirit also raises up, through whom God raises up, for it is written: 'He shall quicken also your mortal bodies, because of his Spirit dwelling in you.'[16] Yet, that you may not think this a weak grace, hear that the Spirit also raises up, for the Prophet Ezechiel says: 'Come, spirit, and blow upon these dead, and they will live. And I prophesied as he had commanded me; and the spirit of life came into them, and they lived, and they stood up upon their feet, an exceeding great assembly.' And below, God says: 'You shall know that I am the Lord, when I shall open your sepulchres, to bring my people out of their graves, and I shall put my spirit in you, and you shall live.'[17]

(150) Surely, when He mentioned His Spirit, did He name any one else besides the Holy Spirit? For neither would He have mentioned His Spirit as produced by blowing, nor would this Spirit have been able to come from the four corners of the world, because this blowing of the winds which we see is partial not universal, and this spirit by which we live is partial not universal, but it is characteristic of the Holy Spirit to be both above all and in all. Thus, according to the

---

13 Cf. Phil. 2.9,10.
14 Cf. Matt. 28.19.
15 John 5.21.
16 Rom. 8.11.
17 Cf. Ezech. 37.9-10; 13-14.

words of the Prophet we may observe how the bones, after the framework of the resolved members had long since been dispersed, return into the form of a revived body under the quickening of the Spirit, and how the ashes grow into their limbs, animated by a disposition to come together, before they were formed anew in the likeness of the living.

(151) Do we not in the likeness of the deed recognize the oneness of the divine power? Thus, the Spirit raises up, just as the Lord also raised at His own passion, when in the twinkling of an eye suddenly the tombs of the dead opened, and the revived bodies arose from their graves,[18] and, after discarding the odor of death and being restored with the scent of life, the ashes of those who perished took on the appearance of those who are alive.

(152) So the Spirit has that which Christ has; He has then what God has, for all things that the Father has, the Son also has, and therefore He said: 'All things whatsoever the Father hath, are mine.'[19]

Chapter 20

(153) And that is not insignificant, our reading that a river goes forth from God. For thus you have it in the words of John the Evangelist: 'And he showed me a river of water of life, clear as crystal, proceeding from the throne of God and of the Lamb. In the midst of the street thereof, and on both sides of the river, was the tree of life, bearing twelve fruits, yielding its fruit every month, and the leaves of the tree for the healing of the nations.'[1]

---

18 Cf. Matt. 27.52.
19 John 16.15.

---

1 Apoc. 22.1,2.

(154) This certainly is the river proceeding from the throne of God, that is, the Holy Spirit, whom he drinks, who believes in Christ, as He Himself says: 'If any man thirst, let him come to me, and drink. He that believeth in me, as the Scripture saith, out of his belly shall flow rivers of living water. Now this he said of the spirit.'[2] Thus the river is the Spirit.

(155) This, then, is in the throne of God, for the water does not wash the throne of God. Then, whatever you understand as that water, David did not say that it was above the throne of God, but above the heavens, for it is written: 'Let all the waters that are above the heavens, praise the name of the Lord.'[3] Let them praise, He said; not, let it praise. For if he had wished the element of water to be understood, surely he would have said: Let it praise, but by speaking in the plural, he wished the Powers to be understood.

(156) And what wonder is it, if the Holy Spirit is in the throne of God, since the kingdom of God itself is the work of the Spirit, as it is written: 'For the kingdom of God is not meat and drink; but justice, and peace, and joy in the Holy Spirit.'[4] And when the Saviour Himself says:[5] 'Every kingdom divided against itself shall be made desolate,' then by adding: 'But if I by the Spirit of God cast out devils, then is the kingdom of God come unto you,' He shows that the kingdom of God is held undivided by Himself with the Spirit.

(157) But what is more foolish than that anyone should deny that the Holy Spirit reigns with Christ, when the Apostle says that we shall reign together with Christ in the kingdom of Christ: 'For if we be dead with him, we shall live also with

---

2 John 7.37,38.
3 Ps. 148.4.
4 Rom. 14.17.
5 Matt. 12.25,28.

him';[6] but we through adoption, He through power; we by grace, He by nature.

(158) The Holy Spirit also, therefore, has participation in the kingdom with the Father and the Son, who is of one nature, of one dominion, also of one power [with them].

Chapter 21

(159) Thus, since He has participation in the Kingdom, what prevents our understanding that it was the Holy Spirit by whom Isaias was sent? For we cannot doubt, since Paul is the author, whose opinion in the Acts of the Apostles Luke the Evangelist so approved as to put in writing. Then, you have it thus, as Paul speaks: 'Well did the Holy Ghost speak to our fathers by Isaias the prophet, saying: Go to this people, and say to them: With the ear you shall hear, and shall not understand; and seeing you shall see, and shall not understand.'[1]

(160) It is the Spirit, then, who sent Isaias. If the Spirit sent him, it is the Spirit surely, whom, when the King Ozias died, Isaias saw, when he said: 'I saw the Lord of Sabaoth sitting upon a throne high and elevated; and the house was full of his majesty; and the Seraphim stood round about him; one had six wings; and the other had six wings, and with two wings they covered his face; and with two they covered his feet; and with two they flew; and they cried one to another, and said, Holy, holy holy, the Lord God of Sabaoth, all the earth, is full of his glory.'[2]

(161) If the Seraphim were standing, how were they

6 2 Tim. 2.11.

1 Acts 28.25-26.
2 Cf. Isa. 6.1-3.

flying? If they were flying, how were they standing? If we cannot comprehend this, how do we wish to comprehend God, whom we do not see?

(162) But just as the Prophets saw a wheel running within a wheel,[3] which certainly has no refence to the likeness of a bodily sight, but the grace of each Testament, because the life of the saints is well rounded, and so harmonious with itself that the later parts correspond with the earlier.[4] The wheel, then, within a wheel is life under the Law, life under grace, on this account, because the Jews are within the Church, the Law within grace. For he is within the Church who is a Jew secretly; and circumcision of the heart is a sacrament within the Church. But that Judaea is within the Church, of which it is written: 'In Judea God is known';[5] therefore, as a wheel runs within a wheel, similarly wings stood still, and wings were flying.

(163) In like manner, also, 'the Seraphim with two wings covered His face, and with two they covered His feet, and with two they flew.' For here, also, is a mystery of spiritual wisdom. The times stand, the times fly; those of past stand, those of the future fly; and just as the wings of the Seraphim, so they cover the face or the feet of God; inasmuch as in God, who has neither beginning nor end, all the course of the times, from this knowledge of its beginning and its end is at rest. So the past or the future times stand, the present fly. Do not ask about the secrets of His beginning or end, which are not. You have the present; praise, do not question.

(164) The Seraphim with unwearied voices, praise, and do you strike asunder? When they do this, surely they indicate

---

3 Cf. Ezech. 1.16.
4 St. Ambrose becomes so involved in his thoughts here that he does not complete this sentence.
5 Ps. 75.1.

that God must never be struck asunder by us, but must always be praised. So the Holy Spirit is also the Lord of Sabaoth. Unless, perchance, the Teacher, whom Christ selected, displeases the irreligious, or they can deny that the Holy Spirit is the Lord of powers, who grants whatever powers He himself wishes.

Chapter 22

(165) It is now possible to recognize the oneness of majesty and rule in the Father, Son, and Holy Spirit. For many say that it was God the Father who was seen by Isaias at this time.[1] Paul said it was the Spirit, and Luke approved it; John the Evangelist referred it to the Son. For thus is it written of the Son: 'These things Jesus spoke; and he went away and hid himself from them. And whereas he had done so many miracles before them, they believed not in him, that the saying of Isaias the prophet might be fulfilled, which he said: Lord, who hath believed our hearing? And to whom hath the arm of the Lord been revealed? Therefore, they could not believe; for Isaias said again: He hath blinded their eyes, and hardened their hearts, that they should not see with their eyes, nor understand with their heart, and be converted, and I should heal them. These things said Isaias, when he saw his glory, and spoke of him.'[2]

(166) These words did John say that Isaias had spoken, and he revealed most clearly that the majesty of the Son had appeared to him, but Paul related that the Spirit had spoken these words. How, then, is there this difference?

(167) There is, indeed, a difference of words, but not of

1 Cf. Isa. 6.1.
2 John 12.36-41.

meaning. For, although they spoke different words, no one erred, for both the Father is seen in the Son, who said: 'He that seeth me, seeth the Father also,'[3] and the Son is seen in the Spirit, for, 'no one says the Lord Jesus, but by the Holy Ghost.'[4] Thus, Christ is seen not by the eye of flesh, but by the grace of the Spirit. Therefore, the Scripture also says: 'Rise thou that sleepest, and arise from the dead, and Christ will enlighten thee.'[5] And when Paul had lost his eyesight, how did he see Christ except in the Spirit?[6] Therefore, too, the Lord says: 'For to this end have I appeared to thee, that I may make a minister and a witness of those things in which thou hast seen me, and in which thou shalt see me.'[7] For the Prophets, too, received the Spirit, and saw Christ.

(168) One, then, is the vision; one the right of precept, one the majesty. Or do we deny that the Holy Spirit is also the Lord of majesty,[8] when the Lord of majesty was crucified, who was born of the Holy Spirit from the Virgin Mary? For there is no other Christ, but there is one, born before the ages of the Father, as the Son of God, and in the world born as man by taking on flesh.

(169) But what shall I say, because as the Father and the Son, so, too, the Spirit is without stain and omnipotent,[9] for Solomon called Him in Greek παντοδύναμον, πανεπίσκω-πον, because He is all-powerful and the surveyor of all things, as it was shown above[10] to be read in the Book of Wisdom. Thus, the Spirit also is in honor and in majesty.

---

3 John 14.9.
4 Cf. 1 Cor. 12.3.
5 Eph. 5.14.
6 Acts 9.8.
7 Cf. Acts 26.16.
8 Cf. 1 Cor. 2.12.
9 Cf. Wis. 7.22.
10 Cf. Ch. 18.135.

(170) Consider now lest, perchance, something not befit Him, or, if this displeases you, O Arian, take Him out of His association with the Father and the Son. But if you do take Him out, you will see the heavens turn upon thee, for all their power is from the Spirit.[11] If you wish to take Him out, your hand must first be laid upon God, for God is the Spirit.[12] But how will you take Him out who searcheth the profound things of God?[13]

---

11 Cf. Ps. 32.6.
12 Cf. John 4.24.
13 Cf. 1 Cor. 2.10.

THE SACRAMENT OF
THE INCARNATION OF
OUR LORD

INTRODUCTION

HE TITLE SEEMS TO BE THAT USED by St. Ambrose, judging from Chapter 63 of the work itself. Paulinus, St. Ambrose's biographer, speaks of the work as *The Incarnation of Our Lord,* as does also Cassiodorus. Leo the Great and some others use the first title with the addition of the words 'against the Apollinarists.'

This work in one book is not dated with certainty. Most scholars agree in placing it after *De fide,* to which St. Ambrose refers in Chapters 62, 81, and 100 of this *Sacrament of the Incarnation of Our Lord,* and even after the *De Spiritu.* It is to be noted that this work is sometimes described in the manuscripts as Book IV of *De Spiritu* or Book IX of the whole work: *De fide, De Spiritu,* and *De Incarnatione.* The earliest possible date seems to be late in the year 381.

The occasion of the work was a challenge hurled at St. Ambrose by two Arian chamberlains of the emperor, who took exception to certain expressions used by Ambrose in a sermon on the Incarnation. They were to meet publicly on the following day in the Portian Basilica. The story is told by

Paulinus (Chapter 18). Ambrose accepted the challenge and was on hand promptly. The chamberlains decided to go for a ride in a traveling--carriage first, and met their death in an accident. Meanwhile, Ambrose, unaware of all this, thought that they were planning to make a late and sudden appearance so as to confuse him. So as not to keep his congregation waiting, Ambrose began to preach, but he did not at once approach the topic of discussion. He discussed, rather, the Biblical story of the sacrifice of Cain and Abel, pointing out that God's words to Cain were applicable to all heretics, and hoping that meanwhile the chamberlains would put in an appearance. When they did not do so, he commenced his real sermon, refuting the Arians who denied the proper divinity of our Lord, and also refuting the Docetae and Apollinarians who denied our Lord's true humanity.

The sermon, according to a common practice of the day, was taken down by shorthand writers and was later transcribed. St. Ambrose then revised and amplified it. Even after the sermon was prepared for publication, Ambrose added an appendix (Chapters 79-116), consisting of an answer to an objection raised by Palladius of Ratiara after the Council of Aquileia, and referred to Ambrose by Gratian.

Thus, the work is divided into three main parts: Part 1 (Chapters 1.1 through 2.13), the introduction, including the discussion of the sacrifices of Cain and Abel; Part 2 (Chapters 3.14 through 7.78), the sermon proper on the Incarnation; and Part 3 (Chapters 8.79 through 10.116), the reply to the objections of Palladius of Ratiara.

THE SACRAMENT OF
THE INCARNATION OF OUR LORD

Chapter 1

RETHREN, I WISH MY DEBT TO BE PAID, but I do not find my creditors of yesterday, unless, perchance, they thought we must be disturbed by their sudden arrival, but true faith is never disturbed.

(2) Perhaps until they do come, let us turn our attention to those farmers who have been proposed,[1] of whom this one, that is, Cain, offered the Lord a sacrifice from the fruits of the land; the other, namely, Abel, offered one of the first-born of his flocks. I find no complaint to make as to the kind of gifts, except that Cain knew that his gifts gave displeasure, and the Lord said: 'If you offer rightly, but do not divide rightly, you have sinned.'[2]

(3) Where, then, is the crime? Where the fault? Not in the offering of the gift, but in the disposition of the mind with

---

1 The Bible story of the sacrifice of Cain and Abel had just been read as the 'prophetic lesson' in the Mass.
2 Cf. Gen. 4.3,4,7.

which the offering is made. There are some who rightly think that one had selected what he should offer, the other offered the cheaper things that he had. But there is in us no such lack of understanding of spiritual sacrifice as to think that the Lord sought a corporal sacrifice, not a spiritual one. And so He added: 'Be still,' signifying that it is more tolerable to abstain from offering gifts than to offer a gift with a zeal lacking faith. For he who knows not how to divide, knows not how to judge; 'but the spiritual man judgeth all things.'[3] And so Abraham divided the sacrifice which he offered.[4]

(4) Abel also knew how to divide, who offered a sacrifice from 'the firstlings of his flock,'[5] teaching that the gifts of the earth, which had degenerated in the sinner, will not please God, but those in which the grace of the divine mystery shone forth. Thus he prophesied that we were to be redeemed from fault through the passion of the Lord, of whom it is written: 'Behold the Lamb of God; behold, he who taketh away the sin of the world.'[6] Thus, too, he made an offering from the firstlings, that he might signify the First-born. Therefore, he shows that God's true sacrifice would be us, of whom the Prophet says: 'Bring to the Lord the offspring of rams.'[7] And worthily is he confirmed by the judgment of God.

(5) But to that reprobate it is said: 'Be still,' and this general sentence I think has been passed on all who are outside the Church. For here I perceive a figure of many peoples whom the divine sentence comprehends, whose gifts He already refused at that time in the gift of Cain.[8]

---

3 1 Cor. 2.15.
4 Cf. Gen. 15.10.
5 Gen. 4.4.
6 John 1.29.
7 Ps. 28.1.
8 Cf. Gen. 4.5.

Chapter 2

(6) For this is the general sentence against all impious men. And so, if a Jew, who separates the Son of the Virgin Mary from God the Father, makes an offering, it is said to him: 'If you offer rightly, but do not divide rightly, you have sinned; be still.'[1]

(7) If a Eunomian,[2] who on coming from the spring of Arian impiety slips in the copious mire of his perfidy as he asserts that the generation of Christ, which is above all things, is to be gathered from the traditions of philosophy, when surely the reasoning of creatures is one thing and the power of divine secrets another, makes an offering, it is said also to him: 'If you offer rightly, but do not divide rightly, you have sinned; be still.'

(8) This is said to a Sabellian,[3] who confuses the Father and the Son. This is said to a Marcionite,[4] who thinks that there is one God of the New and another of the Old Testament. This is said to Manichaeus[5] and to Valentinus,[6] who

---

1 Cf. Gen. 4.7.

2 A follower of Eunomius, Arian bishop of Cyzicus, in 360.

3 Sabellius, the doctor of Monarchianism, at the beginning of the third century. Monarchianism, or Modalism, taught that the Son and the Holy Ghost were modes of the Father.

4 Marcion was born toward the end of the first century at Sinope in Pontus. Although the son of the bishop of that city, he became a rich merchant and spread his doubts of the truth of Christianity, which later became the heresy of Marcionism. He broke with the Church in 144. He taught that there is no connection between Judaism and Christianity, and so the God of the Old Testament and the God of the New Testament are different. Thus Christ, the Redeemer, is not the same as the Jewish Messias, who has not yet come.

5 Manichaeus, or Manes, was the founder of Manichaeism, and was born in Babylonia about 215. Manichaeism is essentially dualism, two eternal and opposing principles, one good, the other evil, Light and Darkness, God and Matter.

6 Valentinus was the most influential leader of Gnosticism, an intellectual and intricate kind of doctrine that took various forms in the course of its history.

did not think that the true flesh of man had been assumed by
Christ. Also Paul of Samosata[7] and Basilides[8] are numbered
in the same kind of opinion.

(9) Similarly, also, by the authority of the same opinion
they[9] are condemned who have denied the divinity of the
Holy Spirit. For certain others are either Arian Jews or Jewish
Arians, for just as the former separate the Son from the
Father, so the latter also separate the Spirit from God the
Father and the Son of God.

(10) Also to Novatus[10] and Donatus[11] and all who strove
to divide the body of the Church, it is said individually: 'If
you offer rightly, but do not divide rightly, you have sinned.'[12]
For that is a sacrifice of the Church which is offered to God,
to which Paul said: 'I exhort you, therefore, brethren, by the
mercy of God, to present your bodies as a sacrifice, living,
holy, pleasing to God.'[13] Badly, then, did they divide the
sacrifice by tearing asunder the members of the Church.

(11) That opinion also smites those who separate the

---

7 Paul, born at Samosata, succeeded Demetrianus as Bishop of Antioch
   in 260. His teachings were essentially Monarchianism.
8 Basilides was born in the latter part of the first century, the place of
   his birth being unknown. He was one of the leading Gnostics of the
   second century.
9 The Pneumatomachi, the heretics who denied the divinity of the Holy
   Ghost. Ambrose wrote his treatise on the Holy Spirit against these.
10 Novatus, a priest of the Roman church, in the middle of the third
   century refuted Modalism and Adoptionism by affirming the divinity
   of Christ, but in doing so he fell into error. He never speaks of the
   human soul of Christ, although he affirms that other men are composed
   of body and soul. He also denies that the Son is equal to the Father,
   and considers the divine attributes as personal qualities. His teachings
   resulted in a schismatic church and the doctrine of Novatianism.
11 Donatus was the heretical bishop of Carthage in 315, and the founder
   of Donatism, a schism which arose ostensibly over the question of
   rebaptizing the lapsed.
12 Cf. Gen. 4.7.
13 Rom. 12.1.

rational soul from the sacrament of the Lord's Incarnation[14] by desiring to separate the nature of man from man.[15] And perhaps these do offer rightly to the Trinity, but they do not know how to distinguish the character of human from that of divine nature; for God's is a simple nature, man consists of a rational soul and a body. If you take away one, you have destroyed the entire nature of man.

(12) Thus that sentence is against all heresies, which under the name of brotherhood in an unbrotherly fashion persecute the Church, since under the option of the Christian name and a kind of nominal brotherhood of faith they desire to wound us with parricidal swords. For our conversion is to them,[16] and sinners rule over us in the world for the sinner dominates in the world but the just man rules in the kingdom of God.

(13) Therefore, let us beware lest anyone attempt to separate us from the abode of the eternal King and from the bosom of Mother Church, to which that soul in the Canticle of Canticles[17] indicates that she had led the Word of God. Let us beware lest we separate the substance of the hidden nature of the only begotten Son from the bosom of the Father and from, as it were, His paternal womb. And by these words on which is based the truth of the Incarnation which was assumed, let us strive to bring decisions for the divine generation, lest it be said, also, to someone of us: 'If you offer rightly, but do not divide rightly, you have sinned; be still,' that is, if we do not know how to distinguish

---

14 A reference to Apollinaris of Laodicea and his followers. He joined Athanasius in combating Arianism but fell into the opposite heresy. He denied that Christ had a rational human soul, saying that it was replaced by His divinity. He thus founded Apollinarism.

15 That is, the Man-God.

16 An allusion to Gen. 3.16 (Septuagint).

17 Cant. 3.4.

the things that are characteristic of eternal divinity and the Incarnation, if we confuse the Creator with His works; if we say that the Author of time began after time. For it cannot be that He, through whom all things are, is one of all things.

Chapter 3

(14) I do not wish that credence be given us; let the Scripture be quoted. Not of myself do I say: 'In the beginning was the Word,'[1] but I hear it; I do not feign but I read what we all read, but do not all understand. And when it is read, we all hear, and all do not hear [i.e., understand]. 'For the heart of some has been hardened, and their ears have heard heavily,'[2] that is, the ears of interior disposition. For the flesh does not err, which performs its function and receives what is heard, but the mind is a perverse interpreter of good hearing, which refuses to hear what is said, and to understand what is read. Why do you stop your ears as with wax and lead, and yet you cannot shut out the benefits of the Lord and the functions of nature? You hear unwillingly, you hear disdainfully, you hear, so that you cannot make an excuse for what you have not heard.

(15) So you hear when this is read: 'In the beginning was the Word.' Who says this? Surely, John the fisherman, but he does not say this as a fisherman, but as a fisher of man's disposition. For already he was not catching fish but was quickening men.[3] These words are not his, but His who granted him the power of quickening. For the fisherman was more silent than the fish which he formerly used to catch, and with respect to the divine mysteries he was more dumb who

1 John 1.1.
2 Cf. Acts 28.27.
3 Cf. Luke 5.10.

did not know the author of his own voice; but he who is quickened by Christ has heard the voice in John, has recognized the Word in Christ.

(16) Accordingly, full of the Holy Spirit, since he knew that the beginning was not of time, but above time, he left the world, and ascending in spirit above all beginning, he says: 'In the beginning was the Word,' that is, let the heavens remain, for they were not yet, since 'in the beginning was the Word.' For, although the heavens have a beginning, God does not have one. Finally, 'in the beginning God made heaven and earth.'[4] 'Made' is one thing; 'was' another. What is made has a beginning; what was, does not receive a beginning, but comes before. Let time also remain, because time is after the heavens. Let also the angels and the archangels remain. And if I do not discover their beginning, yet there was a time when they were not. For they were not who at some time began. If, then, I cannot discover the beginning of those who certainly had a beginning, how can I discover the beginning of the Word, from whom all beginning, not only of creatures, but also of all our thoughts springs.

(17) Thus had John clearly declared the everlasting divinity of the Word, but yet, lest anyone might separate the eternity of the Word from the Father, that we might believe that it is the same for the Word as for the Father, the good fisherman added: 'And the Word was with God'. This that he said is to be understood thus: 'The Word was just as was the Father; since He was together with the Father, He was also in the Father, and He was always with the Father. Surely, just as we read 'He was' of the Father, thus also we read 'He was' of the Word.

(18) Why do you discern what is understood, who does

---

4 Cf. Gen. 1.1.

not discern what is heard? It is. of the Word to be with the
Father; it is of the Father to be with the Word, for we read
that 'the Word was with God.' So, if, according to your
opinion, there was a time when He was not, then, according
to your opinion, He too was not in the beginning with whom
was the Word. For through the Word I hear, through the
Word I understand that God was. For, if I shall believe that
the Word is eternal, which I do believe, I cannot doubt about
the eternity of the Father, whose Son is eternal. If I think
His generation to be temporal, He begins to have fellowship
with us, so that the Father seems to have begun to be; but
if you do not doubt about the Father, because it is not of
God to begin to be, you do not doubt about the Father, because it is of God to have eternal perfection. Lest, perchance,
you slip in the use of human speech, when you say 'Word' and
'Son,' he accordingly added: 'And the Word was God.'

(19)   Surely He has what the Father has, because He was
God. How do you deny the eternity of Him who together
with the Father has the one name of God? Let not the sound
and the similarity of the expression deceive you. The word
which is temporal, which is put together with syllables and is
composed of letters, is one thing; the Son is not such a Word,
because the Father of the Word is not such.

(20)   We must be on our guard lest here also we seem
to bring in the question of corporeal speech. God is incorporeal; surely, one who is incorporeal does not have corporeal
speech. If corporeal speech is not in the Father, neither is the
Son corporeal word. If body is not in the Father, neither is
time in the Father. If time is not in the Father, surely it is
not in the Word. But, if there is no time of beginning in the
Word, surely there is neither number nor degree of the Word.
For if there is number in the Word, then there are many

words. If there are many words, there are also many sons. But there is one Word, who excludes both degree and number, one according to nature.

(21) Do not ask about the kind of nature. I am far more ignorant of this than I know. This only do I know well, that I do not know what I cannot know. 'What we have seen and what we have heard,' says John.[5] This only he said that he knew well, what he heard and what he saw, he who leaned on the bosom of Christ.[6] Thus, for him it was enough to have heard; is this not enough for me?

(22) But what he heard, this he has told me, and what he has heard from Christ, this I cannot deny is the truth about Christ. So, what he has heard, I have heard; and what he saw, I have seen. For he saw what he saw, certainly not divinity which cannot be seen according to its nature. But because He could not be seen according to His nature, He took on what was outside the nature of divinity, that He might be seen according to the nature of the body. Finally, the Holy Spirit also was seen in outward appearance, as a dove,[7] because divinity could not be seen in the truth of its splendor.

Chapter 4

(23) Therefore, do not you also interpret according to nature what is outside the nature of divinity. For, although you believe that true flesh was assumed by Christ, and you offer His body to be transfigured on the altar, yet if you do not distinguish between the nature of His divinity and that of His body, to you also is it said: 'If you offer rightly; but

---

5 1 John 1.3.
6 Cf. John 13.23.
7 Cf. Luke 3.22.

do not divide rightly, you have sinned.'[1] Divide what is mine; divide what is His of the Word. I did not have what was His; He did not have what is mine. He assumed what is mine, that He might share what is His. He assumed it not to confuse, but to complete it. If you believe the assumption, and invent confusion, you have ceased to be a Manichaean, but you have not begun to be a son of the Church.

(24) If you believe the assumption of the body, and join compassion to divinity, surely you have shunned a portion of perfidy, not perfidy; for you believe what you presume to be of benefit to you, you do not believe what is worthy of God.

(25) Again, if you believe that the God of both the New and the Old Testament is the same, but premise times and moments to His Word, Valentinus is more tolerable, who does not think that the ages are before God, but are gods, because the ages are. For it is less of a sacrilege that the ages are joined to divinity than that they are preferred to it.

(26) Furthermore, if you believe that Christ did not assume beginning from the Virgin, but yet you think there is some beginning before Christ, there is a difference in time, a striving for contention; for you have denied that He is the equal of the Virgin, not of time. Moreover, I will not deny that He is the equal of the Virgin according to the assumption of the body, and I will confess Him to be the Creator of time. For what does it profit you if you say that Christ is this or that creature? A creature changes; divinity is not adored.

(27) Christ did not wish Himself to be known thus, nor to be judged only by those merits which are superhuman. Finally, when He had asked: 'Whom do men say that I am?'[2] when some said 'Elias,' others 'Jeremias,' or one of the Proph-

---

1 Cf. Gen. 4.7.
2 Cf. Matt. 16.13.

ets, He took no note of the opinion of anyone; when Peter had said: 'Thou art the Christ, the Son of the living God,'[3] this one alone did He praise, not without merit.

(28) Thus John speaks, Peter speaks, Christ has approved, and do you not approve, O Arian? Do you think that John and Peter are not to be believed, whom even alone our Lord Jesus Christ believed to be abundant as evidence of His glory unto the faith of all? Finally, as if for the evidence of the Old and the New Testaments, Moses is joined with Elias, and Peter is frequently quoted with John.[4]

(29) Peter says: 'Thou art';[5] he does not say: 'Thou hast begun to be.' Peter says: 'Thou art the Son of God';[6] he does not say: 'Thou art a creature.' John has said this. If thus far you have not believed, because you did not understand the mystery of him leaning upon Wisdom,[7] Peter repeated it. Christ commended both, one for his judgment, the other for the mystery. For John added this, that you might read that he was leaning on the bosom of Christ, and that you might understand that his head, in which is the chief of all the senses, was filled with a sort of secret wisdom. If you do not think that the mystery is to be believed, at least do not impugn the judgment. Peter is praised because he believed that the one whom he saw was the Son of God, because he separated himself from the still rude opinions of an ignorant people. Finally, when the Lord asked what men thought of the Son of God, when the opinion of the crowd was stated, Peter was silent.

(30) You are silent then, Simon, and, although others

---

3 Matt. 16.16.
4 Cf. Matt. 17.1.
5 John 13.23.
6 Matt. 16.16.
7 Cf. John 13.23.

reply, you still are silent. Since you yourself are the first, who, even though not questioned, asks questions, do you not fear that you be reprimanded by the Lord, because you do not reply to Him when He asks a question? 'For this reason,' he says, 'I do not reply, because I am not asked my opinion but that of others. For I have read: "That my mouth may not speak the works of men."[8] Moreover, it is the work of the iniquitous to preach iniquities. Therefore, I am still silent, because not yet am I asked what I think; I shall not utter with my lips what my mind has not approved. The time will come when I shall reply. I, too, shall be asked what I think; then at last I shall reply what is mine [to reply]; for it is mine to speak the faith, to declare my devotion, to proclaim grace.'

(31) Therefore, not as if rather dull of mind nor slow of speech is he silent, nor as if disdainful does he put off the homage of his word, but as a cautious person does he avoid the danger of general opinion, as one who does not avoid the danger to his salvation. Finally, later on you have it that he jumped from the ship to meet the Lord, not in a desire for glory but overeager to obey.[9]

(32) He, then, who before was silent, to teach us that we ought not to repeat the words of the impious, this one, I say, when he heard: 'But who do you say I am,'[10] immediately, not unmindful of his station, exercised his primacy, that is, the primacy of confession, not of honor; the primacy of belief, not of rank. That is to say: 'Now let no one outdo me; now is my role; I ought to compensate for my silence; the fact that I was silent ought to be of benefit. My tongue does not have perplexities; faith should come forth without difficulty. While some were casting forth filth, although the

8 Cf. Ps. 16.4.
9 Cf. Matt. 14.29.
10 Matt. 16.15.

filth of another's impiety but proclaimed by them, who said that Christ was either Elias, or Jeremias, or one of the prophets; for that voice had filth, that voice had perplexities; while some, I say, are washing away this filth, while in some these perplexities are being eradicated, let our voice resound that Christ is the Son of God. My words are pure, in which expressed impiety has left no perplexities.'

(33)   This, then, is Peter, who has replied for the rest of the Apostles; rather, before the rest of men. And so he is called the foundation, because he knows how to preserve not only his own but the common foundation. Christ agreed with him; the Father revealed it to him. For he who speaks of the true generation of the Father, received it from the Father, did not receive it from the flesh.[11]

Chapter 5

(34)   Faith, then, is the foundation of the Church, for it was not said of Peter's flesh, but of his faith, that 'the gates of hell shall not prevail against it.'[1] But his confession of faith conquered hell. And this confession did not shut out one heresy, for, since the Church like a good ship is often buffeted by many waves, the foundation of the Church should prevail against all heresies.

(35)   The day will fail me sooner than the names of heretics and the different sects, yet against all is this general faith—that Christ is the Son of God, and eternal from the the Father, and born of the Virgin Mary. The holy Prophet David describes him as a giant for the reason that He, one, is

11 Cf. Matt. 16.16,17.

1 Cf. Matt. 16.18.

of double form and of twin nature, a sharer in divinity and body, who 'as a bridegroom, coming out of his bride-chamber, hath rejoiced as a giant to run the way.'[2] The bridegroom of the soul according to the Word, a giant of earth, because in going through the duties of our life, although He was always God eternal, He assumed the sacrament of the Incarnation, not divided, but one, because He, one, is both, and one in both, that is, as regards both divinity and body. For one is not of the Father, and the other from the Virgin, but the same is of the Father in the one way, and from the Virgin in the other.

(36) His generation is not prejudicial to generation, nor His flesh to divinity, for neither was the pledge[3] prejudicial to the Father, nor the will to the Passion, nor the Passion to the will. For the same one suffered and did not suffer; died and did not die; was buried and was not buried; rose again and did not rise again; for the body proper took on life again; for what fell, this rose again; what did not fall, did not rise again. He rose again, therefore, according to the flesh, which, having died, rose again. He did not rise again according to the Word, which had not been destroyed on earth, but remained always with God.

(37) Thus, He died according to the assumption of our nature, and did not die according to the substance of eternal life; and He suffered according to the assumption of the body, that the truth of the assumption of the body might be believed, and He did not suffer according to the impassible divinity of the Word which is entirely without pain. Finally, the same one said: 'O God, my God, look upon me; why

2 Ps. 18.6.
3 That is, Christ, since through the Incarnation, the Son of God was pledged to the redemption of mankind.

hast thou forsaken me?'[4]—for, according to the flesh, He was forsaken, who according to divinity could have been neither deserted nor forsaken.

(38) The same one also says: 'Far from my salvation are the words of my sins,'[5] that is, let him not be deceived, who hears: 'Why hast thou forsaken me?'—but let him understand that these words are said according to the flesh, which are very foreign to the fullness of His divinity, for the words of sins are foreign to God, since the sins of words are also foreign to Him; but since I[6] have assumed the sins of others, I have assumed also the words of others' sins, so that I say that I, who am always with God, have been forsaken by God the Father.

(39) Therefore, He was immortal in death, impassible in His Passion. For just as the sting of death did not seize Him as God, hell saw Him as man. Finally, 'He yielded up the ghost,'[7] and yet as master of putting off and of assuming a body, He yielded up the ghost; He did not lose it. He hung upon the cross, and threw all into disorder. He trembled on the cross, before whom this whole world trembled. He was in the midst of tortures, He received wounds, and He donated the heavenly kingdom. Having become the sin of all men, He washed away the sins of the human race. At last He died, and a second and a third time in exultation and in joy I say, He died, so that His death might become the life of the dead.

(40) But not even His tomb is without a miracle. For, when He had been anointed by Joseph, and while buried in the latter's tomb,[8] He himself by a kind of new operation, though dead, opened the tombs of the dead; and indeed His

---

4 Ps. 21.1.
5 Ps. 21.1.
6 That is, Christ.
7 Matt. 27.50.
8 Cf. Luke 23.53.

body lay in the tomb, yet He himself was free among the dead; He bestowed remission upon those placed in Hell by loosing the law of death. There was then His body in the sepulchre, but His power operated from heaven. It was shown to all through the true body that the flesh was not the Word, but the flesh was of the Word. The flesh indeed tasted death, but the power of God was impassible; and if He put off the body, yet there was no loss to God with respect to the body.

(41) Why do you attribute the calamities of the body to divinity, and connect the weakness of human pain even with divine nature? 'Now my soul,' He says, 'is troubled.'[9] His soul, not His wisdom, is troubled; for His wisdom remained immutable, although it was encompassed by a cloak of flesh. For in that form of a servant there was the fullness of true light; and when the form emptied itself, there was the light. Then he said: 'Walk whilst you have the light.'[10] And when He was in death, He was not in the shadow. Then, too, He poured the light of eternal life even upon those who were in limbo. The true light of wisdom shone even there; it illumined hell, but was not shut up in hell. For what is the place of wisdom? Then the just man says: 'But where is wisdom to be found, and where is the place of understanding? Man knoweth not its way, neither is it found among men.'[11]

(42) Wisdom, therefore, is neither in time nor in place, so that time also means to be. But how is it in time, which was in the beginning? How in place, which was with God? If the only-begotten Son is sought, according to the sense of the Gospel He is found in the bosom of the Father. Do you think that the bosom of the Father is a place? And do you

9 John 12.27.
10 John 12.35.
11 Cf. Job. 28.12,13.

seek how Wisdom was born, when the man of prophecy says: 'Man knoweth not its way.'[12] And do you think that its origin is according to men, when Job says that it is not found among men? And do you attribute death to Wisdom, of which 'the depth saith: It is not in me: and the sea saith: It is not with me'?[13] Heaven does not say: 'It is not in me,' but 'the depth saith: It is not in me.' For not to the depth, but to the Father did it[14] say: 'Into thy hands I commend my spirit.'[15] Even though His soul was in the depth, it is no longer there, for it is written: 'Because thou wilt not leave my soul in hell, nor wilt thou give thy holy one to see corruption.'[16]

(43) Therefore, the sea says: 'It is not with me,' that is, our life speaks troubled by the waves of the world. For His flesh is not among men, because we no longer know Christ according to the flesh.[17] The earth says: 'It is not with me,' because He has risen. Then the angel says: 'Why seek you the living among the dead?'[18] And well did the sea say: 'It is not with me,' because He was above the sea. Then He walked even with corporeal footsteps on the sea, when, after calming the sea, He ordered Peter to walk upon the sea;[19] and, although he faltered, yet he faltered not through the weakness of Him who ordered but through the weakness of himself who was obeying.

(44) Therefore, do not mingle the darkness of our nature with the splendor of His glory; do not spread the cloud of human flesh over His light. Again, if, while proclaiming His passion, you by no means recognize that which is passible,

---

12 Job. 28.13.
13 Job. 28.14.
14 Wisdom.
15 Luke 23.46.
16 Ps. 15.10.
17 Cf. 2 Cor. 5.16.
18 Luke 24.5.
19 Cf. Matt. 14.26-29.

you have disproved the love of God, you have denied your own salvation. Therefore, we should consider them demented who, on hearing the Son of God say: 'Why strikest thou me?'[20] have thought that He was subjected to injury according to His divine nature. For He said: 'Why strikest thou me?' but His divine nature did not feel the stroke. He said: 'I have given my back to the strikers, and my cheeks to their hands; but I have not turned away my face from the confusion of the spitters.'[21] He said: 'back' and 'cheeks' and 'face,' that is, parts of the human body. For what the flesh of the Word suffered, even while remaining in the flesh, the Word of God suffered by the flesh, as it is written: 'Since Christ has suffered in the flesh.'[22] He surely referred to Himself according to His assumption of a body, in order that He might take upon Himself what is ours and might cloak the human with His own.

(45) Rightly, then, did His flesh suffer according to its nature, and the nature of the Word was not changed by this suffering of the body; for our resurrection is in truth, and thus Christ's Passion is proclaimed in truth.

Chapter 6

(46) He did not, as some say, suffer in phantasm, because He did not walk upon the sea in phantasm, as the disciples in the Gospel are said to have thought.[1] But they are excused, 'for as yet the spirit was not given; because Jesus was not yet glorified.'[2] But for us Christ has already been crucified and

---

20 John 18.23.
21 Cf. Isa. 50.6.
22 1 Peter 4.1.

1 Cf. Matt. 14.26.
2 John 7.39.

has risen; for us the Spirit has already been given, who is the teacher of truth. To be sure, the disciples erred at that time, that we on our part might not be able to err later. Thus their error is of benefit to us. As men they erred; as disciples they believed.

(47) Those, then, who proclaim that Jesus came in phantasm we should condemn, as well as those who in directing their line of error say that the Son of God is not one and the same, but that He who was born of God the Father was one, He who was sprung from the Virgin another, although the Evangelist says that 'the Word was made flesh,'[3] so that you should believe in one Lord Jesus, not two.

(48) Some also believed that the Word of God was one, the Son of God another, although the Evangelist testifies that He who in the beginning was the Word with God the Father came unto His own.[4] Yet there are some who have thought that, just as the Word was made unto one of the Prophets, so it was made unto Christ, not that He was the Word of God. But of none of the Prophets was it said: that 'the Word was made flesh.' No one of the Prophets took away the sins of the world. Of no one else was it said: 'This is my beloved Son in whom I am well pleased.'[5] Of no one of the Prophets do we read that He is the Lord of glory, which the Apostle said of Christ, namely: 'The Jews crucified the Lord of glory.'[6]

(49) But while we are refuting these, others emerge who say that the flesh and divinity of the Lord are of one nature. What infernal places have vomited so great a sacrilege? Indeed, the Arians are more tolerable, the strength of whose

---

3 John 1.1.
4 Cf. John 1.11.
5 Matt. 3.17.
6 Cf. 1 Cor. 2.8.

perfidy is increased through such men, so that they assert with greater vigor that the Father and the Son and the Holy Spirit are not of one substance, since those attempted to say that the divinity and flesh of the Lord are of one substance. Then, when they say that the Word was turned into flesh and hair and blood and bones, and was changed from its proper nature, an opportunity is given to the Arians to distort the weakness of the flesh into the weakness of the divinity, by bringing about a kind of change in the divine nature.

(50) There are also some who have proceeded to such a degree of impiety as to think that the divinity of the Lord was circumcised; that from being perfect it was made imperfect; and that on the cross hung not flesh but that divine substance, creative of all things, coagulated in a likeness of flesh. But who does not shudder at this? Who gives heed to this, that the Word of God made passible flesh for Himself not from the Virgin Mary but from the divine substance? By asserting this they err to the point that they contend that the body of the Lord was assumed not in time but was always coeternal with the Word of God.

(51) Of all these errors they are the authors who have said that the divinity and flesh of the Lord were of one nature. For I have read what I would not have believed, if I myself had not read them. I have read, I say, what is laid down in the books of a certain author,[7] that both the tongue and He by whom the tongue was moved, were of one nature in Christ. Accordingly, I have put this down, so that the name of the author may be detected from his writing, and that they may note that the force of truth cannot be deduced by arguments and words however fine and ornate.

(52) And this author frequently reminds me that he is

---

7 Apollinaris of Laodicea.

holding to the tractate of the Council of Nicea. But in that
tractate our fathers have said that not the flesh but the Word
of God is of one substance with the Father; and indeed they
confessed that the Word proceeded from the substance of the
Father, but that the flesh was of the Virgin. How, then, is the
name of the Council of Nicea alleged and new statements
introduced which our ancestors never thought, since surely
the Scriptures say that Christ suffered according to the flesh,
not according to the divinity;[8] the Scriptures say that 'a virgin
shall receive in her womb and shall bring forth a son'?[9] For
she did receive the power, and did bear a Son, whom she herself assumed from herself.

(53) Then Gabriel also declares this in proper words, saying: 'The Holy which shall be born of thee shall be called
the Son of God.'[10] 'Of thee,' he says, that you might know
that He was born of her according to man, for Mary produced
from herself, in order that what was produced from her, in
Him, the prerogative of the Lord's production being preserved,
there might be the true nature of the body. But Paul also says
that he was predestined for the Gospel of God. 'Which he had
promised before,' he says, 'by His prophets concerning His
Son, who was made to him of the seed of David, according
to the flesh.' And to the Galatians he says: 'But when the
fullness of time was come, God sent His Son, made of a
woman.' And to Timothy he said: 'Be mindful that the Lord
Jesus Christ is risen from the dead, of the seed of David.'[11]

(54) So He received from us what He offered as His own
for us, that He might redeem us from our own, and that He
might confer upon us what was not our own from His divine

---

8 Cf. 1 Peter 1.2.
9 Cf. Isa. 7.14.
10 Luke 1.35.
11 Cf. Rom. 1.2,3; Gal. 4.4.; 2 Tim. 2.8.

liberality. According to our nature, then, He offered Himself, that He might do a work beyond our nature. From that which is ours is the sacrifice, from His is the reward; and many things will you find in Him both according to nature and beyond nature. For, according to the condition of the body He was in the womb, He was born, He was nursed, He was placed in the crib, but beyond this condition the Virgin conceived, the Virgin bore Him, that you might believe that it was God who renewed nature, and it was man who was born of man according to nature.

(55) For not, as some have concluded, was the very nature of the Word changed, which is always unchangeable, as He himself said: 'See me, see me, that it is I, and I am not changed.'[12] But Paul also said: 'Jesus Christ yesterday, and today, and the same forever,'[13] that is, who is not changed according to the nature of the flesh, but who remained unchangeable even in the changeable quality itself of human condition.

(56) So you have learned that He offered the sacrifice from our nature. For what was the cause of the Incarnation except that flesh which had sinned might be redeemed through itself? Therefore, that which had sinned was redeemed. The divinity of the Word, then, was not immolated, because the divinity of the Word had not sinned; and so the nature of the Word was not turned into the nature of the flesh, because divinity immune from sin was not obliged to offer itself for sin which it had not committed. For Christ offered in Himself that which He put on, and He put on what He did not have before. He did not, then, put on the divinity of His own divinity, in which was the fullness of eternal divinity, but He

12 Mal. 3.6.
13 Heb. 13.8.

assumed flesh that He might put off the covering of the flesh, and might both crucify in Himself the spoils of the Devil and erect the trophies of virtue.

(57) Therefore, if the flesh of all, even in Christ, was subject to injury, how do you say that it is of one substance with His divinity? For if the Word is of one substance with the flesh, which has its nature from earth, why is it asserted that the Word is of one substance with the soul, which Christ received perfect for His human nature? Moreover, the Word is of one substance with God according to the declaration of the Father and the assertion of the Lord himself, who says: 'I and the Father are one.'[14] Thus the Father is proclaimed to be of one substance with an earthly body. And are you still indignant with the Arians, because they say that the Son of God is a creature, when you yourselves say that the Father is of one substance with creatures?

(58) But what else are you doing when you say this than either comparing the slime of Adam and our earth with the divine substance, or at any rate transferring divinity to the injury of earthly corruption? For by saying that the Word became flesh and bones you say that He was changed into earth, for flesh and bones are of earth.

(59) Thus it is written, they say: 'The Word was made flesh.'[15] It is written. I do not deny it. But consider what follows, for there follows: 'And dwelt among us,' that is, that Word which took on flesh, this Word dwelt among us, that is, dwelt in human flesh, and so He is called Emmanuel, that is 'God with us.'[16] So this statement, 'The Word was made flesh,' stands for that which took place, He became man. Even as

---

14 John 10.30.
15 John 1.14.
16 Matt. 1.25.

He said in Joel: 'I will pour out of my Spirit upon all flesh,'[17] for the future pouring out of spiritual grace is promised not for irrational flesh but for men.

(60) But if you hold to the letter, so as to think from what is written, namely the Word was made flesh, that the Word of God was turned into flesh, do you not deny that it is written of the Lord, that He did not make sin, but was made sin?[18] So, was the Lord turned into sin?[19] Not so, but, since He assumed our sins, He is called sin. For the Lord is also called an accursed thing, not because the Lord was turned into an accursed thing, but because He himself took on our curse. He says: 'For he is accursed that hangeth on a tree.'[20] Do you wonder, then, that it is written: 'The Word was made flesh,' since flesh was assumed by the word of God, when of the sin which He did not have, it is written that He was made sin, that is, not by the nature and operation of sin, namely, made into the likeness of sin of the flesh; but that He might crucify our sin in His flesh, He assumed for us the burden of the infirmities of body already guilty of carnal sin.

(61) Therefore, let them cease to say that the nature of the Word was changed into the nature of the body, lest by a like interpretation the nature of the Word seem to have been changed into the contagion of sin. For the fact that He assumed is one thing; what was assumed is another. Power came upon the Virgin, as the Angel also said to her: 'The power of the most High shall over-shadow thee.'[21] But a body was born of the Virgin, and thus, indeed, we have a heavenly

17 Cf. Joel 2.28.
18 Cf. 2 Cor. 5.21.
19 Cf. Gal. 3.13.
20 Cf. Deut. 21.23.
21 Luke 1.35.

descent, but a human conception. So the nature of the flesh and of divinity could not have been the same.

Chapter 7

(62) I might have gone on more extensively, but I fear lest these very words may seem to some either superfluous or drawn out. For some one perchance may say: 'Had you not promised that you would complete [your treatment] of the divinity of the Father and the Son in those five books[1] which you have written? But what shall I do, when every day they bring forth new questions? My promise does not escape me, but objections compel [me to speak]. For how can there be an end to replying, when there is no limit to objecting?

(63) And yet I had promised to bring my reply on the divinity of the Father and the Son to an end in my earlier works, but in this book the treatment of the mystery of our Lord's Incarnation[2] has been made fuller as it should have been. For, when that which the Lord says: 'My soul is sorrowful even unto death,' and later, 'O my Father, if it is possible, let this chalice pass from me. Nevertheless, not as I will, but as thou wilt,'[3] is referred not to the suffering of the Holy Spirit but to His assumption of a rational soul and to the affection of a human nature, it follows that in the assertion of the Lord's sacrament we add also that there was also the fullness of human nature in Christ, and that we separate the Holy Spirit from a judgment of weakness. For he is not subject to weakness, who is not subject to suffering.

(64) I ask, then, how certain men[4] think a soul was not

---

1 Of *De fide.*
2 Here Ambrose gives us the full title of this treatise.
3 Matt. 26.38,39.
4 The Arians.

assumed by our Lord Jesus, whether it is because they fear lest Christ might have erred in a human sense? For they do say that concupiscence of the flesh fights back against the law of the mind.[5] But he who says this is so far from having thought that Christ could have been led by the law of the flesh into the bonds of sin that he himself in the stress of human frailty believed that help could be rendered him through Christ, saying: 'Unhappy man that I am: who shall deliver me from the body of this death? The grace of God by Jesus Christ our Lord.'[6] Could He, then, who saved others from the hazardous condition of the flesh have feared lest He Himself also be overcome by the domination of this flesh?

(65) Yet, as they wish it, He did fear the snares of this flesh. Then He ought to have declined the assumption of flesh, lest He be dragged to the hazardous condition of sin. But how could He have feared the hazardous condition of sin, who had come to remit sin? And so, when He took on the flesh of man, it follows that He took on the perfection and fullness of the Incarnation, for there is nothing imperfect in Christ. So He took on flesh, that He might raise it up again; He took on a soul, but He took on and received a perfect soul, rational and human.

(66) For who can deny that He received a soul, when He himself says: 'I lay down my life for my sheep,' and again, 'Therefore doth the Father love me, because I lay down my life, that I may take it up again.'[7] This is not said by means of a parable, nor with perfunctory meaning, in which one thing is said, and another understood, as is this: 'The new moons and your sabbaths my soul will not abide,'[8]

---

5 Cf. Rom. 7.23.
6 Rom. 7.24,25.
7 John 10.15,17.
8 Cf. Isa. 1.13.

although this also could be referred to the soul of Christ, which was laid down for this purpose, to abolish the error of Jewish superstition, and to establish the truth of one sacrifice.

(67) But let them doubt this prophecy; they cannot refute this Gospel spoken with reference to the quality of the soul. After mention is made of the death and resurrection of the Lord, He then adds: 'No man taketh it away from me: but I lay it down of myself, and I have power to lay it down: and I have power to take it up again.'[9] He lays down, then, the same as He has taken up. 'He has taken up,' I say, for the very Word of God was not made living in His flesh in the place of our soul, but just as He has taken up our flesh, so too He has taken up our perfect soul by the assumption of human nature. He has assumed, I say, the soul, that He might bless it with the sacrament of His incarnation; He has taken up my disposition of mind to emend it.

(68) But what need was there to take up flesh without a soul, since, surely, insensible flesh and an irrational soul is neither responsible for sin nor worthy of reward? So He has taken up for us that which in us was in greater danger. Moreover, what does it profit me, if He has not redeemed me entirely? But He has redeemed me entirely, who says: Are you angry at me, because I have healed the whole man on the sabbath day?'[10] He has redeemed me entirely, because the faithful one rises again into the perfect man not in part, but entirely.

(69) Therefore, let those pitiful ones cease to fear lest Christ was unable to direct His flesh or perfect soul or human feeling, who had sat upon the foal of an ass, upon whom no one before had sat.[11] 'He that planted the ear, shall he

---

9 John 10.18.
10 John 7.23.
11 Cf. Luke 12.30.

not hear?'[12] Was not He who ruled others able to rule himself? Did He who pardoned sins Himself commit sin? Let those overly solicitous persons, as if tutors of Christ, cease to fear lest also in Him concupiscence of flesh overcame the law of the mind, which did not overcome in Paul, but only fought back.[13] The athlete of Christ counts the victories of his mind. Do these men fear lest the flesh wavered in the Lord which conquered in the servant?

(70) Christ does not wish us to fear for Him; the Lord does not wish us to weep for Him. So He says: 'Daughters of Jerusalem, weep not over me; but weep for yourselves.'[14] And He says to them: Fear not for me; fear for yourselves. Or have you not heard David saying:[15] 'The Lord is my light and my salvation, whom shall I fear? The Lord is the protector of my life, of whom shall I be afraid?' And elsewhere: 'I will not fear what man can do unto me.' And elsewhere: 'I will not fear what flesh can do against me.'

(72) Therefore, He says: 'I was unable to fear the fall of human nature, which man himself did not fear. Therefore, I, God before the flesh, God in the flesh, assumed the perfection of human nature, I have taken on the senses of man, but I have not been puffed up by the senses of the flesh. By the senses of man I said that my soul was disturbed; by the senses of man I hungered; by the senses of man I petitioned, who was accustomed to heed petitioners; by the senses of man I increased, as it is written: 'And Jesus increased in wisdom, and age, and grace with God and men.'[16]

(72) How did God's wisdom increase? Let the order of

---

12 Ps. 93.9.
13 Cf. Rom. 7.25.
14 Luke 23.28.
15 Ps. 26.1; 107.6; 55.5.
16 Luke 2.52.

words teach you, He increased in age and increased in wisdom, that is, human wisdom. So the Evangelist placed 'age' first, that you might believe that it was said, according to man; for age does not belong to divinity but to the body. So, if He advanced in the age of man, He advanced in the wisdom of man, but wisdom advances according to the senses, because wisdom is from the senses. But Jesus advanced in age and in wisdom. What senses advanced? If the human senses, then these, too, were taken on; if the divine, then they are changeable through advancement. For what advances, surely is changed for the better, but what is divine is not changed. So, what is changed is surely not divine. Therefore, the human senses advanced; thus, He took on the human senses.

(73) And that we may know that he spoke according to man, the Evangelist spoke above by way of preface, saying: 'And the child grew, and waxed strong, full of wisdom; and the grace of God was in him.'[17] And 'child' is the name of our age. The power of God could not wax strong, nor could God grow, nor could the depth of God's wisdom nor the plenitude of His divinity be fulfilled. What then was fulfilled was not God's wisdom but ours. But how was He fulfilled who descended to fulfill all things?[18]

(74) In what sense, moreover, did Isaias say that the child knew not Father or mother? For it is written: 'Before the child know how to call his father and his mother, the strength of Damascus and the spoils of Samaria shall be taken away before the king of the Assyrians.'[19] For future and hidden things do not escape the wisdom of God, but childhood, lacking knowledge, through human ignorance, of course, does not know what he has not yet learned.

---

17 Luke 2.40.
18 Cf. Eph. 4.10.
19 Isa. 8.4.

(75) 'But,' you say, 'it is to be feared lest, if we attribute two principal senses or a twofold wisdom to Christ, we divide Christ.' When we adore both His divinity and flesh, do we divide Christ? When we adore the image of God in Him and the cross, do we divide Him? Surely the Apostle, who said of Him: 'For though He was crucified through weakness, yet he liveth by the power of God,'[20] said that Christ was not divided. Again, do we divide Him when we say that He took on a rational soul also capable of our understanding?[21]

(76) For God the Word himself was not in His body in place of a rational soul, also capable of understanding, but God the Word taking on a soul rational, capable of understanding, and itself human and of the same substance of which are our souls, and flesh like ours, and of the same substance as is our flesh, was also a perfect man, yet without any taint of sin, because He did not commit sin, but became sin for us, 'that we might be made the justice of God in Him.'[22] Thus, His body and soul are of the same substance as are our soul and body.

(77) I do not fear lest I seem to introduce a tetrad;[23] for we, who assert this, truly worship the Trinity alone. For I do not divide Christ when I distinguish the substance of His flesh and divinity; but I proclaim one Christ with the Father and the Spirit of God, and I shall demonstrate that those rather who say that the flesh of Christ is of one substance with His divinity introduce a tetrad. For what is of the same substance is not one person, but one thing, for surely those who confessed the Son of the same substance with the Father in the tract of the Nicean Council did not believe in one Person, but in one divinity in Father and Son.

---

20 2 Cor. 12.4.
21 Cf. 1 Cor. 1.13.
22 2 Cor. 5.21.
23 An objection made by the Apollinarists.

(78) Therefore, when they say that His flesh was of the same substance as was the Son of God, they themselves run into the absurdities of the vain assertion which they throw up to us, namely, dividing Christ. And so they introduce a fourth uncreated being for us to adore, when the divinity of the Trinity is alone uncreated.

Chapter 8

(79) I had concluded this work,[1] but it was a matter of conscience not to seem to have passed by what we could not solve. For, when some time ago, certain ones listened as we said that the Son of God, who was generated, could not be unequal to the Father who generated, despite the fact that the Son was generated and the Father himself was the generator because generating is a matter not of power but of nature, they thought that my voice was silenced before that question, but in this instance with a damnable twist in the argument they turn their track, so that people may think that a change in the question was made by a change in the wording, saying: 'How can the unbegotten and the begotten be of one nature and substance?'

(80) Therefore, most kind Emperor, to reply to the question proposed to me by you: first of all, I find nowhere in the divine Scripture 'unborn';[2] I have not read it, I have not heard it. Of what changeableness, then are such men as say that we usurp what has not been written? When we state what is written, they throw up to us what has not been written. Do they not contradict themselves, and deprive their calumny of authority?

---

1 From this point to the end is an appendix added by Ambrose in reply to an objection raised by Palladius of Ratiarea after the Council of Aquileia. The Emperor Gratian referred the objection to Ambrose.
2 *Ingenitus.*

(81) Indeed, they say that it is not written that there is a substance and nature of God, although Scripture surely testifies that the Son is the splendor of the glory of God the Father, and the figure of His substance,[3] and we have shown most fully in another work[4] that many others have spoken of the divine substance.

(82) Who will also deny His divine nature, when the Apostle Peter wrote this in his letter,[5] saying that through the passion of the cross the mercy of the Lord brought it about that He made us partakers of the divine nature? But Paul elsewhere also wrote: 'But then, indeed, not knowing God, you served them who by nature are not gods.'[6] For thus also we find it in the Greek versions, whose authority is greater.[7]

(83) What, then, are they doing, who deny that there is a divine nature by calumniating not only the Son but the Father, also? For if He is denied to be God by nature, then, He is God through grace like men, or surely He is believed in falsely, like the demons whose images are given the name of God. But let us follow the apostolic authority, and say that in images there is no divine nature. If, then, divine nature is not in images, is not in demons, it remains that divine nature and substance be in God.[8]

(84) Therefore, we have taught by apostolic authority that it is rightly said of God the Father that He is God by nature. Let them now accept that the nature of God the Father is the same as that of the Son, is the same also as that of the Holy Spirit, lest, perchance, they likewise say: 'We have indeed read that there is a divine nature, but we have

---

3 Cf. Heb. 1.3.
4 Cf. *De fide* 3.4.
5 Cf. 2 Peter 1.4.
6 Gal. 4.8.
7 An interesting admission by St. Ambrose.
8 Cf. 1 Cor. 10.

not read of the unity of divine nature.' But when the Son himself said: 'I and the Father are one,'[9] He proved the unity of the divinity. When He said: 'All things whatsoever the Father hath are mine,' and later: 'Father, all mine are thine, and thine are mine,'[10] He affirmed the unity. When He said: 'But the Father who abideth in me, He also doeth the works which I do,'[11] He most clearly declared the unity.

(85) Then Peter shows that the one nature is divine, saying: 'That He might make us partakers of the divine nature.'[12] For He could have said the following if He had thought otherwise; He could have said, I say, the following: 'That He might make us partakers of the divine natures, especially when through the Son we pass over into a participation of divine nature. Can He grant anything that He does not have? Then there is no doubt that He grants from that which He has, and so He has divine nature who grants participations in divine nature.

(86) The Apostle Paul, also, by saying: 'Who by nature are no gods,'[13] shows that the nature of the true God is one. For he also could have said: 'Who by their natures are no gods,' if he knew that there was a plurality of divine nature, so that there was one in the Father, another in the Son, another in the Holy Spirit. By saying, then: 'By nature are no gods,' he expressed the unity of divine nature.

(87) Moreover, what is to be God by nature, if not to be true God? Just as he said to the Thessalonians: 'How were you converted to God from idols, to serve the living and true God?'[14] For they are represented as being gods, but God by

9 John 10.30.
10 John 16.15; 17.10.
11 Cf. John 14.10.
12 Cf. 2 Peter 1.4.
13 Gal. 4.8.
14 Cf. 1 Thess. 1.9.

nature is living and true. For in our own experience there is the adoptive son and the true Son. We do not say that the adoptive son is son by nature but we do say that He is Son by nature, who is His true Son.

(88) So we have proved by Holy Writ that both the nature and the substance are divine; also, apostolic authority has indicated that unity, not plurality belongs to divine nature.

Chapter 9

(89) Now, let them assert where they have read that the Father is unbegotten. But, if in the manner of dialectics they demand that it be granted them to take as read what has not been read, they disclose that they are being distracted by a zeal for contention, that they are not seeking knowledge of the truth. For in dialectics, if that is not conceded which they demand be conceded to them, in which they desire to find an approach to contention, they cannot find a beginning of disputing. And this is true here, where there is contention more about the subtleties of argument than about the consideration of truth. For this is the glory of dialecticians, if they seem to overpower and refute the truth with words. On the other hand, the definition of faith is that truth not words be weighed. Finally, the simple truth of the fishermen excludes the words of philosophers.

(90) What is the meaning of my statement, in which I say, if I do not grant them the word 'unbegotten,' they cannot find a beginning for their assertion? Let them point out, then, where they have read it.

(91) It had slipped my mind. Now I recall it. It was written, they say, for Arius said that the Father was unbegotten, the Son both begotten and created. Behold by what author

they contend against the writings of the Apostles, yet let them contend, provided they confess that they are disciples of Arius. For how do they deny their master, whose inventions they follow?

(92)   But, if they say what Arius said, I more justly should say what the Apostle said.[1] For he mentioned the Father, he did not call Him unbegotten; he mentioned the Son, and mentioned Him as begotten. What I have read I do not deny; rather, I gladly make use of it; what I have not read I should not make use of. But yet let them make use of that which we did not do in dialectics, unless, perchance, they say that, since we have not read the Father as begotten like the Son, we should on that account consider Him unbegotten.

(93)   This is understood; therefore, it is not read. But, if it is understood, neither have I read that the Holy Spirit is begotten. Therefore, the Spirit, also, since He is not begotten, is surely to be called unbegotten according to your opinion. If, then, you say that the unbegotten and the begotten cannot be of one substance, it remains for you not to deny with reference to the Father and the Holy Spirit unity of divine nature and substance, since we have read that neither the Father nor the Holy Spirit is begotten. For, if the entire force of your disputation is in this: that the unbegotten and the begotten cannot be of one nature—then He who is not begotten is of one nature and substance with Him who is not begotten. If then you think the Father to be greater, because He is not begotten, is not the Holy Spirit greater than the Son?

(94)   Many and innumerable examples can be supplied that what is not begotten may be spoken of as unbegotten. For most men have said that the world is unbegotten, and they have declared that the matter of all things, which the

---

1 Cf. Eph. 3.14.

Greeks call ὕλη, as if wood-matter, is unbegotten. They see, thus, that in this word there cannot be a kind of prerogative of power, unless, perchance, by this word they seem to themselves to honor God, with whom the philosophers think the world ought to be endowed. So, then, is the Father unbegotten as the world? God forbid. Or is this word alone befitting God, when God is beyond the scope of all words. Then there is nothing precious for God in this word which can be shared with others.

(95) But yet, just as you wish, let there be an inestimable prerogative in this word, which is not indicated by any authority, but is estimated by your own judgment. Of what profit, then, is this, your wishing to make a difference in nature and a difference in power between the Father and the Son? It is said: 'Unbegotten and begotten cannot be of one nature and substance,' or, as they sometimes say, the unwrought and the made are not of one nature. For they make no distinction between the unbegotten and the unwrought, and they do not wish that there be a difference between the begotten and the created, provided that they say that the Son is a creature.

(96) Therefore, they say that the Father exceeds all cause, that is, αἰτία, as the Greeks say, since He is not created from another, is not a son, since, indeed, there is no substance from which He is, having no beginning or cause from any source. And so, they say, there can be no other such substance, since all things have the cause of their subsisting from God the Father. Thus, they say that it is unlikely that the Son, since He is from the Father, and since He does not have the cause of His being from Himself but from the Father, is like the Father; for the Father does not have His cause from another, but the Son, as they allege, could not have been, unless He received His very existence from the Father.

(97)   And so they say that unbegotten and begotten are unlike, as if, indeed, as I have already often said elsewhere, generation belongs to power, not to nature. For when I say 'begotten,' I have expressed, not a property of nature, but a signification of generation; and this I shall prove by rather clear examples. For if in a general way I say 'son,' and do not add whose son, he can be understood as the son of a man, the son of iniquity, the son of pestilence, and the son of the Devil, as Scripture testifies[2] about the Jews, and, as is customary, the offspring of cattle and the young of pigeons. Thus, in the name of son, no expression of nature has been indicated. But if I desire to designate nature, I shall indicate a man, or I shall name a horse, or I shall speak of a bird, so that the nature can be understood.

(98)   So then, if I wish to designate divine nature, I ought to name the true God. Moreover, when I say 'Son,' I signify begotten; when also I say 'Father,' I declare that He has begotten. Here, then, you do not make a distinction of nature, since this is significant of one begetting and one begotten; moreover, such significations express quality of substance, for, as I have said, there are many sons, but a diversity of sons; one through nature, another through grace.

(99)   There are many creatures, invisible and visible; invisible, as the Principalities and the Powers, the Thrones and the Dominations; visible, as the sun, the moon, the stars, man, the earth. So there are different species, and different substances of creatures. Thus, if you wish to express the property of some creature, you will name either the sun, or the moon, or the stars; and so it is understood what it is, what you thought ought to be signified.

(100)   But if you say 'made' or 'created,' which they some-

2 Cf. John 8.44.

times say of the Son, since many things have been made and created, you do not seem to have signified a property of substance, but a species of quality. For substance is one thing, quality another. Then we have said also elsewhere that the Latins so interpreted οὐσία as to mean 'substance.' But when οὐσία of God is expressed, what else is signified than that God always is? This the very letters express, for divine power οὖσα ἀεί, that is, since it is always, is called οὐσία, the order of one letter being changed for the sake of the sounds and for brevity and embellishment of speech. So οὐσία signifies that God always is, but the appellation of unborn or born, as you wish, declares how He is, that is, that the Father is from no one else, nor is the Son from *Himself*. Here the species seems to be different. Surely the species is distinct, but the divinity is indistinct.

(101) Do you ask how this can be proved? Even in creatures I shall show that there is a difference in species, that there are different beginnings in many, and that there is one substance, and I shall offer examples from Scriptures. Thus, if in these things which are mortal, this can be proper, how can they impose a law of a kind of necessity upon the divinity of the Father and the Son and the Spirit?

(102) All fowls, of course, which seem of the same genus, are, to be sure, also of the same nature, just as there is one genus and one nature of eagles, similarly of vultures, and of the rest of fowls according to their genus. But however the fowls began to be, we find three species, and we read that the causes of their origin are different. For it is written that God said: 'Let the waters bring forth the creeping creature having life and the fowls that may fly.'[3] And a little later when God had made paradise and had placed man in it, it is written

---

3 Gen. 1.20; cf. 2.19.

that God formed out of the ground the beasts of the earth, and the fowls of the heavens. So the fowls in this passage are indicated as having been formed out of the earth. Above, also, you have read that God said to the birds: 'Increase and multiply,'[4] undoubtedly ordering increase of generating through the union of male and female. And so we notice, also, that beings that are of the one genus began to be in different ways. Some from the waters, some from the earth, and some from the generation of male and female, and yet that these are of one nature, and do not have a dissimilarity of substance.

(103) What, now, is so much of one nature as our flesh with the true body of the Lord? Yet they have both been brought forth by different causes, have arisen from different beginnings. For the flesh of the Lord, generated when the Spirit came to the Virgin, did not await the customary intercourse of male and female union; but our flesh, unless the male and female sex bring genital seed to the natural channels, cannot be formed within the maternal womb; and yet, although the cause of generation was different, nevertheless the flesh of Christ is of one nature with all men.

(104) For childbirth did not change the nature of the Virgin, but established a new method of generating. So flesh was born of flesh. Thus the Virgin had of her own what she gave; for the mother did not give something of another, but she contributed her own from her womb in an unusual manner, but in a usual function. Therefore, the Virgin had the flesh, which by customary right of nature she transferred to the fetus. Therefore, the nature of Mary, who gave birth, and that of the Begotten are the same according to the flesh, and not unlike His human brethren, because Scripture says: 'In all things to be made like to his brethren.'[5] Surely the Son of God is like to

---

4 Gen. 1.22.
5 Heb. 2.17.

us not according to the fullness of divinity but according to our rational soul, and, to speak more clearly, according to the truth of our human body.

(105) Now what shall we say of Adam himself, who, when he was fashioned of the slime of the earth, certainly begot sons as sharers of his nature and partakers of his genus, heirs to his succession?[6] Different, certainly, were the beginnings of the sons and the parent, but one nature of man's condition, and yet the dissimilarity of origin was not injurious to similarity of substance. So also is the Son like the Father in those things, which on account of the weakness of the condition of man could not have fullness of similarity. How, then, is the true Son unlike to God the Father?

Chapter 10

(106) But many, following the same sect, think that they differ in their kind of argument from those who say that the Son is unlike the Father in all things. So, let us discuss the absurdities also of those who say that the Son is like the Father but not of one substance with the Father.

(107) But things which are not of one nature are certainly of a different and distinct nature, and those which are of a distinct nature cannot consequently be similar, unless, perchance, you say that they are like in appearance, but actually unlike. For there is the same appearance of color in the whiteness of milk and of snow and of a swan, but it preserves the difference of a distinct nature, and the difference of natures is not affected by the similarity of appearance.

(108) How, then, can these men say that the Father and

6 Cf. Gen. 2.17.

the Son are similar, who deny their unity of substance? Or
do they think that they are similar in form and shape and
color? But these are characteristic of the body; they indicate
a kind of composition. But how do we adapt similarity according to color and form to the invisible? Or how can a creature
be similar to the uncreated? How [can Christ be] the splendor
of his glory and the figure of His substance,[1] if, as they say,
there is a different glory, a different substance.

(109) The Son, they say, is similar in glory and operation
to God, and thus the Son is said to be the image of God. If,
then, He is similar in some respects, He is not in all; partly
similar, partly dissimilar. Moreover, the consequence of this
proposition is that, if He is partly similar, not entirely so,
the image of God is partly composite, and by this it follows
that He also seems to be composite whose image is composite.
Moreover, if His composite image preserves a similarity only
in part, it cannot be similar in part.

(110) But those who deny that Christ is similar to the
Father in unity of nature think that He is like Him in other
respects. For they are accustomed to say: 'Why do you think
that Scripture gave much to the Son, because it called Him
an image, when God himself said to men: "Be ye holy, because I am holy,"[2] and when the Son said: "Be ye perfect, as
also your heavenly Father is perfect"?'[3] They do not understand that this is added: that not in part but in the fullness
and perfection of divinity the Son is like the Father. Then, if
many are alike, why is the Son alone called the image of the
invisible God, and the mark of His substance, unless because
in Him there is the unity of the same nature and the expression of His majesty?

1 Cf. Heb. 1.3.
2 Cf. Lev. 19.2.
3 Matt. 5.48.

(111) For one likeness is according to imitation, another according to nature, which the words also of the examples proposed indicate. For Scripture says: 'Be ye holy,' that man may become so through imitation. So to men it is said: 'Be,' because they are not, but of Himself God says: 'Because I am holy,' surely not by a proficient process but by permanent nature. Then Wisdom says: 'Be you perfect,' that men may begin to have what they do not have. But of the Father it says: 'As your Father, who is in heaven, is perfect.' So the Father, who always is, is perfect. Therefore, either His οὐσία in Greek, which is always, or in Latin that which is permanent in His own and does not subsist with the help of another, is called His substance.

(112) Therefore, holy Father and perfect Father, also holy and perfect Son, as it were the image of God. Moreover, the image of God, because all things which belong to God, are seen in the Son, that is, eternal divinity, omnipotence, and majesty. Then, such as is God is seen in His image. Therefore, you ought to believe that His image is such as is God. For, if you detract from the image, this surely will also seem to have been detracted from Him of whom He is the image. If you believe the image lesser, God will appear lesser in the image. For such as you consider the image, such will He seem to you, of whom, the Invisible, the image is. The image said: 'He that seeth me seeth the Father also'.[4] And such as you consider Him, whose image you believe the Son to be, such necessarily must the Son be considered by you. Thus, since the Father is uncreated, the Son also is uncreated; since the Father is not lesser, the Son is not lesser; since the Father is omnipotent, the Son is omnipotent.

(113) It is said, then, that, even if they employ what they

---

4 John 14.9.

do not read, so as to say 'unbegotten,' nevertheless we are not prevented by this word from believing that Christ is of one nature and substance with the Father. But, if He is of one nature, surely He is of one power.

(114) This passage is by no means more difficult for refuting the contentions of the faithless. For how do they deny the omnipotent Christ, which is written, who wish to employ what they teach which is not written? For we have taught before[5] that Christ is omnipotent, and it is indicated in the Apocalypse of John the Evangelist, and in the prophecy of Zachary, and in the Gospel. If anyone thinks that these matters should be reviewed, let him turn back and seek again what was said above.

(115) Nevertheless, what I almost passed over there on account of the mass of testimony, let them say about what they think Amos's prophecy was said, for these are the words: 'The Lord who toucheth the earth, and moves it, and all that dwell therein shall mourn. And it shall rise up as the river of Egypt, because He buildeth His ascension in heaven, and hath founded His bundle upon earth; who calleth the waters of the sea, and poureth them out upon the face of the earth; the omnipotent Lord is His name.'[6] Do they not understand that all these things befit the Son, who descended and touched the earth, who in His passion shook the earth, ascended into heaven from earth, and descended upon earth from heaven, just as He Himself had promised?

(116) But why do I labor so about the Son, when Scripture testifies that the Spirit also is omnipotent? For it is written: 'By the word of the Lord, the heavens were established; and all the power of them by the spirit of His mouth.'[7]

---

5 *De fide* 2.3-4.
6 Amos 9.5,6.
7 Ps. 32.6.

And of Wisdom it is written that she has in herself the omni-potent Spirit; for Solomon says: 'For wisdom, which is the worker of all things, taught me.'[8] For there is in her the Spirit of intelligence, holy, one, multiple, subtle, easily movable, eloquent, immaculate, manifest, inviolable, loving the good, acute, provident, powerful, bountiful, kind, stable, perfect, without solicitude, who can do all things, seeing all things, and penetrating through all the thoughts of intelligent spirits.

8 Wis. 7.12.

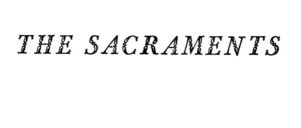

THE SACRAMENTS

INTRODUCTION

S T. AMBROSE'S WORK, *The Sacraments,* has been regarded by many, notably by H. Dudden, as not of
Ambrosian origin. Recently, its authenticity has been
stoutly defended, among others, by J. R. Palanque, and most
recently by Otto Faller, S. J., in the prologomena of Volume
73 of the CSEL (Vienna 1955).

The Sacraments is a work in six books, consisting of six
short addresses delivered by a bishop to the newly baptized,
on six successive days, from Tuesday of Easter week through
the following Sunday. In content it is very similar to *The
Mysteries,* but it is in general a more detailed presentation.
Among other illustrations we cite the more exact description
of the rites of baptism and the fuller account of the Eucharist.
Moreover, *The Sacraments* contains a very interesting expo-
sition of the Lord's Prayer and a discussion of the parts of
prayer which are entirely lacking in *The Mysteries.*

Fr. Faller's chief arguments in favor of St. Ambrose's
authorship of *The Sacraments* are as follows:

1. All the manuscripts in which the name of the author is

given, including all the very ancient ones, with the exception of Sangallensis 188, which includes a collection of sermons of various authors, are obviously falsely handed down under the name of Augustine, show no other name than that of Ambrose. This agreement of manuscripts of diverse sources cannot be explained except by the conclusion that their archetypes written no later than the seventh century all agreed in this fact.

2. All mediaeval writers of the earlier centuries without exception agree on St. Ambrose as the author of *The Sacraments*.

The unanimity of the evidence cited above cannot be contradicted without the very strongest arguments.

3. An argument on the basis of style has been raised against the authenticity of this work. This is very weak, since it is obvious that these sermons are the notes taken down by shorthand written as Ambrose delivered them to the recently baptized and transcribed and published after Ambrose's death. They were never transcribed and polished by Ambrose himself, as was the case with his other sermons. They remain in the very simple language of Ambrose's instructions. Ambrose himself never intended to publish these sermons which were delivered before he wrote *The Mysteries,* but from these Ambrose composed and published *The Mysteries.*

4. Some claim the practice of the washing of the feet, a custom contrary to that of the church in Rome, as an indication of non-Ambrosian authorship, whereas it is a proof of the very opposite. From the year 381, in which St. Ambrose wrote the prologue of *De Spiritu Sancto,* until his last work, *Explanatio Psalmorum XII,* he repeatedly explains and defends this very rite in Milan.

5. These sermons were definitely written in the fourth

century and at Milan, for the greater number of the baptized were adults, whereas in the fifth century, when the churches were fighting Pelagianism, the baptizing of infants prevailed. Besides, the listeners live among pagans (*inter gentiles*), who up to that time dominate public life. None of the Christian sects except Arianism is mentioned, although the speaker depicts the dangers of their age in vivid colors. In *The Sacraments* the same rite of *nox paschalis* is treated as is discussed in *The Mysteries,* and this is Milanese.

6. Although certain familiar Ambrosian expressions are lacking, a great many of them are present. (Fr. Faller lists them at great length on pp. 25-26).

Fr. Faller sums up his view of the matter by saying: 'He who knows Ambrose, after a more careful reading of the work *On the Sacraments,* cannot do otherwise than find Ambrose in every corner, if I may say so, of its manner of speech.'

Although indications generally in *The Mysteries* and *The Sacraments* point to 390 or 391 as the date of composition, it is quite certain that both works were written before the year 392, that is, before the composition of *De institutione virginis ad Eusebium,* in which (5.39) is contained a certain imitation of a passage (7.36) of the *De mysteriis.*

THE SACRAMENTS: I

Chapter 1

I APPROACH A SERMON on the sacraments which you have received, whose scope should not have been presented to you before. For in the Christian man faith is first. Thus, even in Rome they are called 'the faithful' who have been baptized, and our father Abraham was justified by faith, not by works. So you have received baptism, you have believed. Surely it is unfitting that I consider anything else; for you would not have been called to grace if Christ had not judged you worthy of His grace.

(2) What have we done on the Sabbath? 'The opening,' of course. These mysteries of 'the opening' were celebrated when the priest touched your ears and nostrils. What does this signify? In the Gospel, our Lord Jesus Christ, when the deaf and dumb man was presented to Him, touched his ears and his mouth: the ears, because he was deaf; the mouth, because he was dumb. And He said: 'Effetha.'[1] This is a Hebrew word, which in Latin means *Adaperire* (Open). Therefore, the priest has touched your ears, that your ears may be opened to the sermon and exhortation of the priest.

---

1 Mark 7.34.

(3) But you say to me: 'Why the nostrils?' In the one case, because he was dumb, He touched the mouth in order that, since he was unable to speak the heavenly sacraments, he might receive the power of speech from Christ; and in the other case, because the person was a man! In this case, because women are being baptized, and there is not the same purity on the part of the servant as with the Lord—for, since One pardons sins, and sins are forgiven for the other, what comparison can there be?—thus, because of the grace of the work and of the favor, the bishop does not touch the mouth but the nostrils. Why the nostrils? In order that you may receive the good odor of eternal piety, that you may say: 'We are the good odor of Christ,'[2] just as the holy Apostle said, and that there may be in you the full fragrance of faith and devotion.

Chapter 2

(4) We have come to the font; you have entered; you have been anointed. Consider whom you have seen, what you have said; consider; repeat carefully. A Levite[1] meets you; a priest meets you; you are anointed as an athlete of Christ, as if to contend in the contest of this world. You have professed the struggles of your contest. He who contends has what he hopes for; where there is a struggle, there is a crown. You contend in the world, but you are crowned by Christ. And for the struggles of the world you are crowned, for, although the reward is in heaven, the merit for the reward is established here.

---

2 Cf. 2 Cor. 2.15.

---

1 That is, a deacon.

(5) When you were asked: 'Do you renounce the devil and his works?'—what did you reply? 'I do renounce.' 'Do you renounce the world and its pleasures?'—what did you reply? 'I do renounce.'[2] Be mindful of your words, and never let the sequence of your bond be broken. If you give a man surety, you are held responsible, so that you may receive his money; you are held bound, and the lender binds you if you resist. If you refuse, you go to a judge and there you will be convicted by your own bond.

(6) Consider where you promised, or to whom you promised. You saw the Levite, but he is the minister of Christ. You saw him minister before the altar. Therefore, your surety is held, not on earth, but in heaven. Consider where you receive the heavenly sacraments. If the body of Christ is here, here, too, are the angels established. 'Wheresoever the body shall be, there shall the eagles also be,'[3] you have read in the Gospel. Wheresoever the body shall be, there shall the eagles also be, who are accustomed to fly so as to escape the earthly and to seek the heavenly. Why do I say this? Because men, too, are angels, whoever announce Christ and seem to be received into the place of angels.

(7) How? Observe: John the Baptist was born of a man and a woman. Yet give heed, because he himself also is an angel: 'Behold, I send my angel before thy face, who shall prepare thy way before thee.'[4] Observe again. Malachias the Prophet says: 'For the lips of the priest shall keep knowledge and they shall seek the law at his mouth: because he is the angel of the Lord of hosts.'[5] These words are spoken for this

2 From the liturgy of baptism.
3 Cf. Matt. 24.28; Luke 17.37.
4 Matt. 11.10; cf. Mal. 3.1.
5 Mal. 2.7.

reason, that we may proclaim the glory of the priesthood, not that something may be arrogated to personal merits.

(8) So you have renounced the universe; you have renounced the world; be solicitous. He who owes money always considers his bond. And you who owe Christ faith keep faith, which is much more precious than money; for faith is an eternal patrimony, money a temporal one. And do you, therefore, always remember what you have promised; you will be more cautious. If you keep your promise, you will also keep your bond.[6]

Chapter 3

(9) Then you approached nearer; you saw the font; you also saw the priest above the font. I cannot doubt that that could not have fallen upon your mind, which fell upon that Syrian Naaman, for, although he was cleansed, yet he doubted first.[1] Why? I shall tell; observe:

(10) You entered; you saw water; you saw the priest; you saw the Levite. Lest, perchance, someone say: 'Is this all?'—yes, this is all, truly all, where there is all innocence, where there is all piety, all grace, all sanctification. You have seen what you were able to see with the eyes of your body, with human perception; you have not seen those things which are effected but those which are seen. Those which are not seen are much greater than those which are seen, 'For the things which are seen are temporal, but the things which are not seen are eternal.'

---

6 The play on words here, *cautior* ('more cautious') and *cautio* ('bond'), cannot very well be brought out in the English.

1 Cf. 4 Kings 5.1ff.

Chapter 4

(11) Therefore, let us say first—Hold the bond of my words and exact it—'We marvel at the mysteries of the Jews, which were handed down to our fathers, first the age of the sacraments, then the sanctity of those who vouch for them.' This I assure you, that the sacraments of the Christians are more divine and earlier than those of the Jews.

(12) What superiority is there over the people of the Jews having passed through the sea,[1] that meanwhile we may speak of baptism? Yet the Jews who passed through, all died in the desert. But he who passes through this font, that is from the earthly to the heavenly—for there is a passage here, thus Easter, that is, 'His passage,'[2] the passage from sin to life, from fault to grace, from defilement to sanctification—he who passes through this font does not die but rises.

Chapter 5

(13) Naaman[1] then was leprous. A girl said to his wife: 'If my master wishes to be made clean, let him go to the land of Israel, and there he will find him who can rid him of leprosy.' She told her mistress, and the wife told her husband, Naaman the king of Syria, who sent him, as one most acceptable to himself, to the king of Israel. The king of Israel heard that he had been sent to him to be cleansed of leprosy, and rent his garment. Then Eliseus the Prophet commands him: 'Why is it that you have rent your garment, as if there were

1 Cf. Exod. 14.1-15; John 6.49.
2 Cf. Exod. 12.10.

1 Cf. 4 Kings 5.1-14.

no powerful God to cleanse the leper? Send him to me.' He sent him. When he approaches, the Prophet says: 'Come, go down to the Jordan, dip and you will be cured.'

(14) He began to ponder with himself and say: 'Is this all? I have come from Syria to the land of Judaea and I am told: "Come to the Jordan and dip and you will be cured," as if the rivers in my own country were not better.' His servants said to him: 'Lord, why do you not do the word of the prophet? Rather, do it and try.' Then he went to the Jordan, dipped, and, arose cured.

(15) What, then, does this mean? You have seen water: not all water cures, but the water which has the grace of Christ cures. One is an element, the other a consecration; one an opus, the other an operation. Opus belongs to water; operation belongs to the Holy Spirit. Water does not cure unless the Holy Spirit descends and consecrates that water, as you have read that, when our Lord Jesus Christ gave the form of baptism, He came to John, and John said to Him: 'I ought to be baptized by thee; and comest thou to me?' Christ replied to him: 'Suffer it now: for so it becometh us to fulfill all justice.'[2] Behold that all justice is established in baptism.

(16) Therefore, why did Christ descend, except that that flesh of yours might be cleansed, the flesh which he took over from our condition? For no washing away of His sins was necessary for Christ, 'who did no sin,'[3] but it was necessary for us who remain subject to sin. Therefore, if baptism is for our sakes, the form has been established for us, the form of our faith has been set forth.

(17) Christ descended;[4] John stood by, who baptized,

---

2 Matt. 3.14,15.
3 1 Peter 2.22.
4 Cf. Matt. 3.16,17; Mark 1.10,11; Luke 3.22.

and behold! the Holy Spirit descended as a dove. Not a dove descended, but 'as a dove.' Remember what I said: 'Christ took on flesh, not 'as flesh,' but that true flesh of yours; Christ truly took on flesh. But the Holy Spirit in the likeness of a dove, not as a real dove, but in the likeness of a dove descended from heaven.' So John saw and believed.[5]

(18) Christ descended; the Holy Spirit also descended. Why did Christ descend first, the Holy Spirit afterwards, when the form and practice of baptism includes this: that the font be consecrated first, then that he descend who is to be baptized. For, when the priest first enters, he performs the exorcism according to the creation of water; afterwards he delivers an invocation and prayer, that the font may be sanctified and that the presence of the eternal Trinity may be at hand. But Christ descended first, and the Spirit followed. For what reason? Not that the Lord Jesus himself might seem to be in need of the mystery of sanctification, but that He himself might sanctify, that the Spirit also might sanctify.

(19) So Christ descended into the water, and the Holy Spirit descended as a dove; God the Father also spoke from heaven: You have the presence of the Trinity.

Chapter 6

(20) Moreover, the Apostle says that in the Red Sea there was a figure of this baptism, in these words: 'All our fathers were baptized in the cloud and in the sea,'[1] and he added: 'Now all these things happened to them in figure,'[2]

---

5 Cf. John 1.34; 20.8.

---

1 1 Cor. 10.1,2.
2 1 Cor. 10.11.

but to us in reality. Then Moses[3] held the twig. The people of the Jews were shut in. The Egyptian approached with armed men. On one side the Hebrews were shut in by the sea. They were unable to cross the sea or to turn back against the enemy. They began to murmur.

(21) Behold, let it not provoke you that they were heard. Although the Lord heard, yet they are not without fault who murmured. It is your duty, when you are restrained, to believe that you will go forth, not to murmur: to invoke, to question, not to express a complaint.

(22) Moses held a twig and led the people of the Hebrews by night in a pillar of light, by day in a pillar of a cloud. What is light but truth, since it gives forth an open and clear brightness? What is a column of light but the Lord Christ, who has dispelled the shadows of infidelity, has infused the light of truth and grace into human inclinations? But surely the column of a cloud is the Holy Spirit. The people were in the sea and the column of light went ahead, then the column of a cloud followed like the shadow of the Holy Spirit. You see that by the Holy Spirit and by the water He displayed a figure of baptism.

(23) In the flood,[4] also, already at that time there was a figure of baptism, and still, of course, there were no mysteries among the Jews. If, then, the form of this baptism preceded, you see that the mysteries of the Christians are older than were those of the Jews.

(24) But, meanwhile, in consideration of the weakness of my voice and reasons of time, let it suffice today to have tasted the mysteries even from the sacred font. On tomorrow, if the Lord grants the power of speaking or the opportunity,

---

3 Cf. Exod. 14.9-15.21; 13.21ff.
4 Cf. Gen. 6.12; 9.17.

I shall go into the matter more fully. There is need of your sanctity[5] having ears prepared and minds more ready so as to be able to grasp what we can gather from the series of Scriptures and shall go into, that you may have the grace of the Father and of the Son and of the Holy Spirit, to which Trinity is the everlasting kingdom from the ages and now and always, and forever and ever. Amen.

------

5 Since they had just been baptized.

THE SACRAMENTS: II

Chapter 1

(1) Yesterday we began to discuss that in the flood, also, a figure of baptism had preceded. What is the flood except where the just is reserved for the seminary of justice, and where sin dies? So the Lord, seeing that the sins of men were flourishing, reserved the just man alone with his progeny, but ordered the water to go out even above the mountains. And thus in that flood all corruption of the flesh perished; only the stock and the kind of the just remained. Is not this a flood, which baptism is, in which all sins are washed away, only the mind and grace of the just are raised up again?

(2) The Apostle[1] proclaims many kinds of baptism, but *one baptism*. Why? There are the baptisms of the Gentiles, but they are not baptism. They are baths, but they cannot be baptisms. The flesh is bathed; fault is not washed away; rather, in that bath fault is contracted. There were baptisms among the Jews, some superfluous, others in figure. And the

1 Eph. 4.5.

279

figure itself was of benefit to us, since it is an indication of the truth.[2]

Chapter 2

(3) What was read yesterday? It said: 'An angel of the Lord went down at a certain time into the pond, and, as often as the angel went down, the water was moved. And he that went down first into the pond, after the motion of the water, was made whole of whatsoever infirmity he lay under.'[1] This signifies the figure of our Lord Jesus Christ about to come.

(4) Why 'angel'?—for He Himself is the angel of great counsel; 'at a certain time,' which was saved for the last hour, that at the very setting he might overtake the day and defer the setting.[2] So, 'as often as the angel went down, the water was moved.' Perchance you say: 'Why now is it not moved?' Give heed why: 'Signs for the incredulous, faith for those who believe.'[3]

(5) 'He that went down first was made whole of every infirmity.' Why is 'first'? In time or in honor? Understand both! If in time, 'he that went down first' was made whole beforehand, that is, of the people of the Jews rather than of the people of nations. If in honor, 'he that went down first,' that is, who had fear of God, zeal for justice, grace, charity, affection for chastity, he himself rather was made whole. Yet at that time one was saved; at that time, I say, in a figure 'he that went down first' alone was cured. How much greater is the grace of the Church in which all are saved, whoever go down!

2 Cf. Mark 7.4,8; Heb. 6.2; 9.10.

1 Cf. John 5.4.
2 Cf. Jos. 10.12-14.
3 Cf. 1 Cor. 14.22.

(6) But see the mystery: Our Lord Jesus Christ comes to the pond. Many sick were lying there. And easily were many sick lying there, where only one was cured. Then He said to the paralytic: 'Go down.' He said: 'I have no man.'[4] Behold where you are baptized, whence the baptism is, if not from the cross of Christ, from the death of Christ. There is all the mystery, because He suffered for you. In Him you are redeemed; in Him you are saved.

(7) He says: 'I have no man.' That is: 'Because by a man came death and by a man the resurrection,'[5] he was not able to go down, he was not able to be saved, who did not believe that our Lord Jesus Christ had taken on flesh from a virgin. But this man who was awaiting the mediator of God and men, the man Jesus, expecting Him of whom it was said: 'And the Lord will send a man who will make them whole,'[6] said: 'I have no man,' and so he deserved to come to good health, because he believed in Him coming. Yet he would have been better and more perfect if he had believed that He had already come whom he hoped would come.

Chapter 3

(8) Now, behold the incidents one by one. We said that a figure had preceded on the Jordan, when the leprous Naaman was cleansed. That girl of the captives, who is she but one who had the likeness of the Church and represented a figure? For the people of the nations was captive; I do not mean captivity established under some enemy, but I mean

4 Cf. John 5.3,6,7.
5 Cf. 1 Cor. 15.21.
6 Cf. Isa. 19.4.

that captivity which is greater, when the Devil with his own dominates with cruel power and subjects the captive necks of sinners to himself.

(9) So you have one baptism, another in the flood; you have a third kind, when the fathers were baptized in the Red Sea; you have a fourth kind in the pond, when the water was moved. Now I ask you whether you should believe that you have the presence of the Trinity at this baptism, with which Christ baptizes in the Church.

Chapter 4

(10) Thus the same Lord Jesus in His Gospel says to the Apostles: 'Go ye, baptize the nations in the name of the Father, and of the Son, and of the Holy Spirit.'[1] These are the words of the Saviour.

(11) Tell me, O man, Elias[2] invoked fire from heaven, and fire went down; Eliseus[3] invoked the name of the Lord, and from the water the head of the axe, which had been submerged, came up. Behold, another kind of baptism. Why? Because every man before baptism is pressed like the head of the axe and submerged; when he has been baptized, not as the head of an axe but as a lighter kind of productive wood, he is raised. Thus, here also is another figure. It was an axe with which pieces of wood were cut. The handle fell from the axe, that is, the head was submerged. The son of the Prophet did not know what he was doing, but this alone he knew, that he besought Eliseus the Prophet and asked for a remedy. Then Eliseus threw a piece of wood, and the head

---

1 Cf. Matt. 28.19.
2 Cf. 3 Kings 18.36-38.
3 Cf. 4 Kings 6.5-7.

of the axe was raised. So do you see that in the cross of Christ the infirmity of all men is raised?

(12) Another example—although we do not keep an order; for who can grasp all the accomplishments of Christ, as the Apostles have related?—When Moses[4] had come into the desert and the people were thirsty and the people had come to the fountain of Mara and wished to drink, because, when he first took a swallow, he tasted a bitterness and began to be unable to drink, on this account Moses cast a stick into the fountain, and the water, which was bitter before, began to grow sweet.

(13) What does this signify except that every creature subject to corruption is water bitter for all? Although sweet for a time, a creature who cannot cast off sin is bitter. When you drink, you will thirst; when you take the sweetness of the drink, again you taste the bitterness. So the water is bitter, but when it has received the cross of Christ, when the heavenly sacrament, it begins to be sweet and pleasant, and worthily sweet, in which fault is withdrawn. So, if in a figure baptisms have such great power, how much more power does baptism have in reality?

Chapter 5

(14) Now, then, let us take thought. A priest comes; he says a prayer at the font; he invokes the name of the Father, the presence of the Son and of the Holy Spirit; he uses heavenly words. The words are heavenly, because they are Christ's, that we baptize 'in the name of the Father and of the Son and of the Holy Spirit.'[1] If, then, at the words of men, at the

4 Cf. Exod. 15.22-25.

1 Matt. 28.19.

invocation of a holy man, the Trinity was present, how much more is the Trinity present there where eternal words operate? Do you wish to know that the Spirit came down? You have heard that He came down as a dove. Why as a dove? That the unbelievers might be called to faith. In the beginning there ought to have been a sign; in later generations there ought to be perfection.

(15) Accept another example: After the death of our Lord Jesus Christ the Apostles were in one place and they were praying on the day of Pentecost, and suddenly there came a great sound, as of a mighty wind coming, and there appeared cloven tongues as it were of fire.[2] What does this signify except the coming down of the Holy Spirit. He wished to show Himself to the unbelievers even corporeally, that is, corporeally by a sign, spiritually by a sacrament. So the testimony of His coming is manifest, but upon us the privilege of faith is now conferred, because in the beginning signs were made for the unbelievers;[3] now in the fullness of the Church, not by a sign, but by faith must we gather the truth.

Chapter 6

(16) Now let us examine what it is that is called baptism! You came to the font; you went down into it; you gave heed to the highest priest; you saw the Levites (deacons) and the priest at the font. What is baptism?

(17) In the beginning our Lord God made man so that, if he had not tasted sin, he would not have died the death. He contracted sin; he was made subject to death; he was

2 Cf. Acts 2.1,3.
3 Cf. 1 Cor. 14.22.

ejected from paradise. But the Lord, who wished his benefits
to endure and to abolish all the snares of the serpent, also to
abolish everything that caused harm, first, however, passed.
sentence on man: 'Dust thou art and into dust thou shalt
return,'[1] and He made man subject to death. It was a divine
sentence; it could not be resolved by a human condition. A
remedy was given: that man should die and rise again. Why?
That that also, which before had ceded to a place of damna-
tion, might cede to a place of benefit. What is this except
death? Do you ask how? Because death intervening makes an
end to sin.[2] For when we die, surely we have ceased to sin.
The satisfaction of the sentence seemed to be that man, who
had been made to live, if he had not sinned, began to die.
But that the perpetual grace of God might persevere, man died,
but Christ found resurrection, that is, to restore the heavenly
benefit which had been lost by the deceit of the serpent. Both,
then, are for our good, for death is the end of sins and resurrection is the reformation of nature.

(18) However, lest in this world the deceit and snares of
the Devil might prevail, baptism was found. Hear what Scripture—rather, the Son of God—says about this baptism, that
the Pharisees, who did not wish to be baptized by John's
baptism, 'despised the council of God.'[3] Then baptism is the
council of God. How great is grace, where there is the council
of God!

(19) Listen then: For, that in this world, also, the grip of
the Devil might be loosened, there was discovered how man
alive might die and alive might rise again. What is 'alive'?
That is: the living life of the body, when it came to the font,
and dipped into the font. What is water but of earth? So it

---

1 Cf. Gen. 2.7.15-17; 3.6-24.
2 Cf. Heb. 9.15,16.
3 Luke 7.30.

satisfies the heavenly sentence without the stupor of death.
Because you dip, that sentence is resolved: 'Thou art dust and
into dust thou shalt return.'[4] When the sentence has been fulfilled, there is opportunity for heavenly benefit and remedy.
So water is of earth, but the potentials of our life did not permit
that we be covered with earth and rise again from earth. Then
earth does not wash, but water washes. Therefore, the font
is as a sepulture.

Chapter 7

(20) You were asked: 'Do you believe in God the Father
almighty?' You said: 'I do believe,' and you dipped, that is:
you were buried. Again you were asked: 'Do you believe in
our Lord Jesus Christ and in His cross?' You said: 'I do
believe,' and you dipped. So you were also buried together
with Christ.[1] For who is buried with Christ rises again with
Christ. A third time you were asked: 'Do you believe also in
the Holy Spirit?' You said: 'I do believe,' you dipped a third
time, so that the threefold confession absolved the multiple
lapse of the higher life.

(21) Finally, to furnish you an example, the holy Apostle
Peter,[2] after he seemed to have lapsed by the weakness of
his human condition, who had before denied, afterwards, that
he might wipe out and resolve the lapse, is asked a third time
if he loved Christ. Then he said: 'Thou knowest that I love
thee.' He said it a third time, that he might be absolved a third
time.

(22) Thus, then, the Father dismisses sin; thus the Son

4 Gen. 3.19.

1 Cf. Rom. 6.4; Col. 2.12.
2 Cf. John 18.25-27; 21.15-18.

dismisses it; thus, too, the Holy Spirit. But do not marvel that we are baptized in one name, that is, 'in the name of the Father, and of the Son, and of the Holy Spirit,'[3] because He said one name, in which is one substance, one divinity, one majesty. This is the name of which it is said: 'Whereby we must be saved.'[4] In this name you all have been saved; you have returned to the grace of life.

(23) So the Apostle exclaims, as you heard in the reading of the Gospel today, that whoever is baptized is baptized in the death of Jesus.[5] What is 'in the death'? That, just as Christ died, so you also taste of death; just as Christ died to sin and lives unto God,[6] so you, too, died to the former allurements of sins through the sacrament of baptism and rose again through the grace of Christ. So death is, but not in the reality of corporal death but in likeness. For when you dip, you take on the likeness of death and burial, you receive the sacrament of that cross, because Christ hung on the cross and His body was transfixed with nails. You then are crucified with Him;[7] you cling to Christ, you cling to the nails of our Lord Jesus Christ, lest the Devil be able to take you from Him. Let the nail of Christ hold you, whom the weakness of human condition recalls.

(24) So you dipped; you came to the priest. What did he say to you? He said: 'God the Father Almighty, who regenerated you by water and the Holy Spirit and forgave you your sins, Himself will anoint you unto life everlasting.' See, unto what you were anointed, he said: 'Unto life everlasting.' Do not prefer this life to that life. For example, if some enemy rises

---

3 Cf. Matt. 28.19.
4 Cf. Acts 4.12.
5 Cf. Rom. 6.3.
6 Cf. Rom. 6.10.
7 Cf. Gal. 2.19.

up, if he wishes to take away your faith, if he threatens death, that someone may prevaricate, beware what you choose. Do not choose that in which you are not anointed, but choose that in which you are anointed, so that you prefer eternal life to temporal life.

THE SACRAMENTS: III

Chapter 1

(1) Yesterday we discussed the font, whose likeness is as a kind of sepulchre into which, believing in the Father and Son and Holy Spirit, we are received and dipped and rise, that is, are resuscitated. Moreover, you receive myrrh, that is, ointment upon the head. Why upon the head? Because 'the eyes of a wise man are in his head,' Solomon says.[1] For wisdom without grace grows cold, but when wisdom has received grace, then its work begins to be perfect. This is called regeneration.

(2) What is regeneration? You have it in the Acts of the Apostles,[2] for that line which is mentioned in the second psalm,[3] 'Thou art my Son, this day have I begotten thee,' seems to refer to the resurrection. For the holy Apostle Peter[4]

---

1 Eccle. 2.14.
2 Acts 13.33.
3 Ps. 2.7.
4 A lapse of memory because of the similarity of Paul's prayer (Acts 13.15-41) and Peter's prayer (Acts 2.14-36).

in the Acts of the Apostles thus interpreted, that at that time, when the Son rose from the dead, the voice of the Father resounded: 'Thou art my Son, this day have I begotten thee.' Therefore, He is also called 'the first-born from the dead.'[5] So, what is resurrection other than we rise from death unto life? Thus, then, even in baptism, since it is a likeness of death, undoubtedly, when you dip and rise again, it becomes a likeness of resurrection. Thus, according to the interpretation of the Apostle,[6] just as that resurrection was a regeneration, so that resurrection from the font is a regeneration.

(3) But why do you say that you dip in water? For this reason do you roam about; for this reason does uncertainty hold you? Indeed, we read: 'Let the earth bring forth fruit from itself, and the earth bring forth yielding fruit.'[7] Similarly, too, you have read about water; 'Let the waters bring forth creatures having life,'[8] and creatures having life were born. They indeed were in the beginning of creation, but for you it was reserved for water to regenerate you unto grace, just as water generated other creatures unto life. Imitate the fish, which indeed has obtained less grace, yet should be an object of wonder to you. It is in the sea and is upon the waters; it is in the sea and swims upon the floods. A tempest rages in the sea, storms shriek, but the fish swims; it is not submerged, because it is accustomed to swim. So even for you this world is a sea. It has diverse floods, heavy waters, severe storms. And do you be a fish, that the water of the world may not submerge you. Moreover, beautifully does the Father say to the son: 'This day I have begotten thee.'[9] That is: 'When you re-

---

5 Col. 1.18.
6 Cf. Rom. 6.3-11.
7 Cf. Gen. 1.11,12.
8 Cf. Gen. 1.20,21.
9 Cf. Acts 13.33 (Ps. 2.7).

deemed the people, when you called them to the kingdom of heaven, when you fulfilled my will, you proved that you were my son.'[10]

(4) You came up from the font. What followed? You heard the reading. The girded priest—for, although the presbyters also do this, the highest priest, girded, I say, washed your feet. What mystery is this? Surely, you have heard[11] that the Lord, after He had washed the feet of the other disciples, went to Peter, and Peter said to Him: 'Do you wash my feet?' That is: 'Do you, Lord, wash the feet of a servant; do you without stain wash my feet; do you, the author of the heavens, wash my feet?' You have this also elsewhere:[12] He went to John and John said to Him: 'I ought to be baptized by thee, and cometh thou to me?'[13] I am a sinner, and have you come to a sinner, that you who have not sinned may put aside your sins? Behold all justice,[14] behold humility, behold grace, behold sanctification. He said: 'If I wash not thy feet, thou shalt have no part with me.'[15]

(5) We are not unaware of the fact that the Church in Rome does not have this custom, whose character and form we[16] follow in all things. Yet it[17] does not have the custom of washing the feet. So note: perhaps on account of the multitude this practice declined. Yet there are some who say and try to allege in excuse that this is not to be done in the mystery, nor in baptism, nor in regeneration, but the feet are to be washed as for a guest. But one belongs to humility, the other

10 Cf. Exod. 15.13.
11 Cf. John 13.4-11.
12 Cf. Matt. 3.14.
13 Cf. 1 Peter 2.22.
14 Matt. 3.15.
15 Cf. John 13.8.
16 In Milan.
17 The Church in Rome.

to sanctification. Finally, be aware that the mystery is also sanctification: 'If I wash not thy feet, thou shalt have no part with me.' So I say this, not that I may rebuke others, but that I may commend my own ceremonies. In all things I desire to follow the Church in Rome, yet we, too, have human feeling; what is preserved more rightly elsewhere we, too, preserve more rightly.

(6) We follow the Apostle Peter himself; we cling to his devotion. What does the Church in Rome reply to this? Surely for us the very author of this assertion is the Apostle Peter, who was the priest of the Church in Rome, Peter himself, when he said: 'Lord, not only my feet, but also my hands and my head.'[18] Behold faith: That he first pleaded an excuse belonged to humility; that he afterwards offered himself belonged to devotion and faith.

(7) The Lord answered him, because he had said 'hands and head': 'He that is washed, needeth not to wash again, but to wash his feet alone.'[19] Why this? Because in baptism all fault is washed away. So fault withdraws. But since Adam was overthrown by the Devil,[20] and venom was poured out upon his feet, accordingly you wash the feet, that in this part, in which the serpent lay in wait, greater aid of sanctification may be added, so that afterwards he cannot overthrow you. Therefore, you wash the feet, that you may wash away the poisons of the serpent. It is also of benefit for humility, that we may not be ashamed in the mystery of what we disdain in obedience.

---

18 John 13.9.
19 Cf. John 13.10.
20 Cf. Gen. 3.1-6.15.

Chapter 2

(8) There follows a spiritual sign which you heard read today, because after the font there remains the effecting of perfection, when at the invocation of the priest the Holy Spirit is poured forth, 'the spirit of wisdom, and of understanding, the spirit of counsel, and of virtue, the spirit of knowledge, and of godliness, the spirit of holy fear,'[1] as it were, seven virtues of the Spirit.

(9) All virtues, of course, pertain to the Spirit, but these are, as it were, cardinal; as it were, principal. For what is so principal as godliness? What so principal as knowledge of God? What so principal as virtue? What so principal as counsel of God? What so principal as fear of God? Just as fear of this world is infirmity, so fear of God is great fortitude.

(10) There are seven virtues, when you are signed. For, as the Holy Apostle[2] says, because the wisdom of our Lord is manifold, he says, and the wisdom of God is manifold,[3] so is the Holy Spirit manifold, who has diverse and various virtues. Therefore, He is called the 'God of hosts,'[4] which can be applied to the Father and the Son and the Holy Spirit. But this belongs to another discussion, to another time.

(11) After this what follows? You are able to come to the altar. Since you have come, you are able to see what you did not see before. This is a mystery that you have read in the Gospel;[5] if, however, you have not read it—certainly you have heard it: A blind man presented himself to the Saviour to be cured, and He who had cured others only by a word and

---

1 Cf. Isa. 11.2,3.
2 Cf. 1 Cor. 12.4-11.
3 Eph. 3.10.
4 Ps. 79.5.8.15.20 et passim.
5 Cf. John 9.1-7.

speech, and by His power restored the sight of eyes, yet in the book of the Gospel which is written according to John, who truly before the rest saw great mysteries and pointed them out and declared them, wished to prefigure this mystery in him. Surely, all the Evangelists were holy, all the Apostles; all were holy except the betrayer. Yet St. John, who was the last to write his Gospel, as if a friend required and chosen by Christ, poured forth the eternal mysteries by a kind of greater trumpet. Whatever he has said is a mystery. Another[6] said that the blind man was cured. Matthew said it, Luke said it, Mark said it. What does John alone say?—'He took clay and spread it upon his eyes and said to him: Go to Siloe. And rising he went and washed and he came seeing.'[7]

(12) Do you also consider the eyes of your heart. You saw the things that are corporeal with corporeal eyes, but the things that are of the sacraments you were not yet able to see with the eyes of the heart. So, when you gave your name, he took mud and besmeared it over your eyes. What does this signify? That you confessed your sin, that you examined your conscience, that you performed penance for your sins, that is, that you recognize the lot of human generation. For, even if he who comes to baptism does not confess sin, nevertheless by this very fact he fulfills the confession of all sins, in that he seeks to be baptized so as to be justified, that is so as to pass from fault to grace.

(13) Do not think it a matter of indifference. There are some—I know for certain that there was someone who said it—when we said to him: 'In this age you ought rather to be baptized,' he said: 'Why am I baptized? I have no sin; I have

---

6 Cf. Matt. 9.27-30; 12.22; 20.30-34; 12.14; Luke 18.35-43; Mark 8.22-25; 10.46-52.
7 Cf. John 9.7.

not contracted sin, have I?' This one did not have the mud, because Christ had not besmeared him, that is, He had not opened his eyes; for no man is without sin.

(14) He who takes refuge in the baptism of Christ recognizes himself as human. So, too, He placed mud upon you, that is, modesty, prudence, consideration of your frailty, and said to you: 'Go to Siloe.' 'Which,' he says, 'is interpreted sent.' That is: Go to that font, at which the cross of Christ the Lord is preached; go to that font, at which Christ redeemed the errors of all.

(15) You went, you washed, you came to the altar, you began to see what you had not seen before. That is: Through the font of the Lord and the preaching of the Lord's passion, your eyes were then opened. You who seemed before to have been blind in heart began to see the light of the sacraments.

So, most beloved brethren, we have come all the way to the altar, to the richer discussion. And thus, since this is a matter of time, we cannot begin the whole disputation, since the discussion is more comprehensive. What has been said today is enough. Tomorrow, if it pleases the Lord, we will discuss the sacraments themselves.

THE SACRAMENTS: IV

Chapter 1

(1) In the Old Testament the priests were accustomed to enter the first tabernacle frequently;[1] the highest priest entered the second tabernacle once a year. Evidently recalling this to the Hebrews, the Apostle Paul[2] explains the series of the Old Testament. For there was manna in the second tabernacle;[3] there was also the rod of Aaron, that had withered and afterwards blossomed, and the censer.[4]

(2) To what does this point? That you may understand what the second tabernacle is, in which the priest introduced you, in which once a year[5] the highest priest is accustomed to enter, that is, the baptistry, where the rod of Aaron flourished. Formerly it was dry; afterwards it blossomed: 'And

1 Cf. Exod 30.10; Lev. 16.2-34; Heb. 9.6-7.
2 Cf. Heb. 9.1-7.
3 Cf. Heb. 9.3-4.
4 Cf. Num. 17.2-10.
5 Heb. 9.7.

you were dried, and you begin to flower by the watering of the font.'[6] You had become dry by sins, you had become dry by errors and transgressions, but now you began to bring forth fruit 'planted near the running waters.'[7]

(3) But perchance you may say: 'What was this to the people, if the rod of the priest had become dry and blossomed again?' What is the people itself, if not of the priest? To these it was said: 'But you are a chosen generation, a royal priesthood, a holy nation,' as says the Apostle Peter.[8] Everyone is anointed into the priesthood, is anointed into the kingdom, but the spiritual kingdom is also the spiritual priesthood.

(4) In the second tabernacle also is the censer.[9] The censer is that which is accustomed to emit good odor. Thus you also now are the good odor of Christ;[10] now there is no lot of transgressions in you, no odor of graver error.

Chapter 2

(5) There follows your coming to the altar. You began to come; the angels observed; they saw you approaching, and that human condition which before was stained with the shadowy squalor of sins they saw suddenly shining bright, and so they said: 'Who is this that cometh up from the desert whitewashed?'[1] So the angels also marvel. Do you wish to know how they marvel? Hear the Apostle Peter saying that

---

6 Cf. Vergil, *Georgics* 4.32.
7 Ps. 1.3.
8 1 Peter 2.9.
9 Cf. Heb. 9.4.
10 Cf. 2 Cor. 2.15.

---

1 Cf. Cant. 8.5.

those things have been conferred on you which the angels also desired to see.[2] Hear again. It says: 'The eye hath not seen, nor ear heard what things God hath prepared for them that love him.'[3]

(6) Then recognize what you have received. The holy Prophet David saw this grace in figure and desired it. Do you wish to know how he desired it? Again hear him as he says: 'Thou shalt sprinkle me with hyssop, and I shall be cleansed; thou shalt wash me, and I shall be made whiter than snow.'[4] Why? Because snow, although it is white, quickly grows dark with some filth and is corrupted; that grace which you have received, if you hold fast what you have received, will be lasting and perpetual.[5]

(7) You came, then, desiring; inasmuch as you had seen so much grace, you came to the altar desiring to receive the sacrament. Your soul says: 'And I will go in to the altar of God, to God who giveth joy to my youth.'[6] You laid aside the old age of sins, you took on the youth of grace. The heavenly sacraments have bestowed this upon you. Finally, again, hear David as he says: 'Thy youth will be renewed like the eagle's.'[7] You have begun to be a good eagle, which seeks heaven, disdains earthly things. Good eagles are about the altar, for 'Wheresoever the body shall be, there shall the eagles also be gathered together.'[8] The form of the body is the altar, and the body of Christ is on the altar; you are the eagles renewed by the washing away of transgression.

---

2 Cf. 1 Peter 1.12.
3 Cf. 1 Cor. 2.9.
4 Ps. 50.9.
5 Cf. Apoc. 3.11.
6 Ps. 42.4.
7 Ps. 102.5.
8 Matt. 24.28; Luke 17.37.

Chapter 3

(8) You have come to the altar; you have seen to the sacraments placed on the altar; and indeed you have marveled at the creature itself. Yet the creature is customary and known.

(9) Perchance someone may say: 'God furnished the Jews so much grace; manna rained upon them from heaven; what more has He given His faithful; what more has He allotted to these to whom He promised more?'[1]

(10) Accept what I say: that the mysteries of the Christians are earlier than those of the Jews and the sacraments of the Christians are more divine than those of the Jews. How? Accept. When did the Jews begin to be? Surely from Juda, the great-grandson of Abraham,[2] or, if you wish also to understand it so, according to the Law, that is, when they merited to receive 'the law of God.' Therefore, from the great-grandson of Abraham they were called Jews in the time of holy Moses. Then God rained manna from heaven on the Jews as they murmured.[3] But for you a figure of these sacraments preceded, when Abraham was, when he gathered 318 servants born in his house, and he went, pursued his adversaries, and delivered his great-grandson from captivity.[4] Then he came as a victor; Melchisedech the priest met him and offered bread and wine. Who had the bread and wine? Abraham did not have it. But who had it? Melchisedech. He himself then is the author of the sacraments. Who is 'Melchisedech'? Who is signified as 'king of justice, king of peace'?[5] Who is this king

---

1 Cf. Exod. 16.14,15.
2 Cf. 1 Par. 1.34; 2.1.
3 Cf. Exod. 16.2-36.
4 Cf. Gen. 14.14-18; Heb. 7.1-3.
5 Heb. 7.2.

of justice? Can any man be king of justice? Who, then, can be the king of justice other than the justice of God?[6] Who is the peace of God, the wisdom of God? He who was able to say: 'My peace I give to you, my peace I leave with you.'[7]

(11) So first understand these sacraments which you receive, that they are earlier than the sacraments which the Jews say that they have, and that the Christian people began before the people of the Jews began, but we in predestination, they in name.

(12) Thus Melchisedech offered bread and wine. Who is Melchisedech? 'Without father,' it says, 'without mother, without genealogy, having neither beginning of days nor end of life.' The Epistle to the Hebrews has this. 'Without father,' it says, and 'without mother.' You have 'likened unto the Son of God.'[8] The Son of God was born by heavenly generation 'wihout mother,' because He was born of the only God the Father, and again He was born 'without Father,' since He was born of a virgin. For He was not begotten of the seed of a man, but was born of the Holy Spirit and the Virgin Mary, brought forth from a virginal womb. Melchisedech, also, was a priest in all respects 'likened unto the Son of God,' to whom it is said: 'Thou art a priest forever according to the order of Melchisedech.'[9]

Chapter 4

(13) Therefore, who is the author of the sacraments but the Lord Jesus? Those sacraments came down from heaven, for all counsel is from heaven. Moreover, truly a great and

---

6 Cf. 1 Cor. 1.30.
7 Cf. John 14.27.
8 Heb. 7.3.
9 Ps. 109.4; Heb. 7.17.

divine miracle,[1] that God rained manna from heaven upon the people, and the people did not labor and did eat.

(14) You perhaps say: 'My bread is usual.' But that bread is bread before the words of the sacraments; when consecration has been added, from bread it becomes the flesh of Christ. So let us confirm this, how it is possible that what is bread is the body of Christ.

By what words, then, is the consecration and by whose expressions? By those of the Lord Jesus. For all the rest that are said in the preceding are said by the priest: praise to God, prayer is offered, there is a petition for the people, for kings, for the rest.[2] When it comes to performing a venerable sacrament, then the priest uses not his own expressions, but he uses the expressions of Christ. Thus the expression of Christ performs this sacrament.

(15) What is the expression of Christ? Surely that by which all things were made. The Lord ordered,[3] the heaven was made; the Lord ordered, the earth was made; the Lord ordered, the seas were made; the Lord ordered, every creature was generated. You see then how the creating expression of Christ is. If then there is so great force in the expression of the Lord Jesus, that those things might begin to be which were not, how much more creating, that those things be which were, and be changed to something else. The heaven was not, the sea was not, the earth was not, but hear David[4] as he says: 'He spoke and they were made; He commanded and they were created.'

(16) Therefore, to reply to you, there was no body of Christ before consecration, but after the consecration I say

---

1 Cf. Exod. 16.14-36.
2 Cf. 1 Tim. 1.1,2.
3 Cf. Gen. 1.6ff.
4 Ps. 148.5.

to you that now there is the body of Christ. He Himself spoke and it was made; He Himself commanded and it was created. You yourself were, but you were an old creature; after you were consecrated, you began to be a new creature. Do you wish to know how a new creature? It says: 'Every creature is new in Christ.'[5]

(17) Accept, then, how Christ's expression was accustomed to change every creature and changes the designs of nature when He wishes. Do you inquire how? Accept this. And first of all let us take the example of His generation. It is usual that a human being be not generated except of man and woman and by conjugal association. But because the Lord wished, because He chose this sacrament, Christ was born of the Holy Spirit and a virgin, that is, the 'Mediator of God and men, the man Christ Jesus.'[6] You see, then, that contrary to designs and order a man was born, born of a virgin.

(18) Accept another example.[7] The people of the Jews were hard pressed by the Egyptians; they were shut off by the sea. By divine order Moses touched the seas with a rod and the water divided, not of course according to the practice of its nature, but according to the grace of heavenly power. Accept another example.[8] The people were thirsty; they came to a fountain. The fountain was bitter; holy Moses cast a twig into the fountain, and the fountain, which was bitter, was made sweet, that is, it changed the usual state of its nature; it took on the sweetness of grace. Accept also a fourth example.[9] The iron head of an axe fell into the water, as iron, according to its practice, it dipped; Eliseus cast a stick, im-

---

5 Cf. 2 Cor. 5.17.
6 1 Tim. 2.5.
7 Cf. Exod. 14.21,22.
8 Cf. Exod. 14.23-25.
9 Cf. 4 Kings 6.5-7.

mediately the iron head was raised and floated upon the waters, surely contrary to the practice of iron, for it is heavier material than is the element of the waters.

(19) From all this, then, do you not understand how great is the operation of heavenly expression? If heavenly expression operated in an earthly fountain, if it operated in other things, does it not operate in heavenly sacraments? Then you have learned that from bread the body of Christ is made. And what is wine, water? It is put in the cup, but it becomes blood by heavenly consecration.

(20) But perhaps you say: 'I do not see the appearance of blood.' But it has the likeness. For just as you took on the likeness of death, so, too, you drink the likeness of precious blood, that there may be no horror of blood and yet the price of redemption may be effected. You have learned then that what you receive is the body of Christ.

Chapter 5

(21) Do you wish to know how it is consecrated with heavenly words? Accept what the words are. The priest speaks. He says:[1] 'Perform for us this oblation written, reasonable, acceptable, which is a figure of the body and blood of our Lord Jesus Christ. On the day before He suffered He took bread in His holy hands, looked toward heaven, toward you, holy Father omnipotent, eternal God, giving thanks, blessed, broke, and having broken it gave it to the Apostles and His disciples, saying: "Take and eat of this, all of you; for this is my body, which shall be broken for many".'[2] Take note.

---

1 Canon of the Mass.
2 Cf. Matt. 26.26; Mark 14.22; Luke 22.19; 1 Cor. 11.24.

(22) 'Similarly also, on the day before He suffered, after they had dined, He took the chalice, looked toward heaven, toward thee, holy Father omnipotent, eternal God and giving thanks He blessed it, and gave it to the Apostles and His disciples, saying: "Take and drink of this, all of you; for this is my blood".'[3] Behold! All these words up to 'Take' are the Evangelist's, whether body or blood. From them on the words are Christ's: 'Take and drink of this, all of you; for this is my blood.'

(23) Look at these events one by one. It says: 'On the day before He suffered, He took bread in His holy hands.' Before it is consecrated, it is bread; but when Christ's words have been added, it is the body of Christ. Finally, hear him as He says: 'Take and eat of this, all of you; for this is my body.' And before the words of Christ, the chalice is full of wine and water; when the words of Christ have been added, then blood is effected, which redeemed the people. So behold in what great respects the expression of Christ is able to change all things. Then the Lord Jesus Himself testified to us that we receive His body and blood. Should we doubt at all about His faith and testification?

(24) Now return with me to my proposition. Great and venerable indeed is the fact that manna rained upon the Jews from heaven. But understand! What is greater, manna from heaven or the body of Christ? Surely the body of Christ, who is the Author of heaven. Then, he who ate the manna died; he who has eaten this body will effect for himself remission of sins and 'shall not die forever.'[4]

(25) So you say not indifferently 'Amen,' already confessing in spirit that you receive the body of Christ. Therefore, when you ask, the priest says to you: 'the body of Christ,'

---

3 Cf. Matt. 26.27,28; Mark 14.23,24; Luke 22.20.
4 Cf. John 6.49.58; 11.26.

and you say: 'Amen,' that is, 'truly.' What the tongue confesses let the affection hold. That you may know, moreover: 'This is a sacrament, whose figure went on before.'

Chapter 6

(26) Next, realize how great a sacrament it is. See what He says: 'As often as you shall do this, so often will you do a commemoration of me, until I come again.'[1]

(27) And the priest says: 'Therefore, mindful of His most glorious passion and resurrection from the dead and ascension into heaven, we offer you this immaculate victim, a reasonable sacrifice, an unbloody victim, this holy bread, and chalice of eternal life.[2] And we ask and pray that you accept this offering upon your sublime altar through the hands of your angels, just as you deigned to accept the gifts of your just son Abel and the sacrifice of our patriarch Abraham and what the highest priest Melchisedech offered you.'

(28) So, as often as you receive, what does the Apostle say to you? As often as we receive, we proclaim the death of the Lord.[3] If death, we proclaim the remission of sins. If, as often as blood is shed, it is shed for the remission of sins, I ought always to accept Him, that He may always dismiss my sins.[4] I, who always sin, should always have a remedy.

(29) Meanwhile, today also we have explained according to our ability. But tomorrow, on the seventh day and Sunday we shall speak about the order of prayer, as we are able. May our Lord God keep for you the grace which He gave, and

---

1 Cf. 1 Cor. 11.25,26.
2 Cf. Rom. 12.1.
3 Cf. 1 Cor. 11.26.
4 Cf. Matt. 26.28.

may He deign to illuminate more fully the eyes which He gave you, through His only-begotten Son, King and Saviour, our Lord God, through whom He has, with whom He has praise, honor, glory, magnificence, power, together with the Holy Spirit, from the ages and now and always, and forever and ever. Amen.

THE SACRAMENTS: V

Chapter 1

(1) Yesterday our sermon and tractate was brought up to the sacraments of the holy altar. And we learned that the figure of these sacraments preceded the times of Abraham, when holy Melchisedech offered a sacrifice, 'having neither beginning of days nor end.'[1] Hear, man, what the Apostle Paul says to the Hebrews! Where are they who say that the Son of God is of time? As for Melchisedech, it is said that he has neither beginning of days nor end. If Melchisedech does not have beginning of days, could Christ have had it? Yet it is not more a figure than truth. You see, then, that He himself is both the first and the last:[2] first, because He is the author of all; last, not because he finds the end, but because He includes all things.

(2) We have said, then, that the chalice and bread are placed on the altar. What is put in the chalice? Wine. And what else? Water. But you say to me: 'How, then, did Mel-

---

1 Cf. Heb. 7.3.
2 Apoc. 1.17.

chisedech offer wine and bread? What does the admixture of water mean?' Accept the reason!

(3) First of all ,the figure which preceded in the time of Moses, what does it mean? For, when the people of the Jews were thirsty and murmured, because he could not find water, God ordered Moses to touch the rock with a twig. He touched the rock, and the rock poured forth a great deal of water, just as the Apostle says: 'And they drank of the rock that followed, and the rock was Christ.'[3] It was not an immovable rock that followed the people. And do you drink, that Christ may follow you. See the mystery: 'Moses,' that is, the Prophet, 'with a twig,' that is, with the word of God—The priest with the word of God touches the rock, and water flows, and the people of God drink. Then the priest touches the chalice, water abounds in the chalice, the people of God spring up into eternal life and drink, who acquired the grace of God.[4]

(4) Have you learned this, then? Accept another example.[5] At the time of the Lord's passion, when the great sabbath was approaching, because our Lord and the thieves were living, men were sent to beat them. They came and found our Lord Jesus Christ dead. Then one of the soldiers touched His side with a lance, and from His side flowed water and blood. Why water, why blood? Water, that He might cleanse; blood, that He might redeem. Why from the side? Because from where fault comes, from there also comes grace: fault through a woman, grace through our Lord Jesus Christ.[6]

3 Cf. 1 Cor. 10.4.
4 Cf. John 4.14.
5 Cf. 19.31-34.
6 Cf. John 1.17.

Chapter 2

(5) You have come to the altar; the Lord Jesus calls you —both your soul and the Church—and He says: 'Let him kiss me with the kiss of his mouth.'[1] Do you wish to prepare for Christ? Nothing is more pleasing. Do you wish to do so for your soul? Nothing is more pleasant.

(6) 'Let him kiss me.' He sees that you are clean of all sin, because transgressions have been wiped away. Thus He judges you worthy of the heavenly sacraments, and thus invites you to the heavenly banquet. 'Let Him kiss me with the kiss of His mouth.'

(7) Yet on account of the following—both the condition of man and the Church—your soul sees that it is cleansed of all sins, that it is worthy so as to be able to approach the altar of Christ—for what is the altar of Christ but a form of the body of Christ—it sees the marvelous sacraments and says: 'Let him kiss me with the kiss of His mouth,' that is, 'Let Christ impress a kiss upon me.'

(8) Why? 'For thy breasts are better than wine,'[2] that is, your perceptions are better, your sacraments are better than wine, than that wine which, although it has sweetness, has pleasure, has agreeableness, yet in it is worldly pleasure, but in you is spiritual delight. Already at that time Solomon introduces the marriage either of Christ and the Church or of the spirit and the flesh or of the spirit and the soul.

(9) And he added: 'Thy name is as oil poured out; therefore, young maidens have loved thee.'[3] Who are these young maidens but the souls of individuals who have put aside the old age of this body, renewed through the Holy Spirit?

---

1 Cant. 1.1.
2 Cant. 1.1.
3 Cant. 1.2.

(10) 'Draw us; let us run after the odor of thy ointments.'[4]
See what he says: 'You cannot follow Christ, unless He himself draws you.' Finally, that you may know He says: 'If I be lifted up, I will draw all things to myself.'[5]

(11) 'The king has brought me into his bedchamber'—the Greek has 'into his storeroom' or 'into his pantry'[6]—where are good libations, where good odors, sweet honey, diverse fruits, where various dishes, that your meal may be made pleasant by a great many dishes.

Chapter 3

(12) So you have come to the altar; you have received the body of Christ. Hear again what sacraments you have obtained; hear holy David as he speaks. And he in spirit foresaw these mysteries and rejoiced and said that nothing was lacking to him. Why? Because he who shall receive the body of Christ shall never thirst.[1]

(13) How often have you heard Psalm 22 and have not understood it! See how it is applicable to the heavenly sacraments: 'The Lord feeds me and I shall want nothing; He hath set me in a place of pasture; He hath brought me upon the water of refreshment; He hath converted my soul. He hath led me on the paths of justice for His own name's sake. For though I should walk in the midst of the shadow of death, I will fear no evils, for thou art with me. Thy rod and thy staff, they have comforted me.' Thy rod is power, the staff suffering, that is, the eternal divinity of Christ, but also cor-

---

4 Cant. 1.3.
5 Cf. John 12.32.
6 Cf. Cant. 1.3.

---

1 Cf. John 6.35.

poreal suffering; the one created, the other redeemed. 'Thou hast prepared a table before me against them that afflict me. Thou hast anointed my head with oil; and my chalice which inebriateth me how goodly it is!'[2]

(14) You have come, then, to the altar; you have received the grace of Christ; you have obtained the heavenly sacraments. The Church rejoices in the redemption of many, and is glad with spiritual exultation that the members of her household are at hand dressed in white. You have this in the Canticle of Canticles. Rejoicing, she invokes Christ, having prepared a banquet, which seems worthy of heavenly feasting. And so she says: 'Let my beloved come into His garden and eat the fruits of His apple trees.'[3] What are these apple trees? You were made dry wood in Adam, but now through the grace of Christ you flower as apple trees.

(15) Gladly did the Lord Jesus receive and with heavenly dignity reply to His Church. He says: 'I am come into my garden, I have gathered my myrrh with my aromatical spices, I have eaten my bread with my honey, I have drunk my wine with my milk.' 'Eat, He says, 'my brethren, and be inebriated.'[4]

(16) 'I have gathered my myrrh with my aromatical spices.' What is this gathering? Recognize the vineyard, and you will recognize the gathering. He says: 'Thou hast brought a vineyard, out of Egypt,'[5] that is, the people of God. You are the vineyard, you are the gathering, planted, as it were, as a vineyard, you are the gathering, who have yielded fruit. 'I have gathered myrrh with my aromatical spices,' that is, 'unto the odor, which you have received.'

---

2 Ps. 22.1-5.
3 Cant. 5.1.
4 Cf. Cant. 5.1.
5 Ps. 79.9.

(17) 'I have eaten my bread with my honey.' You see that in this bread there is no bitterness, but there is all sweetness. 'I have drunk my wine with my milk.' You see that such is the gladness that it is polluted by the filth of no sin. For as often as you drink, you receive the remission of sins and you are inebriated in spirit.[6] Therefore, the Apostle also says: 'Be not drunk with wine, but be ye filled with the Holy Spirit.'[7] For he who is inebriated with wine totters and sways; he who is inebriated with the Holy Spirit is rooted in Christ. And so, glorious is ebriety which effects sobriety of mind. So much have we gone over briefly regarding the sacraments.

Chapter 4

(18) There is nothing more, is there, but the prayer? And do not think that it is an ordinary virtue to know how to pray. The holy Apostles said to the Lord Jesus: 'Lord teach us to pray, as John taught his disciples.'[1] Then the Lord said the prayer: 'Our Father, who art in heaven, hallowed be thy name. Thy kingdom come. Thy will be done on earth as it is in heaven. Give us this day our daily bread, and forgive us our debts as we forgive our debtors, and lead us not into temptation, but deliver us from evil.'[2]

You see how brief the prayer is, and how full of all virtues. Of what great charm is the first sentence!

(19) O man, you did not dare to raise your face to heaven; you directed your eyes toward earth; and suddenly you

---

6 Cf. Matt. 26.28; 1 Cor. 11.26.
7 Eph. 5.18.

1 Luke 11.1.
2 Matt. 6.9-13.

received the grace of Christ; all your sins were forgiven. From an evil servant you became a good son.[3] So presume not from your own operation but from Christ's grace. 'By grace,' He says, 'you are saved'; so the Apostle[4] says. There is no arrogance here, but faith. To preach what you have received is not pride but devotion. So raise your eyes to the Father, who begot you through the laver,[5] to the Father, who redeemed you through His Son,[6] and say: 'Our Father.' A good presumption, but moderate. As if a son you call Him Father, but do not lay claim to anything specially for yourself. He is the special Father of Christ alone, for all of us He is Father in common, because He begot Him alone, He created us. You, too, then say 'Our Father' through grace, that you may deserve to be His son. In the sight and consideration of the Church do you commend yourself!

(20) 'Our Father, who art in heaven.' What is 'in heaven'? Hear the words of Scripture: 'The Lord is high above all heavens.'[7] And everywhere you have it that the Lord is above the heaven of the heavens.[8] As if even the angels were not in the heavens, as if also the dominations were not in the heavens! But in those heavens of which it is said: 'The heavens show forth the glory of the God.'[9] Heaven is there where fault has ceased; heaven is there where shameful deeds are idle; heaven is there where there is no wound of death.

(21) 'Our Father, who art in heaven, hallowed be thy name.' What is 'hallowed be'? As if we wish Him to be

---

3 Cf. Matt. 25.26; Gal. 4.7.
4 Eph. 2.5.
5 Of baptism.
6 Cf. Titus 3.5; James 1.18.
7 Cf. Ps. 112.4.
8 3 Kings 8.27; Ps. 8.2.
9 Ps. 18.2.

hallowed who says: 'Be ye holy, because I am holy,'[10] as if
something may be added to Him by our prayer for hallowedness! No, but let Him be made hallowed in us, that His
hallowedness may be able to come to us.

(22) 'Our Father, who art in Heaven, hallowed be thy
name, thy kingdom come.' As if the kingdom of God were
not eternal! Jesus himself says: 'For this I was born,'[11] and
you say to the Father: 'Thy kingdom come,' as if He had not
come. But then the kingdom of God has come, since you have
obtained His grace. For He Himself says: 'The kingdom of
God is within you.'[12]

(23) 'Thy kingdom come, thy will be done, on earth as
it is in heaven; give us this day our daily bread.' By the blood
of Christ all things were pacified both in heaven and on
earth;[13] heaven is hallowed; the Devil is cast down. He turns
there, where the man also is whom he deceived. 'Thy will be
done,' that is, let there be peace on earth as there is in
heaven.[14]

(24) 'Give us this day our daily bread.' Remember my
words, when I discussed the sacraments. I have told you that
what is offered before the words of Christ is spoken of as
bread; when the words of Christ have been brought forth,
no longer is it spoken of as bread, but is called body. Why,
then, in the Lord's prayer, which follows afterwards, does He
say 'our bread'? Surely He has spoken of it as bread, but as
ἐπιούσιον (sufficient for the day), that is, substantial. That
is not the bread that enters the body,[15] but that is the bread
of eternal life, which supports the substance of our soul.[16]

---

10 Cf. Lev. 19.2.
11 John 18.37.
12 Luke 17.21.
13 Cf. Col. 1.20.
14 Cf. Luke 2.14.
15 Cf. Mark. 7.19.
16 Cf. John 6.35-58.

So in Greek it is spoken of as ἐπιούσιος. Moreover the Latin has spoken of this bread as daily (*cottidianum*), because the Greeks speak of τὴν ἐπιούσιαν ἡμέραν, the coming day. Thus what the Latin has said and what the Greek, both seem useful. The Greek has signified both in one word; the Latin has spoken of it as daily.

(25) If bread is daily, why do you take it after a year, as the Greeks in the East are accustomed to do? Receive daily what is of benefit to you daily! So live that you may deserve to receive it daily! He who does not deserve to receive it daily does not deserve to receive it after a year. In this manner holy Job offered sacrifice for his sons daily, lest, perchance, they had committed some sin either in heart or in speech. Then do you hear that, as often as the sacrifice is offered, the death of the Lord, the resurrection of the Lord, the elevation of the Lord, is signified, and the remission of sins, and do you not take this bread of life daily? He who has a wound requires medicine. The fact that we are under sin is a wound; the medicine is the heavenly and venerable sacrament.

(26) 'Give us this day our daily bread.' If you receive daily, daily is today for you. If today is Christ for you, today for you He rises. How? 'Thou art my son, this day I have begotten thee.'[17] Today then is when Christ arises. 'He himself is yesterday and today,' the Apostle Paul says; but elsewhere he says: 'The night is passed, and the day is at hand.'[18] Last night has passed; this day is at hand.

(27) There follows: 'And forgive us our debts, as we forgive our debtors.'[19] What is a debt but a sin? So, if you had not accepted the money of a stranger's interest, you would not be poor, and so sin is imputed to you. You had money with which you would have been born rich. You had been

17 Ps. 2.7.
18 Cf. Heb. 13.8; Rom. 13.12.
19 Matt. 6.12.

made rich in the image and likeness of God.[20] You lost what you had, that is humility; when you desire to assume arrogance, you have lost money. Like Adam, you were made naked.[21] You accepted a debt from the Devil which was not necessary. And thus you were free in Christ, were made a debtor of the Devil. An enemy held your bond, but the Lord impaled it and destroyed it with His blood.[22] He took away your debt, returned liberty.

(28) Well then does He say: 'And forgive us our debts, as we also forgive our debtors.' See what you say: 'As I forgive, so do you forgive me.' If you have forgiven, you accost Him well, that you be forgiven. If you do not forgive, how do you accost him?

(29) 'And suffer us not to be led into temptation, but deliver us from evil.'[23] See what He says: 'And suffer us not to be led into temptation,' which we cannot endure. He does not say 'Lead not into temptation,' but like an athlete He wishes such temptation as human nature and that of each one can endure, that He be delivered 'from evil,' that is, from sin.

(30) Moreover, the Lord is able, who has taken away your sin and has forgiven your transgressions, to guard and protect you against the snares of the opposing Devil,[24] that the enemy, who is accustomed to create fault, may not surprise you. But he who commits himself to God does not fear the Devil. For, 'if God be for us, who is against us?'[25] So praise and glory be to Him from the ages and now and always, and forever and ever. Amen.

---

20 Cf. Gen. 1.26.
21 Cf. Gen. 3.7.
22 Cf. Col. 2.14.
23 Matt. 6.13.
24 Cf. Eph. 6.11.
25 Rom. 8.31.

THE SACRAMENTS: VI

Chapter 1

(1) Just as our Lord Jesus Christ is the true Son of God, not as man through grace, but as the Son of God from the substance of the Father, thus He is true flesh, as He himself said, which we receive and is His true drink.[1]

(2) But perchance you say what the disciples of Christ also said at that time when they heard Him say: 'Unless one eat my flesh and drink my blood, he will not abide in me and will not have eternal life'[2]—perchance you say: 'How true [flesh]? Certainly I see a likeness, I do not see true blood.'

(3) First of all, I told you about the words of Christ which operate so as to be able to change and transform the established orders of nature. Then, when His disciples did not tolerate the words of Christ, but hearing that He gave His flesh to eat and gave His blood to drink, went back, and yet Peter alone said: 'Thou hast words of eternal life, and whither shall I go back from you?'[3]—lest, then, more might say that

---

1 Cf. Heb. 1.2,3; John 6.55.
2 Cf. John 6.54-61.
3 Cf. John 6.69.

they go, as if there were a kind of horror of the blood, but as if the grace of redemption did abide, thus indeed in likeness you receive the sacraments, but obtain the grace and virtue of true nature.

(4) 'I am the living bread,' He says, 'which came down from heaven.'[4] But flesh did not come down from heaven, that is, He took on flesh on earth from a virgin. How, then, did bread come down from heaven and living bread? Because our same Lord Jesus Christ is a sharer of both divinity and body, and you who receive the flesh participate in that nourishment of His divine substance.

Chapter 2

(5) Therefore, you received of the sacraments; most fully do you know all. Because you have been baptized in the name of the Trinity, in all that we have done the mystery of the Trinity has been preserved. Everywhere the Father, the Son, and the Holy Spirit, one operation, one sanctification, although they seem to be, as it were, certain special things.

(6) How? God, who anointed you, and the Lord sealed you, and placed the Holy Spirit in your heart.[1] Therefore, you have received the Holy Spirit in your heart. Take another example, as the Holy Spirit is in the heart, so also is Christ in the heart. How? You have this in the Canticle of Canticles, Christ saying to the Church: 'Put me as a seal upon thy heart, as a seal upon thy arm.'[2]

(7) Therefore, God anointed you, Christ sealed you. How? Because you were sealed unto the form of the cross itself,

---

4 John 6.41.

1 Cf. 2 Cor. 1.21,22.
2 Cant. 8.6.

unto His passion. You have received the seal unto His likeness, that you may rise again unto His form, may live unto His figure, who was crucified to sin and liveth unto God. And your old man is dipped in the font, was crucified unto sin, but arose again unto God.[3]

(8) Then you have elsewhere a special thing, that God has called you; in baptism, moreover, as if you were crucified in a special way unto Christ, then as if something special, when you receive the spiritual seal. You see that there is a distinction of persons, but a mystery of the Trinity all connected.

(9) Then what did the Apostle say to you, as it was read clearly and concisely? 'Now there are diversities of graces, but the same spirit; and there are diversities of ministries, but the same Lord, and there are diversities of operations, but the same God, who worketh all in all.'[4] He says, God worketh all. But of the Spirit of God also it was read: 'One and the same Spirit, dividing to every one according as He will.'[5] Hear Scripture saying that the Spirit divides as according to His will, not according to obedience. So the Spirit divided grace for you, 'according as He will,' not according as He is ordered, and especially because He is the Spirit of God, the Spirit of Christ. And retain that, that He is the Holy Spirit Himself, the Spirit Himself of God, the Spirit Himself of Christ, the Spirit Paraclete Himself.

(10) The Arians think that they detract from the Holy Spirit if they call the Spirit Paraclete. What is a paraclete but a consoler? As if it were not read of the Father also, that He is the "God of consolation'![6] You see, then, that they think

---

3 Cf. Rom. 6.10,4-6.
4 1 Cor. 12.4-6.
5 1 Cor. 12.11.
6 Cf. 2 Cor. 1.3.

that there must be detraction from the Holy Spirit in this in which the power of the eternal Father is proclaimed with pious affection.

Chapter 3

(11) Now accept how we should pray. There are many virtues in prayer. Where you should pray is not insignificant nor an insignificant question. The Apostle says: 'I will, therefore, that men pray in every place, lifting up pure hands, without anger and strife.'[1] And the Lord says in the Gospel: 'But thou, when thou shalt pray, enter into thy chamber, and having shut the door, pray to thy Father.'[2] Does it not seem to you to be contrary for the Apostle to say: 'Pray in every place,' and the Lord to say: 'Pray within thy chamber'? But it is not contrary. Therefore, let us dismiss this; then let us learn all the following: How you should begin prayer and in what order divide it; what you should add, what bring forward, how conclude the prayer, then for whom you should pray.

(12) First, where you should pray. Paul seems to say one thing, the Lord another. Could Paul have taught anything contrary to the precepts of Christ? Surely not. For what reason? Because He is not contrary to but the interpreter of Christ. He says: 'Be ye followers of me, as I also am of Christ.'[3] What, then? You can pray everywhere, and you can always pray in your chamber; you have your chamber everywhere. Although you are placed among the Gentiles, among the Jews, yet you have your solitude everywhere. Your mind

---

1 1 Tim. 2.8.
2 Matt. 6.6.
3 1 Cor. 11.1.

is your chamber. Although you are placed among the people, yet your secret and solitude you preserve in the interior man.

(13) 'But thou, when thou shalt pray, enter into thy chamber.' Well does he say: 'Enter,' lest you pray as the Jewish people, to whom it is said: 'This people honoreth me with their lips, but their heart is far from me.'[4] Do not, then, let your prayer proceed from the lips alone. Assert it with your whole mind, enter the recesses of your breast, go in wholly. Let Him whom you desire to please not see you perfunctory. Let Him see that you pray from the heart, that He is worthy to see you pray from the heart.

(14) 'But thou, when thou shalt pray, enter into thy chamber.' You have this also elsewhere: 'Go, my people, enter into thy chambers: hide thyself a little, until the wrath of the Lord passes away.'[5] The Lord said this through the Prophet; in the Gospel, however, He says: 'But thou, when thou shalt pray, enter into thy chamber, and, having shut the door, pray to thy Father.'

(15) What is 'having shut the door'? What door do we have? Hear what door you have, what you ought to close, when you pray. Would that the women did hear! Already have you heard; holy David taught you when he said: 'Set a watch, O Lord, before my mouth, and a door round about my lips.'[6] There is a door elsewhere which the Apostle Paul mentions in these words. He says: 'That a door of speech may be opened to me to speak the mystery of Christ.'[7] That is, when you pray, do not shout aloud with words nor scatter your prayer nor toss it about through the people. Pray in your own secrecy, secure that He can hear you in secret, who sees

---

4 Matt. 15.8.
5 Cf. Isa. 26.20.
6 Ps. 140.3.
7 Cf. Col. 4.3.

all and hears everything. 'Pray to thy Father in secret; for thy Father who seeth in secret'[8] hears you as you pray.

Chapter 4

(16) But of what benefit is it, let us inquire, for what reason we should pray in secret rather than with clamor. Give heed. Let us take an example from the practice of men. If you ask someone who hears readily, you do not think there is need of shouting; you ask gently, with a moderate voice. If you ask some deaf person, do you not begin to shout, that he may be able to hear you? He, then, who shouts, thinks that God cannot hear him otherwise than as he shouts, and when he asks Him, he detracts from His power. But he who prays in silence, offers faith and confesses that 'the searcher of hearts and reins is God,'[1] and He hears your prayer before it is poured forth from your mouth.

(17) Therefore, let us see! 'I will, therefore, that men pray in every place.'[2] For what reason did he say 'men'? Surely, prayer is common to both women and men. This I do not ascertain, unless perchance the holy Apostle said 'men' lest the women take cognizance of and misunderstand 'in every place' and begin to clamor everywhere, and these women we cannot endure in a church.

(18) 'I will, therefore, that men,' that is, who can keep the precept, 'pray in every place, lifting up pure hands.' What is 'lifting up pure hands'? Ought you in your prayer to point out the cross of the Lord to the Gentiles? Surely that

8 Cf. Matt. 6.6.

1 Ps. 7.10.
2 1 Tim. 2.8.

sign is for virtue, not for shame. Yet this is how you can pray, not how you point out a figure, but how you raise your acts. If you wish to perform your prayer, you raise pure hands through innocence. You raise them not everyday; once you have raised them, there is no necessity for you to raise them again.

(19) 'I will, therefore, that men pray in every place, lifting up pure hands, without anger and strife.'[3] Nothing is more true. He says: 'Anger ruins even the wise.'[4] Thus on every occasion, as much as it can be done, the Christian man should temper his wrath, especially when he comes to prayer and lest indignation disturb your mind, lest indeed the fury of your anger impede your prayer, approach rather with a placid heart. For why do you become angry? A servant has offended. Do you come to prayer that your delinquencies be forgiven you, and do you become indignant at another. This, then, is without 'anger.'

Chapter 5

(20) Now let us see about 'strife.' Usually a trader comes to prayer, or an avaricious person considers money, another gain, another honor, another desire, and he thinks that God can hear him. And so, when you pray, it befits you to prefer divine to human things.

(21) 'In like manner women,'[1] He says: 'I will to pray without boasting of ornaments and pearls,' says the Apostle Paul. But the Apostle Peter also says: 'The grace of women is of the greatest value, that the affection of her husband may be turned by the good conversation of his wife, and the

---

3 1 Tim. 2.8.
4 Prov. 15.1. (Septuagint).

1 1 Tim. 2.9.

incredulous one may be directed to the grace of Christ.'[2]
The dignity and modesty of a woman and her good conversation have this power, to call her husband to faith and
devotion, which the words of a prudent man frequently effects.
He says: 'Let a woman, then, have her adornment not in the
decoration of the hairs of the head, not in plaited hair,'[3] but
in prayer from a pure heart,[4] where 'is the hidden man of the
heart, who is always rich in the sight of God.'[5] You have then
that, in which you are rich. In Christ are the chastity and
purity of your wealth, the faith of the filet, the devotion, the
compassion. These are the treasures of justice, as the Prophet
reminded.[6]

(22) Hear, then, how you ought to begin. Tell me, if you
wish to make a request of a man and you begin thus: 'Now
give me that which I ask of you,' does not your prayer seem
to be arrogant? Thus prayer should begin with praise of God,
so as to make a request of the omnipotent God, for whom all
things are possible[7] who has the will to perform them. The
supplication follows, as the Apostle taught, saying: 'I desire,
therefore, first of all, that prayers, supplications, intercessions,
and thanksgiving be made.'[8] The first prayer, then, should
have praise of God, the second supplication, the third intercession, the fourth thanksgivings. You ought not as a famished
person begin about food [when asking] for food, but begin
first with praises of God.

(23) Thus the wise who plead have this custom: To
make a judge favorable for themselves they begin with his
praises, so as to make the advocate kind to themselves. Then

2 Cf. 1 Peter 3.1,2.
3 Cf. 1 Tim. 2.9.
4 Cf. 2 Tim. 2.22.
5 Cf. 1 Peter 3.3,4.
6 Isa. 33.6.
7 Cf. Matt. 19.26; Mark 10.27; 14.36.
8 Cf. 1 Tim. 2.1.

they begin gradually to make the request of the judge, that he deign to hear them patiently; thirdly to draw forth his intercession, to express what they seek; fourthly, to end in praise,[9] just as they began with praises of God. Thus everyone of us ought to end in praise of God and in thanksgiving.

(24) You have this in the Lord's prayer: 'Our Father, who art in heaven.' Praise of God, because He is proclaimed Father. In this is glory of piety, praise of God, because He lives in heaven,[10] not on earth. 'Our Father who art in heaven, hallowed be thy name,' that is, that He may make His servants hallowed, for His name is hallowed among us, whenever Christian men are proclaimed. So, 'hallowed be thy name' belongs to one who desires something. 'Thy kingdom come': the request that the kingdom of Christ be in all. If God reigns in us, the adversary can have no place there, fault does not reign, sin does not reign, but virtue reigns, modesty reigns, devotion reigns. Then: 'Thy will be done on earth as it is in heaven. Give us this day our daily bread.' This request is the very greatest of those that are requested. He says: 'And forgive us our debts as we forgive the debts of our debtors.' So accept daily, so that you may request daily indulgence for your debts. 'And do not suffer us to be led into temptation, but deliver us from evil.' What follows? Hear what the priest says: 'Through our Lord Jesus Christ in whom for you and with whom for you is honor, praise, glory, magnificence, power, with the Holy Spirit from the ages and now and always, and forever and ever. Amen.'

(25) Here is another example. Although there is one book of the Psalms of David containing the virtues of prayer which we have mentioned above, yet in general those parts of prayer

---

9 'To end in praise' is suggested by O. Faller to fill in the lacuna of the text at this point.
10 Cf. Ps. 122.1.

are found even in one psalm, as we find them in the eighth psalm. Now it begins thus: 'O Lord, our Lord, how admirable is thy name in the whole earth.'[11] So the first prayer. Then the supplication: 'For I will behold thy heavens, the works of thy fingers'; that is, 'I will behold the heavens'; 'the moon and the stars which thou hast founded.'[12] Surely he did not say: 'I shall see the heaven,' but 'I shall see the heavens,' in which grace begins to grow white with heavenly splendor. Then the Prophet promised that these heavens are given to them who merit heavenly grace from the Lord: 'the moon and the stars which thou has founded,' 'the moon' the Church, 'the stars' the resurging heavenly graces. Then behold his petition. 'What is man that thou art mindful of him? or the son of man that thou visitest him? Thou hast made him a little less than the angels, thou hast crowned him with glory and honour, and hast set him over the work of thy hands. Thou hast subjected all things under his feet, all sheep and oxen; moreover the beasts also of the fields,'[13] and others.

(26) We have taught according to our capacity, perhaps, what we have not learned; as we have been able, we have set it forth. Let your sanctity, informed by sacerdotal instructions, labor to maintain what it has received, that your prayer may be acceptable to God, and your oblation be as a pure victim, and that He may always recognize His sign in you, that you yourselves also may be able to come to the grace and the rewards of virtues, through our Lord Jesus Christ, to whom is honor and glory, praise, perpetuity from the ages and now and always, and forever and ever. Amen.

11 Ps. 8.2.
12 Ps. 8.4.
13 Ps. 8.5-8.

INDEX

GENERAL INDEX

Aaron, 16
Abdemeleck, an Ethiopian, 135, 136
Abel, 218, 219, 306
Abraham, 21 ff., 37, 41, 55, 94, 98, 167, 220, 260, 306, 309
Acholius, Bishop of Thessalonica, xviii
Adam, 55, 258, 292
Adoptionism, 222 n.
Adrianople, xvii
Aemelia-Liguria, viii, xvi
Agricola, martyr, xxi
Alexandria, 42
Altar of Victory, xii, xviii f., altars of heaven, 110
Ambrose of Milan, *passim,* 42 n.
Anamius, Bishop of Sirmium, xvii

Ananias, 57, 131, 172
angels, 18; bread of, 23, 58, 65, 76, 109, 180
Antichrist, 168
Antioch, difficulties at, xviii, 42
Anysius, Bishop of Thessalonica, xviii
Apocalypse, 261
Apollinaris of Laodicea, 223 n., 238 n.
Apollinarianism, 180 n., 223 n.
Apollinarists, 217, 218, 248 n.
Apology, of Rufinus, 32
Apostle, 7, 9, 20, 27, 45ff., 55f., 57, 65, 67, 71, 80; Apostles, 88, 99, 100, 148, 149, 152, 154, 155ff., 180, 181, 203, 204, 231, 237, 253, 270, 279, 284, 287, 293, 305, 314, 315, 324

331

332

Ezechiel, 207

Faith, The, 31, 81
faith, mystic, 19
Faller, Fr. O., S.J., xiv, xxiii, 205
famine in Rome, xvii
Father, God the, 22
fathers, 22
Felix, Pope, xvi, xix f.
fellowship, 82
Flavian, Bishop of Antioch, xviii
fleece, of the Jews, 39
flood, 279
Florence, xx
flower, of the root, 110
footstool, His, 180
fountain, sacred, 27; of Life, 89 f.
Frisch, J. du, xxiii
Fritigil, queen, xxi
fruits, sweet-smelling, 110

Gabriel, 66
Gallus, Emperor, xv
Gedeon, 36, 37, 39, 44, 88
generation, divine, 110
Genesis, 21
Gentiles, 11, 37, 38, 40, 70, 99,
    101, 131, 133, 135, 322, 324
Gervasius, Saint, xiv, xix
gifts of tongues, 150
Gnosticism, 221 n.
Godhead, 70, 74, 79, 83, 87 ff.,
    91, 106, 120, 146, 155, 173, 174,
    180; of the Trinity, 184, 185,

186, 187, 192, 193, 194, 201,
    202, 206
Gospel, 27
Goths, xiii, xvii f.
grace, moral, 19; spiritual, 76,
    79, 82, 100, 110, 118, 119, 147;
    of healings, 150; grace of the
    Lord, 180
Gratian, Emperor, xii, xvi ff., 31,
    218, 249 n.
Greeks, 14
Gregory of Constantinople, 42 n.,
    174 n.

harlots, 95
Hebrew, 9, 22, 91, 204, 276, 297,
    309
Helisaeus, 10
heretics, 112
Hilary of Poitiers, xiv, xv
Hippolytus, x
Holy Eucharist, 3
Holy of holies, 6, 6 n.
Holy Spirit, 9, 12 f., 15, 18, 29;
    The Holy Spirit, 31 ff.
Honorius, xxi
ὕλη, 254
humility, 17
hymnody, Latin, xiv
hyssop, 17

Idacius, Spanish bishop, xviii
Incarnation, 22, 115, 116, 117,
    181, 199, 217, 223, 224, 232 n.,
    232, 243, 244, 245

334

338

339

INDEX
OF HOLY SCRIPTURE

(BOOKS OF THE NEW TESTAMENT)

341

342